RELIGION AND SUSTAINABILITY

RELIGION AND SUSTAINABILITY
Social Movements and the
Politics of the Environment

LUCAS F. JOHNSTON

Published by Equinox Publishing Ltd.

UK: Unit S3, Kelham House, 3 Lancaster Street, Sheffield, S3 8AF
USA: ISD, 70 Enterprise Drive, Bristol, CT 06010

www.equinoxpub.com

First published 2013

ISBN: 978-1-908049-81-0 (hardcover)
ISBN: 978-1-908049-82-7 (paperback)

British Library Cataloguing-in-Publication Data
A catalogue record for this book is available from the British Library.

Library of Congress Cataloging-in-Publication Data

Johnston, Lucas F.
    Religion and sustainability : social movements and the politics of the environment / Lucas F. Johnston.
        p. cm.
    Includes bibliographical references (p.) and index.
    ISBN 978-1-908049-81-0 (hardcover) — ISBN 978-1-908049-82-7 (pbk.)
    1. Environmental ethics. 2. Environmental justice. 3. Sustainability—Religious aspects. 4. Religion and politics. I. Title.
    GE42.J65 2012
    201'.77—dc23

                                              2012022763

Typeset by JS Typesetting Ltd, Porthcawl, Mid Glamorgan
Printed and bound in the UK by MPG Books Group

For my parents, who taught me to ask hard questions, and who instilled in me the desire for a better tomorrow.

CONTENTS

PART III: THE ETHNOGRAPHIC DATA AND SUSTAINABILITY CASES

ACKNOWLEDGMENTS

It is customary to thank those who helped usher along projects such as this one, and I would be remiss if I did not highlight some of these important contributions. Most importantly, this work would not have been possible without the generous people who volunteered their valuable time to explain to me their vision of sustainability. My deepest thanks to all who endured my questions and comments.

Bron Taylor (University of Florida) encouraged me to tackle this project, though it seemed daunting during the planning stages. He also read many early drafts of chapters which came from this research and pointed out some of the blind spots therein. Robin Wright (University of Florida) enriched my understanding of the field of anthropology in significant ways, and much of what is here, particularly sections related to the social sciences, would have been anemic without his contributions. I also had the good fortune to engage with colleagues who shaped my thinking about sustainability and about the fields of religious and environmental studies. Special thanks go to "nature boys" Gavin Van Horn (Center for Humans and Nature), Sam Snyder (Alaska Conservation Foundation), and Joe Witt (Mississippi State), who also read early drafts of some chapters.

Several of my students at Wake Forest University read chapters and provided feedback regarding their appropriateness for undergraduate courses. My thanks to Carrie Stokes, Jordan Garside, David Inczauskis, and Andrew Luisi.

Finally, my thanks to those at Equinox Press who shepherded the book through the publication process: Janet Joyce, who saw its potential value, and Tristan Palmer, who gathered helpful feedback and kept me on task.

Portions of Chapter 6 have appeared in the *Journal for the Study of Religion, Nature and Culture* 4(1), the book *Inherited Land* (Whitney Bauman, Richard R. Bohannon II & Kevin J. O'Brien (eds), Eugene, OR: Wipf & Stock, 2011), and in *The Encyclopedia of Sustainability*, vol. 4 (Gt Barrington, MA: Berkshire Press, 2011).

INTRODUCTION AND READER'S GUIDE

Several people had gathered to hear the Lakota elder talk, and participate with him in a series of ceremonies.[1] I recall that one of the participants commented afterward that it was difficult to believe that—of all people—these Indians and those who supposedly appreciated their ways (enough, at least, to come to see the old man speak and conduct ritual) would use disposable plates and napkins, and eat such high-sugar, high-fat diets (potato chips, soft drinks, and other snacks were often the main fare). This was fascinating to me, for this person was a sustainability *practitioner* (one who implemented sustainability plans in educational environments). Although likely influenced by popularized depictions of the environmentally "noble savage," underlying her comment was a perception that sustainability was ultimately about particular *behaviors* and consumer *choices*. In contrast, many of those in the academy, particularly those who studied sustainability as it related to religious beliefs and practices, perceived that moving toward sustainability was primarily about correcting erroneous worldviews or a shift in consciousness. The American Indians gathered there, particularly those who led the ceremonies, did not often resort to using the word sustainability, but when they did it referred to strengthening their spiritual community in a way that would allow it to persist over time. Moreover, they often talked (without referencing sustainability) about obligations to future generations and to non-human beings. At bottom their perception of "sustainability" had very little to do with paper plates, but rather with their ability to make decisions about their own future that reflected the values they wished to see sustained into the future. Here were three divergent perspectives—sustainability as *enactment*, sustainability as right *perception*, and sustainability as a *community ethos*—that rested on very different value propositions. Yet my

1

hunch was that these communities would often find significant overlap and convergence in the sorts of policies and outcomes they would find preferable in a wide variety of situations.

I began to ponder whether, and how, religious and spiritual discourse informed the cultivation and maintenance of inclusive, adaptive, and sustainable political processes and community formation. Secondary questions included whether there were any differences between the ways in which institutional religious and secular groups, indigenous communities, grassroots organizations and international bodies understood sustainability. Related sub-questions included: Are there any values that obtain across religious and secular sustainability-oriented constituencies? Can understanding the religious dimensions of sustainability aid in reducing human suffering and inter-group conflict? What are the most commonly cited values, or reasons expressed for why movement leaders became engaged in sustainability advocacy? Finally, how are these values expressed to others in the public sphere?

The importance of addressing these questions became clearer still when my home institution began to consider offering an advanced degree in Sustainability. Some suggested that it was impossible to design a program without first concretely defining sustainability, often offering the fetishized definition provided in *Our Common Future* (WCED 1987) without acknowledging that this definition was a restatement of definitions offered long before that book was published (see Chapter 5 for further discussion). Academics often value definitions, often endorsing them as universal, failing to recognize they are relative to their own interests and contexts.

To tackle this problematic disconnect, and to sketch preliminary answers to the above questions, this book sets out to accomplish two things. First, it endeavors to provide an analytical (not exhaustive) history of the concept of sustainability, including reflection on the emergence of the term into various uses that have socio-political, economic, and ecological implications. Second, it provides some targeted ethnographic and case data that explores how non-governmental organizations have used the concept of sustainability, specifically focusing on similarities and differences between religious, interfaith, and secular groups.

While uses of the term sustainability abound in popular culture, business, higher education, government, and development and conservation programs, there has been a dearth of attention to the religious dimensions of sustainability. My conclusions thus far are that historically these religious dimensions of sustainability have been important ingredients in several understandings of sustainability. Moreover, pragmatically, in many cases, the inclusion of religious values in conservation and development efforts facilitates sustainable relationships between people with different value structures, and may increase chances of long-term success. In other cases, though, religious ideologies conflict with resource conservation or ecosystem restoration, or simply cause greater division within explicitly religious constituencies (for example among evangelical Christians) where a small minority of individuals have adopted more sustainable behaviors or environmentalist sentiments. This, I reasoned, was all the more reason for a careful articulation of what specific individuals and groups *mean* when they use the term sustainability.

It is the dizzying variety of understandings and definitions of sustainability that prompted the philosopher Bryan Norton to propose a new "constructive" social science research program, one engaged in developing "a new kind of integrative social science" (Norton 2005: 291). Norton recognized that pluralism inevitably leads to "a range of values from consumptive to transformative to spiritual" (2005: 373). For Norton, however, language related to some values, such as religious values, is relevant only *within* particular communities of accountability and not applicable to public policy debates.[2] A number of the informants who provided input into this research reported that they engaged in deliberation or partnerships with others precisely *because* of their religious beliefs and values, not in spite of them. This goes against the grain of Norton's claim that such commitments to risky partnerships (commitments to negotiate with others outside one's familiar communities) are (or should be) *"independent of the particular beliefs and values of the participants"* (Norton 2005: 285, italics his). In fact, in many cases they are directly related, and hiding this from public eyes may hamper public debate.

When oil companies, international political bodies, the Sierra Club, radical environmentalist and indigenous organizations (and everything in between) can all use sustainability (or some variation of it) to describe their agendas, goals, and activities it is vitally important that there be more focused investigation into particular deployments of the term and the values these uses underwrite. The importance of exposing the values at play in various definitions of sustainability becomes especially clear in a pluralistic global context, where those who provide the funding and institutional support for sustainable development programs have in mind a concept of sustainability that is not only foreign, but often unwelcome to those who are the "targets" of such development. For example, some conservation and development agencies assume that raising standards of living in a sustainable manner requires engagement with the global market. In contrast, the idea of sustainability may be strategically deployed by indigenous or other marginalized groups to resist incorporation into the global market and its attendant values (Trusty 2009; Wright 2009).[3] The current moral "austerity" of environment-related policy-making cannot be overcome without making these values foundations explicit (Gilroy & Bowersox 2002). If sustainability itself is to be a long-term cultural project, these values require more attentiveness, and different communities of accountability require more practice at translating them into the public sphere.

GENERAL OUTLINE AND SUMMARY OF THE STUDY

To provide a brief preview, the arguments advanced here are that religion has historically been a significant part of many visions of sustainability. In addition, the inclusion of religious values in conservation and development efforts has facilitated relationships between people with different value structures. Despite this, little attention has been paid to the interdependence of sustainability and religion, and there have been no significant comparisons of religious and secular sustainability advocacy.

The book is broken into three parts, each of which aims to provide a novel contribution to the sustainability conversation, which spans several academic disciplines and professional schools. The task of Part I is to provide a foundation for the analysis that follows, first by examining why sustainability matters and highlighting what is typically missing from the discourse. Second, it performs the difficult task of constructing the definitions of religion and sustainability that will guide the explorations in the rest of the volume. The novel contributions offered include a schematic definition of sustainability that illustrates the centrality of the concept's religious dimensions. Further, although the *family resemblances* model used to define the other operative term—religion—has been exercised by other scholars (Saler 1993, 2004; Taylor 2007, 2010; Benthall 2008; Vasquez 2008), this exploration of the approach first suggested by Ludwig Wittgenstein takes seriously his notion that polythetic definitions can act as a sort of linguistic therapy. In the case of sustainability, such definitions can act as both linguistic *and* social therapy, offering a means for bringing together disparate communities and their understandings of sustainability. Third, it offers a brief theoretical excursus that provides a model for investigating religion in social movements through the notion of "nested individuals."

Part II analyzes the historical antecedents and contemporary composition of the multi-faceted social movements related to sustainability. The novel contributions here include the elucidation of the religious underpinnings of the earliest uses of the term in resource management, and the important contributions of religious individuals and groups to the development of *sustainability* and *sustainable development*. In addition, it highlights the globalization and institutionalization of these terms, noting the highly affective tropes used to advertise them. Finally, this section reflects on the most common sources of these emotive and often spiritual tropes and metaphors, which include institutionalized political and religious groups, counter-cultural movements, and certain interpretations of the natural and social sciences.

Part III includes the ethnographic data derived from participant observation, dozens of informal interviews, and twenty-five in-depth interviews with thought leaders from religious, interfaith, and secular sustainability-oriented non-governmental organizations. Common threads that run between these disparate groups and their leaders included the idea that core values are an important consideration for any definition of sustainability. Further, many of the high level actors interviewed expressed the importance of approaching their work and particularly the core values of people from disparate constituencies, with humility—what I have called here an ethic of personal risk.

The final chapter offers some reflections on where these widely varied social movements are headed, and offers some areas in which further investigation could prove fruitful. Readers interested primarily in the historical development of sustainability and sustainable development will likely find Parts I and II most helpful. Those who are interested in the ethnographic data would be well served to focus on Parts II and III. Although each part includes novel contributions to the discourse, my hope is that the thread that runs through them helps to clarify why it is important *not* to decide on a particular definition of sustainability before beginning work toward sustainable political and social processes. Indeed, it is through such processes that the meanings of sustainability endorsed by particular people and groups are clarified. Moreover, transparent, inclusive, and deliberative analyses of what sustainability means in specific circumstances can help to cultivate the ability to acknowledge, honor, and hold up for scrutiny the core values of others, an approach that I suggest could be bioculturally adaptive. In the end, sustainability is not a goal or end-point, but something closer to a process of community discernment, and a strategy for engaging with others who do not share the same values or vision of the future. For posterity's sake, my hope is that we are up to the challenge of rethinking sustainability.

DEFINING RELIGION AND SUSTAINABILITY, AND WHY IT MATTERS

Part I offers a brief description of trends that are widely considered unsustainable, and then relates them to analyses of the religious and spiritual dimensions of social movements related to correcting these trends. The academic background for the ethnographic portion of the study is explained, including some of the intellectual tributaries that influenced the method utilized. In addition, some of the common themes that emerged from the ethnography are discussed in greater detail to frame the following chapters on defining the key terms, and finding religion in social movements that are not obviously *all about* religion. Some of the key metaphors and tropes used to advertise sustainability in the public sphere are detailed with an eye to how these highly affective concepts are transmitted through and across cultures.

These first three chapters which comprise Part I are intended to lay the groundwork for the historical and ethnographic work that follows. They also, however, offer some novel contributions. Specifically, a new definition of sustainability, which highlights its religious dimensions and the ways in which it is inextricably tied to broader cultural trends, is offered. The definition of religion utilized in this study, while drawing on earlier scholars, extends their analyses to paint a picture of the ways in which rich and multifaceted terms such as sustainability and religion can be a sort of productive social therapy. Finally, the theoretical approach detailed in Chapter 3 also draws on existing scholarship, but offers a robust portrait of the individual nested within several communities of accountability. While the analysis contained here focuses primarily on scales beyond the individual, the model could provide a possible starting point for further empirical research on the ways in which values relevant to individuals and communities, which operate at various scales, can be fruitfully explored.

CHAPTER ONE

THE STAKES OF SUSTAINABILITY AND ITS RELIGIOUS DIMENSIONS

It is not uncommon in popular media to trace the first inklings of environmental activism to the first photos of earth from space and the accompanying realization that we live on a finite and fragile planet. Many have drawn inspiration from the accounts of astronauts such as Edgar Mitchell ("My view of our planet was a glimpse of divinity"), Alexi Leonov ("The Earth was small, light blue, and so touchingly alone, our home that must be defended like a holy relic"), and James Irwin ("That beautiful, warm, living object looked so fragile, so delicate, that if you touched it with a finger it would crumble and fall apart. Seeing this has to change a man, has to make a man appreciate the creation of God and the love of God") (Kelley [1988] 1991: 24, 52, 38). It is perhaps no coincidence that the first Earth Day celebration in 1970 followed closely on the heels of these first forays into space.

Awareness of environmental scarcity, however, far predates the first space explorations or the counter-cultural environmental movements of the late twentieth century. By the first Earth Day it had long been clear that human cultures were on an unsustainable course. In the postwar period the growth of the interstate system and urban planning schemes built around this new individualized form of transportation had contributed significant amounts of carbon to the atmosphere. Industrial capacity continued to grow exponentially, while the international concern with development allowed increasingly global economic markets access to more resources and labor, and promoted the growth of multinational corporations who possessed the rights of citizens with none of the concomitant obligations. In the 1970s, the term sustainable development was forged as a euphemism for attempts to mitigate these dramatic shifts. By the 1980s such activities were correlated with shifting climatic trends and a dramatically widening gap between the rich and the poor.

At this writing the world population has passed 7,000 million humans, approximately one third of whom suffer from hunger and malnutrition and about one half of which live below the poverty level. Globally wealth inequality continues to increase both in the developing world and within industrialized economies. To illustrate, according to the Gini coefficient (a measure of income disparity) the US ranks 100th out of 140 nations in income inequality, just below Iran and just above Jamaica, Mozambique, and Rwanda. The United Kingdom ranks forty-sixth, while the European Union comes in at twenty-fourth.[1] Meanwhile, an emerging middle class in developing economies such as India and China is driving increased consumption and production of many commodities. Take for example meat production, which has tripled worldwide in the past forty years, and grown 20 per cent in the past ten years alone, creating significant environmental problems related to habitat fragmentation and waste disposal.[2] These emerging economies have literally millions of people making the transition from extreme energy poverty to new energy consumption, while the primary mode of energy production remains the use of fossil fuels, pointing toward worsening ecological ramifications.

The ecological impacts of the prevailing economic and social development policies are well documented, and include the disruption of planetary cycles (i.e. the nitrogen and carbon cycles [Vitousek 1994; Vitousek et al. 1997]) and the radical simplification of biocultural diversity. Most scientists would agree that species are disappearing at a rate at least 1,000 (and some have speculated as high as 10,000) times faster than the background extinction rate. Globally there is a strong correlation between biological and cultural diversity, and as biodiversity is being eroded, so are the traditional cultures that have depended on this natural variety. Cultural groups, their languages and knowledge of their habitats, including various medicinal plants and practices, are also vanishing. The twenty-first century will continue to be characterized by increasingly frequent conflicts over increasingly scarce resources, particularly if societies continue to depend on solving energy poverty with finite reserves of fossil fuels that have only grown more difficult to access, secure, and protect.

These trends are the very definition of unsustainability. Beginning with the first scientific resource management regimes over two hundred years ago, however, several loosely related social movements related to generating more sustainable societies emerged and continue to grow and diversify. As illustrated below, social movements and programs designed for sustainability or sustainable development have from their earliest manifestations been used to channel economic relations, maintain social control, and exert political will. "Like 'motherhood' and 'God,'" the environmental policy expert Michael Redclift notes, "sustainable development is invoked by different groups of people in support of various projects and goals, both abstract and concrete" (in Ghai & Vivian 1992: 25).

Much like the astronauts quoted above, who gained new perspectives on humanity's place in the cosmos, Redclift illustrates that sustainability is increasingly tied to spiritual and highly affective modes of communication in the public sphere. Indeed, as the public intellectual Stephen Prothero argued, "religion is now emerging alongside race, gender, and ethnicity as one of the key identity markers of the twenty-first century" (Prothero 2007: 7). The concept of *sustainability* is also emerging as a popular term that in some cases acts as an identity marker, often used as a shorthand reference to a complex set of socio-politico-economic problems and possible solutions. As sustainability expert and educator Andrés Edwards put it, sustainability is linguistic shorthand that links "the central issues confronting our civilization" (Edwards 2005: 133). In what follows I explore these two contested twenty-first century identity markers: religion and sustainability.[3]

WHAT IS USUALLY MISSING FROM THE DISCOURSE: THE RELIGIOUS DIMENSIONS OF SUSTAINABILITY

Most treatments of sustainability begin by defining what the term means. Some of these definitions of sustainability describe particular approaches to development (WCED 1987), represent alternatives to existing development practices and socio-political arrangements (Sumner 2005; Hawken 2007a), or suggest that sustainability is best measured in terms of empirical data such as biodiversity (Patten 2000; Lovejoy 2002). Development-related definitions, however, too often pay inadequate attention to existing global power imbalances. Counter-hegemonic definitions can make the mistake of dismissing or downplaying the power of nation states to promote social change, a presupposition that, as policy experts Michael Kenny and James Meadowcroft put it, is "rather short-sighted politically, and suspect intellectually" (Kenny & Meadowcroft 1999: 2). Finally, scientific definitions, which often offer preservation of biodiversity or other scientific measurements as central to sustainability, may simply shift the locus of power from nation states and corporate elites to the scientific "experts" who can design and implement policy in a values vacuum.

Such definitions provide narrow lenses through which it may be difficult to see and account for sustainable living arrangements that depend on locally adapted (and historically situated) knowledges, or non-economic variables. In part, this is because these definitions of sustainability, it turns out, have very little to do with what is actually sustainable in particular situations. Disputing such simplistic understandings of sustainability, indigenous activists and scholars and even development entities such as the World Bank and the United Nations have encouraged the investigation of alternative sources of knowledge and locally adaptive social norms, and their application in international agreements. Disciplines such as ethnobotany, ethnobiology, and activist forms of anthropology emerged, at least in theory, from the recognition that the native eye did not see a positive vision in the Western versions of sustainable development.

Counter to these approaches, I will suggest that in some cases sustainability has become a term that mediates a brokering process between different constituencies, their epistemologies, and their visions of the good life. As the anthropologist Scott Atran put it, "Environmental management increasingly involves diverse groups with distinctive views of nature. Understanding the ways in which local cultural boundaries are permeable to the diffusion of relevant knowledge may offer clues to success with more global, multicultural commons" (Atran *et al.* 2002: 422). Sustainability should be imagined as a positive term forged to broker relationships between and across these cultural boundaries and their accompanying views and uses of nature.

Thus, energies expended defining sustainability (WCED 1987; Baker 2006), discerning some so-called central principles (Dresner 2005), or elucidating its foundational ethical tenets should instead be directed at understanding the core values of those who use the term, and the reasons for which it is deployed. Although it has received little attention, this religious dimension, strongly related to core values of particular constituencies, has long been a pervasive feature of sustainability discourse. Moreover, these underlying values, which are often a prominent feature of the religious dimensions of sustainability, are in some cases important to producing successful policy outcomes. But in all cases, to the extent that it acts as a tool for connecting affective states with political issues related to resource utilization, sustainability acts as a political religion.[4]

This is important because rather than creating intractable disputes, religious people and groups, as well as those who generate the more diffuse religious ambiance of much sustainability discourse, have in some cases inspired what I refer to as an ethic of personal risk, which may be an adaptive "meme" to promote.[5] Such an approach entails viewing political, social, or cultural "others" from a standpoint of humility, vulnerable to (or at least willing to empathetically consider) others' worldviews, values, and behaviors. Toward the end of the book the narrative shifts from a descriptive to a normative mode, arguing that when used appropriately such tactics can facilitate sustainable relationships between people with different values, increasing chances of long-term success for some sustainability ventures. Sustainability advocates, in other words, should pay attention to the strategies pioneered by religious groups and secular sustainability advocates who use highly affective and loosely spiritual language. Encouraging an ethic of interpersonal and intercultural risk can be bioculturally adaptive by promoting the peaceful co-existence of cultures and societies even when they differ in their core value commitments.

BACKGROUND AND COMMON THEMES THAT EMERGED FROM THE ETHNOGRAPHY

To gather data I utilized a combination of ethnographic and historical research methods, focusing specifically on a network of actors who occupied high level positions in various sustainability movements, with the aim of comparing the use of religious discourse among religious and secular groups.

The focus here, the *sustainability milieu*, is characterized by a human-centered ethos, the recognition of biological, ecological, or cosmological interdependence, and an ethic of personal empathy, or risk. So the unit of analysis—the sustainability milieu—was no doubt significantly influenced by environmentalism, although it has become a broader and more inclusive sub-population than the environmentalist milieu. The methodology exercised here, however, investigating a particular expert network and analysis of the manner in which they transmit the central themes related to the religious dimensions of sustainability, is rather narrow, and is not intended as an exhaustive study of the remarkable breadth of the sustainability milieu.

The inspiration for this research emerged from my perception of parallel questions (although not yet research convergences) among the methods or theoretical approaches of three distinct academic disciplines. (a) In sustainability studies literature, I noted the contested usefulness of the term. Some believed that sustainability was always counter-hegemonic (Sumner 2005; Hawken 2007a); others noted that the term could be used to generate the illusion of consensus while preserving the status quo (Davison 2001); some thought it was specifically about a set of principles and requisite duties (Dresner 2005); still others thought the term ought to be jettisoned altogether. (b) The attention of cultural anthropologists to sustainable development programs has made traditional ecological knowledge an important topic in global sustainability discourse. Yet, questions are continuously raised about whether these programs actually benefit the people they meant to help (Escobar 1995). Little attention, however, has been paid to the differences between what specific sets of citizens mean when they use the terms sustainability and sustainable development. (c) Religious studies scholars have increasingly been turning toward a methodology that was articulated in the 1990s as the study of "lived religion." This approach to understanding religious life was "radically empiricist," meant to correct a bias in religious studies toward analysis of texts and institutions (Orsi 1997: 8). This more empiricist approach to the analysis of religion-in-culture highlighted the contested and highly political nature of sacred symbols, ideas, and practices (Griffiths & Cervantes 1999; McCutcheon 2005; Wright 2009). The common thread in each of these sets of literature was a focus on contested, and highly affective concepts, and at least two of these approaches were related to long-term sustainable subsistence. Could an empiricist approach to contested ideas and practices be used to help clarify the confusion about the definitions, or usefulness of sustainability as a goal? My tentative answer is yes.

What follows analyzes the emerging sustainability metanarrative, which has manifested in a loosely related set of social phenomena and movements that resist the social, political, or economic status quo. However, added to these "alternative" socio-cultural models are important contributions to sustainability discourse from mainstream corporations and government sectors, who do *not* represent alternatives to the prevailing socio-political arrangements, and who also utilize the discourse of sustainability to describe their own socio-political agendas, and core missions.

Specifically I investigated one particular network of experts spanning religious, interfaith, and secular NGOs located within the United States and western Europe (although in some cases their work is global in scope), noting the religious dimensions of their activism, seeking to understand the sources of religious themes in their public discourse, and tracing how they are used by different groups. The empirical data cited in this study as evidence of the religious dimensions of sustainability includes:

(a) the endorsement of environmentalist aims by some organized religions, and the parallel activities or behaviors in which sustainability advocates and religious adherents engage (i.e. feeding the poor, protecting endangered ecosystems, concern with social justice, etc.);

(b) political leaders' use of religious language in discussing the environment (i.e. the idea that nature is somehow sacred);

(c) scientists' use of language or metaphors related to the sacred to describe their own work or findings;

13

(d)   the opposition by religious adherents and sustainability advocates to capitalism and modernism;

(e)   secular conservation groups' outreach to religious organizations;

(f)   the popularization of spiritualized sustainability-related narratives; and

(g)   the perceptible shift, at least among some demographic sectors in North American and western European societies, toward lifestyles and practices that are more "sustainable" (for example the LOHAS[6] segment of the population, a now widely recognized and powerful consumer group).

To conclude, Chapter 10 provides an analysis of how different theories of individual action in relation to environmental degradation can be integrated into a useful methodological tool for investigating social movements with religious dimensions.

Common themes

Although nearly all of the informants emphasized that the values necessary for achieving a sustainable society were locally-dependent, there were two general commonalities among the themes that ran through the reports of sustainability advocates, one conceptual, and one methodological. First, most resonated with the idea that they possessed a profoundly affective (that is, emotionally evocative) affinity for biological, ecological, or cosmological interdependence. In these cases, the moral sensibilities of these sustainability leaders were informed by this emotively charged affinity. The promotion of amorphous ideas of interconnectedness has been criticized by some scholars who suggest that they are overly romantic, inapplicable to whole populations or sets of religious believers, or obfuscate human exploitation of ecosystem services (see for instance Kalland 2005: 1368–9). Nonetheless, they are frequently used to describe sustainability in the public sphere and should therefore be scrutinized.

Another central idea commonly expressed by sustainability advocates was the importance of translating sustainability-oriented narratives between differing constituencies. In other words, many of the sustainability leaders emphasized the need to approach political, social, or cultural "others" from a standpoint of humility, vulnerable (or at least willing to empathetically consider) others' worldviews, values, and behaviors. This is what I refer to throughout as an ethic of personal risk. An ethic of personal risk is typically focused on engagement between individuals and constituencies regarding their respective central values, motivations, and perceived future goals with the understanding that both sides undertake some sort of risk. This risk might refer to accepting challenges to personal or communal worldviews, production and consumption habits, or social arrangements. I envision this ethic as similar in certain ways to Sharon Welch's "feminist ethic of risk" (Welch 1990), sharing with her vision the notion that engagement with "others" requires relinquishing power over them to some extent, that an ethic of risk is grounded in community, and that the risks taken are strategic (for Welch's definition see 1990: 20). Welch, however, suggests that such engagement is always ultimately grounded in an ethic of resistance. In the cases examined here such an ethic may be undertaken by those in power in an effort to cede power to "others" in a spirit of cooperation. Or on the other hand, it may be used to solidify existing social and economic inequalities.

Sources of language for deploying sustainability themes in the public sphere

The language, metaphor, and imagery utilized when these common themes were deployed in the public sphere generally derived from one of three sources: (a) contributions to sustainability discourse from existing religious groups as well as international political bodies who formulate spiritually-grounded global sustainability ethics (see Chapter 4); (b) contributions from the natural sciences; and (c) the social sciences (see Chapter 5). The messages derived from these sources are vetted and translated within various sustainability-related social movements.

Interestingly, there was some consensus among my respondents regarding the manner in which such religious narratives were expressed. First, the values associated with sustainability are coded into narratives and used strategically to intentionally modify behavior, perception, and policy. Second, nearly all of the central informants believed that core values were of utmost importance to good policy-making (challenging the post-metaphysical social scientific methodology suggested by Norton). Third, at least among the small network of actors analyzed here, telling good stories—about successes and valiant efforts—seemed to be an important and prevalent component in the transmission of the values related to sustainability and the long-term viability of on-the-ground projects. These value-laden stories contribute to the cultivation of a religious metanarrative of sustainability, often grounded in an optimistic, empathetic anthropocentrism. In effect, these stories act as discursive devices, or cognitive tools for the spread of normative sustainability-related ideas.

Transmission of sustainability narratives

Reviewing the transmission of these narrative-grounded cognitive tools, it is clear that they are primarily passed from individual to individual, and that leaders in various sustainability movements (the targets of this fieldwork) are some of the primary "evangelists" who spread the sustainability metanarrative. Such stories are exchanged between subcultures of resistance and mainstream culture, between grassroots-level groups and international organizations, and between religious and secular groups (these themes are more fully developed in Chapters 3, 4, 5, and 8). Tracing some of the networks through which these values-laden stories are transmitted helps to illuminate the *religious work* that such terms are performing by negotiating identity and "forming community, focusing desire, and facilitating exchange" (Chidester 2005a: 18). Even when the language of sustainability advocacy is not explicitly religious, in many cases it reflects core values and deep beliefs of particular individuals, communities, or groups, and when deployed in the public sphere, it is performing religious work.

To unpack the religious dimensions of sustainability, I first have to wrestle with the key terms, religion and sustainability (Chapter 2), and then trace the sources of language used to characterize sustainability in the public sphere (Chapters 4, 5, and 6). I later focus on interviews with elite actors in the NGOs listed in Table 1.1.

Table 1.1 Categories of NGOs examined in this research.

	Religious	Interfaith	Secular
International	Evangelical Environmental Network	Alliance of Religions and Conservation	Conservation International
			Natural Capitalism Solutions
Grassroots/local	Northland Church (Longwood, FL)	Interfaith Power and Light	Northwest Earth Institute

Each of these organizations and the individuals who lead them utilize religious narratives (at least as religion is defined here) in the public sphere in order to further their understanding of sustainability. Despite differences among interviewees regarding the perceived utility of the term "sustainability," such religious values and narratives seem to be present and in many cases important across these various sustainability-oriented constituencies.

CHAPTER TWO

DEFINING THE TERMS: RELIGION AND SUSTAINABILITY

INTRODUCTION

Do terms such as "sustainability" or "religion" lose some of their usefulness if their boundaries are conceived as broad, permeable, and imprecise? No, and on the contrary, their analytic utility expands if defined broadly because deployments of such terms shed light on why a particular set of beliefs, values, or behaviors matters to particular persons. I am specifically interested here in how religion functions in the context of sustainability.

Sustainability is a strategy of cultural adaptation to the dynamic interplay between ecological and social systems that is often tethered to broad-scale narratives that elucidate how to make such survival strategies *meaningful*. Thus, the deployment of sustainability can be a socio-political identity marker since it refers to what it is those who use the term believe is required to live meaningfully over the long term. Spirituality, broadly defined, has been a crucial ingredient in the feedback loops between cultures and their environments historically, and there is some evidence (although debatable) that its inclusion in ecosystem management planning is important for long-term success. Rather than excluding religion from the policy formulation process, it may be more productive to channel its affective power into a more robust reflective phase of policy deliberation. To understand how exercising religious concepts in the public sphere can act as a sort of social therapy, it is necessary to clarify what is meant by the term religion.

USING RELIGION AS A MULTIFACETED, THERAPEUTIC TOOL

Analysis of how religion functions within sustainability movements may be helpful because sustainability is a term that is often used as popular shorthand for referring to a widely variable set of core values and deep beliefs that those who deploy the term would like to see sustained over the long term. Clarifying which of these values is at stake in particular debates and policy decisions may help to generate more sustainable cultures. To begin to understand how religious values inform visions of sustainability it is necessary to gain some clarity regarding what exactly is meant by "religion." Religion has two modes of expression within sustainability movements: (a) it takes the shape of formal, institutionalized religious structures and their members who advocate (and implement) sustainable practices; and (b) it is expressed in various evocations of a "new" ethic, a different concept of the place of humans in the natural world, or alternative model of society. Each of these is considered "new" to the extent that it provides an alternative to traditional development-oriented definitions of sustainability (which are often revealed to promote increasing inequity and ecological degradation), or to the prevailing (and typically loosely defined) paradigm of modernity (which constructs binary oppositions, mechanistic portraits of nature and human nature, and speaks of reality in terms of universals). For examples of this critique of modernity see Merchant (1980), Capra ([1975] 1984), T. M. Berry (1988), and Garè (1998), all of which influenced various sustainability movements. To the extent that these cultural sustainability narratives draw on the language of core values and deep beliefs and trigger emotive responses in people, they are doing religious and political work. Using the analytical term *religious* to describe an often overlooked dimension of sustainability helps to provide a richer assessment of some facets of sustainability movements.

Religion as a non-essentialist, multi-factorial category

Religion, at least within sustainability movements, functions as a multifaceted tool. The way religion is understood and used by particular people in particular places to describe their actions and motivations reveals something about what they hold sacred.[1] When religious metaphor and language are utilized in the public sphere, they chip out sharper portraits of individual and community identity. All invocations of religion, as the religion scholar Russell McCutcheon argued, erect or perpetuate oppositions (i.e. profane/sacred, irreligion/religion, insider/outsider). He noted that such conceptual binaries are useful, but can cause trouble if "understood as normative, self-evident, and naturally privileged rather than as strategically, intellectually, and socially useful" (McCutcheon 1997: 66). The anthropologist Benson Saler made the similar point that religion is instrumental in generating and sustaining community, but in so doing it simultaneously places others outside of that community, however conceived (Saler 1993: 74). Jonathan Benthall concurred when he argued that "the definition of religion is political. It is a legitimating claim, a discursive strategy" (Benthall 2008: 8). Religion, in other words, has no essential element that marks it off as morally significant and spiritually relevant. It is a tactical term used to describe deeply seated values and beliefs and mark them off from others' values, but is also now used to refer to the study of these socio-political dynamics in the academy.

For example, Jonathan Z. Smith investigated the history of the term in academic usage, influentially arguing "'religion' is not a native term; it is a term created by scholars for their intellectual purposes and therefore it is theirs to define" (Smith 1998: 281; see also Smith 1988: 233). Smith meant that rather than a self-evident term self-applied by all communities to describe their rituals, beliefs, and practices, religion should instead be viewed as an analytical term whose meaning depends on the person (or community) using it, and on the questions they use the term to illuminate.[2] As McCutcheon understands Smith's meaning, religion "is part of the data to be explained because as they are commonly defined religious discourses remove something (a claim, an institution, a practice) from history, thereby privileging it over all other historically embedded claims and knowledges" (McCutcheon 2001: 136). According to Smith and McCutcheon religion is not a native term, because its use isolates and authenticates certain practices or features of culture as religious without due recognition that what counts in this category depends upon a particular understanding of the prototypical features of *religion*. These prototypical features, which cast boundaries around what is included in the category "religious," have derived from particularly Western ideas which are not always applicable to the spiritual lives of cultural others.

In other respects then, religion *is* a native term—it is native to Western culture. The term is also used widely now by those outside Western culture, in many cases by people and groups who have adopted it to refer to certain cultural phenomena for the purpose of engaging in cross-cultural dialogue. So while the term is not native to most indigenous peoples, for example, they have adapted it to reflect their own core values and deep beliefs for their own ends. Religion is neither a self-evident set of phenomena, nor a thing that *is* essentially this or that—and yet it is a term that carries tremendous political import, particularly among those for whom it is *not* a native term. Anthropologist Daniel Dubuisson argued:

Religion was intimately linked to the principal events and to the major orientations of our [Westerners'] intellectual history (when it was not literally identified with them) ... because it has contributed for centuries to the discipline of our bodies and our minds, because it has influenced the design and patterning of our cities, because it has cultivated our manner of looking at the world ... and because it has been put at the heart of the principal debates and controversies affecting the definition of humanity as well as the destiny of the world. *So religion, as outlined above, must be considered the locus in which the identity or figure of the West has in principle been constituted and defined.*

(Dubuisson 2003: 36–7, italics mine)

Tomoku Masuzawa's *The Invention of the World's Religions* (2005) advanced a related argument that the emergence of the "comparative religion" research program (made famous by Mircea Eliade, but whose origin lies with the fathers of the social sciences[3]) grew from the cultivation of Western power in the colonial and post-colonial eras. The appearance of the "world's religions," while seemingly a solid step toward pluralism "neither displaced nor disabled the logic of European hegemony—formerly couched in the language of the universality of Christianity—but, in a way, gave it a new lease" (Masuzawa 2005: xiv).

Some scholars who have noted the colonialist roots of the term "religion" may underestimate the agency of those impacted by the imposition of religions, who have intentionally and strategically adopted, adapted, and redeployed the term religion and related religious practices for their own ends. Nonetheless, the points reviewed here are important: religious discourse builds boundaries, facilitates the formation of community, and reflects values and beliefs that are tied in significant ways to cultural mores and behaviors.

Thus, religion is strategically, intellectually, and socially useful in several contexts, both for Westerners and non-Westerners who have adapted the term as a means of explaining their lifeways to others. Some religious studies scholars have adopted a methodology less indebted to exploring what people *believe* than to noting what people *do* with their religious categories. Russell McCutcheon's response to an audience question at a conference is illustrative: following his presentation he was asked whether he meant that religion was "*also* social, biological, political, economic, and so on, or whether [McCutcheon] was saying that religion was *only* social, biological, political, economic, and so on." McCutcheon's answer: "Only. Next question?" (McCutcheon 2001: x). McCutcheon may have been unduly provocative in his response, but his point is significant: that for scholars of religion (not caretakers of the term) analysis should focus not on supposed internal subjective states and beliefs, but on the effects that these beliefs, values, and practices have (through their believers) in the real world. The focus should be *on* their behaviors, and their self-reported (either in print, or in person) values rather than on evaluating *a priori* assumptions.[4]

According to the above scholars, building a bounded definition of religion is less important than learning what it means for particular people.[5] Many have used the term religion to refer to institutional manifestations of religion (those confined by buildings and traditions), as well as more commonplace and everyday experiences of affectively grounded communion with others (even, as religion scholar David Chidester has [2005a], referring to baseball or live music performance). In this broad and porously bounded category of religion, all of these uses of the term "count." As Saler put it, "if we deem admission to a group (as comprehended by the category religion) to be a matter of 'more or less' rather than a matter of 'yes or no,' then an argument can be made for admitting 'secular religions' and 'quasi-religions' as peripheral members" (Saler 2004: 230).[6] Many different communities to which individuals are accountable have religion-resembling features, although none of these particular features is alone *necessary* to trigger the use of the term religion.[7]

Drawing on the above scholars, it is possible to envision the term religion as referring to a host of often overlapping and cross-fertilizing *families* of religious practice, experience, and function. Saler suggested that the term "religion" is an instance of what Wittgenstein called a "concept-word" (Saler 1993: 197; Benthall 2008: 46–80; see also Vasquez 2008).[8] Envisioning "religion" as a concept-word means that it can act as an analytical tool, referring to pools of elements that tend to cluster together in different ways, and which typically are also strongly related to other things that are not religious (Saler 1993: 213). Conceptualizing religion in this way "facilitates going beyond religion [as synonymous with institutional practice and creed] and attending to 'the religious dimension' of much of human life" (214).[9] Religion is intimately intertwined with many facets of human lives that are not themselves essentially or explicitly religious, including sustainability advocacy and conservation behaviors, both of which figure prominently in this research.

Religion as a therapeutic concept

If several of the varied sets of characteristics referred to as religious ought to "count," from "classic" definitions of religion formulated by Friedrich

Schleiermacher ([1799] 1996), Max Müller ([1870] 2002), E. B. Tylor (1871), James Frazer ([1890] 1959), Emile Durkheim ([1912] 1995), Max Weber ([1930] 2005), William James ([1902] 2002), Rudolph Otto (1958), Mircea Eliade (1959), Clifford Geertz (1973), Stewart Guthrie (1993), and Talal Asad (1993), to some newer ones (Saler 1993; Benthall 2006, 2008; Taylor 2010), this allows analysis of a wider range of social phenomena with a religious studies lens than would otherwise be the case. It is possible, for example, to attend to the "religious dimensions," of social movements while withholding judgement about where they fall on the "more to less religious" continuum. Envisioning religion as a pool of loosely related elements allows analysis of how the religious dimensions of social movements help to forge community, facilitate exchange, and focus desire (Chidester 2005a).

For Wittgenstein, concept-words were not important simply because of their flexibility, but because this flexibility allowed for their therapeutic deployment in language games. Wittgenstein thought such games helped to prevent the "freezing" of language by facilitating new relationships between concept-words.[10] For Wittgenstein, "Philosophy is a battle against the bewitchment of our intelligence by means of our language" (Wittgenstein [1953] 2001: 109).[11] Philosophy and language-games are tools for interpreting perceptions and adapting behaviors to the worlds humans find themselves thrown into, a task with which religion is also concerned (Orsi 1997: 8). It is important that scholars in several disciplines who examine religion expand their definition to include many families of religion-resembling activity, but it is perhaps more important that they recognize *which ones* are being deployed by *which groups* for *what ends*. For it is in and around the worded nodes of language-games that language becomes "part of an activity, or of a life-form" (Wittgenstein [1953] 2001: 23). It is in these creative zones that old understandings of words and language are challenged and new ones forged precisely because of the elasticity of meaning in such language.

Parallel to the discussion of how to approach sustainability below, treating the term religion as an element in a cultural (or cross-cultural) language-game can turn critical attention on the ways in which the deployment of such terms (religion and sustainability) create and sustain (or challenge and erode) socio-political relations. In cases where the religious dimensions of sustainability are involved, language-games can really be said to grow into what the anthropologist Scott Atran and his collaborators referred to as "spiritual games," where cultural mores are "played with" and massaged into new meanings for particular communities of accountability. In the cases examined by Atran *et al.*, "players" in spiritual games include the non-economic values of ecological services, social relations, and non-human subjectivities, all of which provide valuable inputs into individual and collective decision-making (Atran *et al.* 2002; see also Benthall 2008: 50–51).[12] The employment of the affective power of religion-resembling cultural features in the name of sustainability can be a therapeutic tool for negotiating identity, community, and belonging in democratic societies. It is from deployments in particular circumstances that any term takes its meaning, and in turn adds layers of meaning to its future uses.[13] Fundamentally, religion, somewhat like sustainability, is about dealing with cultural, ethnic, and ethical "others" in effective ways.[14] Typically, it is by risking something of themselves (not necessarily personally, but on the level of community norms and values) that people are able to achieve success in sustainability through partnership.

For analytical purposes here, then, religion will serve dual roles as it does in folk understandings of the term (Johnson 1993; Benthall 2008: 7–9). On the one hand, it will be used to refer to institutional religions, their authoritative hierarchies, traditions, practices and places. The so-called "world religions" have undoubtedly played a major role in sustainability discourse, and their reach attests to the social and financial pressures they have brought to bear on promoting sustainable practices. On the other hand, the term religion will also describe the growth of religiously tinged sustainability-oriented material culture, spiritual narratives of individual and group experiences, and the use of religious metaphor and ideation in communications between specific communities of accountability and outside groups. Through the interplay of these two modes of religious expression, a third sort of religious production emerges, couched in the metanarrative of sustainability. Simply defined, a metanarrative is a story that justifies another story. The metanarrative of sustainability (conceived of in various ways by different constituencies) acts as a benchmark against which other cultural "stories" can be weighed, for it is within the sustainability metanarrative that these cultural stories are set in the context of the ecological matrix upon which they depend. Analysis of the transfer of religious messages through and across various constituencies, from subcultures of resistance to international political and economic regimes, uncovers something interesting about sustainability movements: they cultivate as an integral part of their sustenance affective and often religious language and metaphor. As will become clearer below, religious language, metaphor, and motivations are the medium through which different constituencies communicate their understanding of their own group-specific values. Thus, analysis of the religious dimensions of sustainability also reveals something interesting about the people who participate in sustainability initiatives.

A better understanding of the religious dimensions of sustainability discourse is a worthwhile endeavor because it can open a window into the diverse underlying values that motivate various groups. Just as the analytical utility of the term religion is maximized by defining it broadly, sustainability—the other important variable under discussion—is best imagined as a flexible and widely variable concept.

SUSTAINABILITY IN THREE DIMENSIONS

There are three common elements that most existing definitions of sustainability typically include: the ecological/environmental dimension, the social equity/justice dimension, and the economic/capital dimension. By way of example, note the ecologists Robert Costanza and Carl Folke's broad goals for sustainably managed ecosystems:

1. ensuring that the scale of human activities within the biosphere is *ecologically sustainable*;
2. *distributing* resources and property rights *fairly*, both within the current generation and for future generations, and between this generation and other species;
3. *efficiently* allocating resources as constrained and defined by numbers 1 and 2 above (1997: 49–50).

Costanza and Folke's concise statement of goals provides one example of how the three dimensions of sustainability are typically deployed together. Educator Andrés Edwards likewise reviews the "three E's" of sustainability: (1) ecology/environment; (2) equity/equality; and (3) economy/employment (Edwards 2005: 21–2).[15] He adds another "E" for "education," but he also acknowledges the centrality of these three "pillars of sustainability," as they are commonly portrayed today.

Separating the idea of sustainability into three dimensions is somewhat artificial (and is often exposed as such when applied to specific real-world situations). But these dimensions can act as valuable heuristic devices for discerning the various streams of sustainability advocacy at work today among the global citizenry and the values that underlie them. Rather than imagining these as discrete, or separate "compartments" for sustainability, perhaps it is more helpful to say that when all three dimensions (regardless of whether they are prioritized or range in degree of importance) are present in a social movement, a community vision, a mission statement, a government policy, a building policy, a business plan, an educational curriculum or standard (or what-have-you), this is evidence of something related to the quest for sustainability.

SUSTAINABILITY IN FOUR DIMENSIONS

The working definition which guided my inquiries into and analysis of sustainability is this: Sustainability is a strategy of cultural adaptation to the limitations imposed by the dynamic interplay of ecological and social systems, couched in large-scale stories that illustrate how to persist within habitats in a manner that provides genuine affective fulfillment now, and for the foreseeable future. It is not merely subsisting within ecological limits. Sustainability cannot, and should not be described as a concrete goal to be "achieved." Rather, it is a conceptual device for connecting core (and often religious) values to community narratives, positing an ideal state toward which political processes, exchange activities, and social formations move. This definition connects the dots between the aforementioned three dimensions of sustainability, but also foregrounds the importance of a fourth dimension: the religious dimension.

As Edwards put it, sustainability discourse helped to unify, at both popular and official levels, four concerns:

> (1) an awareness of the profound spiritual links between human beings and the natural world; (2) a deep understanding of the biological interconnection of all parts of nature, including human beings; (3) an abiding concern with the potential damage of human impact on the environment; and (4) a strongly held commitment to make ethics an integral part of all environmental activism.   (Edwards 2005: 14–15)

Edwards suggested that these four concerns underlie, and manifest positively the "E's" of sustainability (detailed above). More importantly for this analysis, in a mainstream sustainability text whose intended audience included business people and educators the author attached spiritual values to a "deep interconnection" with nature and environmental activism, and suggested that these spiritual values are fundamental to the idea of sustainability. In fleshing out her definition of sustainability, the development expert Jennifer Sumner invoked the notion of interconnectedness and empathetic forms of knowing, saying that achieving sustainability is ultimately dependent upon collectively understanding what the Buddha said in his first sermon: "Everything depends for its origination on everything else at once and in unison" (Sumner 2005: 102). Paul Hawken also suggested that the movement is drawn forward by the "spiritual deeds" that inform and improve the moral imagination (Hawken 2007a: 188), in the end arguing that "what will guide us is a living intelligence that creates miracles every second" (190). These brief examples begin to illustrate the importance of more carefully identifying and characterizing the discursive and physical sites where religion is tied to sustainability. To unpack the claim that this fourth dimension is crucial to understanding sustainability it will be helpful to detail how some others have defined sustainability.

As noted above, there are several definitions of sustainability, the most well known of which describe particular approaches to development, or represent alternatives to them and to existing socio-political arrangements. Others have developed definitions that are either self-consciously adaptive, or that describe flexible sets of sustainability "principles" that can guide the search for sustainability over time (e.g. Norton 2003, 2005; Edwards 2005). These latter definitions have two advantages. First, they prioritize political processes, recognizing that the context and content of political delibera-tion may change over time. Second, such models acknowledge that norma-tive discernment derives from participation in particular communities of accountability, from the familial to the global.[16] These nested communities, to the extent that they offer up values for assessment and revision in the public sphere, contribute to the shape of the metanarrative of sustainability.

The philosopher Bryan Norton, for example, argued that "[sustain-ability's] meaning … is intimately tied to the values of the community that uses the term. This view is contrary of course, to that of economists and others who seek a 'purely descriptive' concept of sustainability" (Norton 2005: 386).[17] Norton offers what he calls a *schematic definition* of sustain-ability, which includes as foci four categories of "sustainability values": (1) community-procedural values; (2) weak sustainability (economic) values; (3) risk-avoidance values; and (4) community identity values (365–71). The first is concerned primarily with the political processes that allow appropri-ate values to be vetted for community analysis and revision. The second attends to economic assessments of values, acknowledging their importance for both human well-being and political traction. The third refers to creat-ing opportunities to increase social resilience when faced with external or internal disruptions. Finally, community identity values are those embraced by particular communities of accountability which are central to what it means to belong to that particular community. Such a schematic definition

> characterizes and relates the key components of a definition [of sustainability] while leaving specification of the substance to those components open. Speaking schematically, we can say that sustainability is *a relationship between generations such that the earlier generations fulfill their individual wants and needs so as not to destroy, or close off, important and valued options for future generations.* (Norton 2005: 363, italics in original)

The plurality of values that might be included in the categories above, Norton argued, include consumptive values, transformative and spiritual values and everything in between, and allows for their variation over space and time (Norton 2005: 373). Thus, filling in the content of these categories with specific (and locally dependent) values is an exercise in solidifying the identity of a particular community and supervising their exchange relations.[18] In short, Norton views sustainability as an active, pragmatic, and comprehensive (politico-socio-economic) philosophy of adaptive management.[19] A schematic definition depends on vague categories of values that by themselves neither exhaust the values invoked in sustainability advocacy, nor stand as *the* central values needed to achieve sustainability. They can instead be considered as nodes in a complex web of sustainability values, called on by different people for deployment in particular situations and times.

The provisional definition of sustainability I offered above resonates most with this adaptive, process-oriented definition with one important exception. For Norton, religious or spiritual values are included in his fourth category of "community identity values." Yet Norton's claim that language related to some community identity values should be confined within communities (and not vetted in the public sphere) is insufficient to account for the deeply affective and politically charged use of religious values in the public sphere. Thus, I am suggesting a fourth dimension be added to the traditional conception of the three dimensions of sustainability to acknowledge that at the very least religious values are important ingredients in defining and implementing sustainability. This religious dimension of sustainability reaches across the other three usually cited dimensions of sustainability, present and in many cases prevalent across sustainability discourses.

Depending on who deploys the term, sustainability may involve: caring for the poor, social advocacy, or civil disobedience; the creation of intentional communities, local purchasing and slow food movements, or back to the land movements; revising methods of economic exchange, micro-lending, or economic restructuring for lower throughputs; protecting indigenous rights, preserving languages, and cultural diversity; restoring denuded ecosystems, rescuing plant and animal regimes, and creating wildlife corridors; sharing cleaner technology and production techniques, alleviating food and water shortages, and planning for increased resilience in the face of future shortages; establishing fair labor laws, ensuring that such labor is meaningful and productive in particular habitats, and management of markets for the local good; encouraging more holistic and transdisciplinary educational arrangements, more sustainable administrative structures, and more ecologically and socially sensitive education, and a host of other activities that attempt to increase ecological, social, and exchange resilience. Institutionalized religious groups have been participants in or advocates of all of these activities, and some scholars have pointed to the spiritual dimensions of many of those that fall outside of the bounds of conventional religions (Taylor 1995; Daly [1973] 1980; Jordan 2003; Gould 2005; Wright 2007; Berkes ([1999] 2008, to name a few). None of these activities or groups is definitive of the sustainability movement, although they all work toward sustainability. These widely variable activities can all be envisioned as "families" of sustainability-related practices, and each has its own sets of values.

These are "fuzzy sets" of sustainability-related activity, distributions of things (concepts, ideas, or practices) that can be understood as belonging to the family of ideas and practices in the category of sustainability. Recalling Wittgenstein, members of a set may resemble more of the prototypical category features than others, but that hardly warrants making the claim that these attributes obtain across all items in that set.[20] The *use* of the term or concept itself is part of a language game—its deployment is partially constitutive of its unfolding meaning in particular situations (Wittgenstein [1953] 2001: 40).[21] Sustainability, then, is multi-factorial, encompassing many meanings with different histories and accompanying values. Identifying which values particular constituencies are invoking when they characterize themselves as involved in the quest for sustainability is the first step to understanding sustainability for that particular situation set.

This multi-factorial approach is productive in defining sustainability because it makes it possible to "see" sustainability in a number of social, economic, political, and other movements and programs, even where they are not explicitly *all about* sustainability (e.g. the Christian constituencies discussed in Chapter 7). This model also allows closer focus upon an element that I believe is significant in sustainability discourse: the importance of meta-ethical debate. As the policy experts Michael Kenny and James Meadowcroft have argued, most definitions of sustainability involve revisiting the "meta-objectives" of a given society, re-calibrating the social trajectory of the society by promoting some scenarios as more desirable and sustainable than others (Kenny & Meadowcroft 1999: 4). For Norton, this reorientation of societal goals occurs within his fourth category of sustainability values: community-identity values. Religious or spiritual values, Norton says, may be vetted within those particular communities, but cannot be reliably translated into the language of democratic politics. Indeed, for Norton, the whole point of focusing on political processes is to ensure that such subjective metaphysical commitments are not needed in formulating public policies that appease the democratic majority (interview 3, January 2008). But if value preferences are to play such an important role in the policy formulation process, why should the deeply felt sources of such preferences, religious values, and motivations, be excluded?[22]

The argument here is that such core values and deep beliefs are extremely important to a fully transparent policy formulation process, and that the moral austerity of environmental decision-making cannot be overcome without making these values foundations explicit. While Norton's analysis utilized hierarchy theory to account for communities of accountability at different scales he did not detail at what level "religious" or "metaphysical" beliefs and values should fall out of the mix of normative information included in adaptive political processes. For example, presumably it would be fine for individual and even family identity to be tied to core religious beliefs and values. But they should not, in Norton's account, play a part in the normative machinations of public policy formulation. One might ask: At what point do these normative, religious values become too cumbersome for an inclusive policy process? If sustainability is to be a long-term cultural project, these values require more attentiveness, and different communities of accountability require more practice at translating them into the public sphere.

Field work within sustainability movements and interviews with dozens of high level actors indicate that Kenny and Meadowcroft are correct: nearly all definitions of sustainability envision a reorientation of the "meta-objectives" of a society, whether it is a new ethic, an alternative anthropology, or a new vision of where humans stand in relation to the rest of the world or cosmos.[23] If this is indicative of these movements generally, then Norton's "community-identity values" may be too limited to characterize what people mean when they talk about a new approach to ethics. To imagine that the ripples of community values extend only within the bounds of a particular community is to miss the richly networked relationships among the various sustainability movements. In many cases insiders are pointing agreed-upon community values outward to critique the larger culture, and its social trajectory. These values, then, may be held by communities, but when they are displayed and dissected in the public eye they inevitably impact popular culture (whether doing so through challenging prevailing paradigms, or reinforcing them).

The fourth, religious dimension of sustainability becomes particularly important for the translation and transformation of values that occurs when different communities and their accompanying value preferences contact each other in political and social worlds. The importance of this additional dimension became increasingly apparent to me as I gathered qualitative data from people in various sustainability movements who cited their own individual and community values *as well as values arising outside their own communities* as generative of a new sort of moral imagination. Far from remaining hidden from the public eye, these are the value sets that should be presented and debated in the public sphere. The explicit claim here is that being honest about core values and deep beliefs in the public sphere can act as a sort of community therapy, invigorating the moral vacuum within which much political decision-making occurs.

This work neither defends the value of religion nor suggests that it is the most important ingredient in the quest toward sustainable societies. Rather, it highlights that people who attend to sustainability in various ways often ascribe their motivation for doing so to core values and deep beliefs, many times describing them in religious language. Thus, while I remain unconvinced that religion is or will be the key variable in motivating sustainable behaviors and lifeways, it is in many cases an important medium for the exchange of deeply held values between various constituencies (between subcultures of resistance and mainstream political bodies, for example).

With this background in place, after a theoretical interlude in Chapter 3, I will examine the development of the concept of sustainability and its intellectual foundations.

CHAPTER THREE

SUSTAINABILITY AS A CONTAGIOUS MEME

OPPOSITIONAL MILIEUS, RELIGION, AND CULTURAL TRANSMISSION

In 1972 philosopher Colin Campbell published a provocative essay about what he called the *cultic milieu* (Campbell 1972). His key insight was that different individuals and groups within oppositional subcultures engaged in a relatively free exchange of motivational metaphors and tropes, although they generally retained distinctive identities and sometimes even anti-thetical beliefs and goals.[1] An edited volume from religion scholars Jeffrey Kaplan and Helen Loow (2002) took up Campbell's idea, highlighting the impacts of increasing globalization on oppositional subcultures. Cults thrive, and freely exchange ideas, however, only within a cultural medium in which the dominant cultural milieu—either structurally, intellectually, or academically—facilitates the emergence of cults (Campbell 2002: 14).[2] Campbell's original analysis and Kaplan and Loow's book focused on par-ticularly rich eras in the emergence of alternative subcultures. In Kaplan and Loow's volume, Bron Taylor adapted Campbell's theory by postulating the existence of a global *environmentalist milieu*, which not only promoted information exchange between environmentalist subcultures but between such subcultures and mainstream individuals and institutions.[3] In a milieu where the characteristics and foci of cults adapt to specific socio-political circumstances, it would be expected that in an age of eco-crisis there would be increasingly strong environmentalist and anti-globalization activity, and hybridity among participants.

The sustainability milieu as a whole, however, is certainly not dark green in the sense that much of the environmentalist milieu is, and in some cases does not appear to be very green at all. Many sustainability advocates do

31

not consider themselves to be outdoor enthusiasts or advocates, and would not immediately or easily connect their understanding of nature to the ideas that the natural world contains intrinsic worth or sacred value. Yet many of these people would unhesitatingly use highly emotive normative or religious language to advocate nature preservation if it promoted their vision of sustainability.[4] Imagine the different constituencies that comprise the sustainability milieu as a series of concentric circles, moving from a dark green center, to light green, to light brown, to dark brown on the outside. The central dark green circle represents those who may resonate with some form of nature-as-sacred religion or ideas about the intrinsic value of nature.[5] Light green sustainability participants are those who, for example, recognize some correlation between social justice and ecological degradation, but who would not assent to the idea that nature itself is sacred or has intrinsic value. This light green group is not biocentric, but could be characterized as being weakly anthropocentric.[6] The light brown circle represents those sustainability advocates who frame their activism in purely human-centered terms (economic or social terms, for example) with little or no consideration of nature having "its own good" or of any human obligations to non-humans. Those outside the sustainability milieu dwell in the dark brown circle, which represents those who typically do not support the central aims of sustainability or have affinity for those who reside within the other portions of the diagram. The sustainability milieu, generally speaking, retains a *human-centered* ethos that focuses on empathetic negotiation and personal and interpersonal responsibility. The focus here on the sustainability milieu extends the above analyses and highlights the presence of similar themes even across groups perceived to be on opposite sides of the sustainability spectrum.

NETWORKS AND CULTURAL TRANSMISSION

The first stage of this research trajectory was an attempt to gather data about the religious language, metaphors, and motivational concepts employed by movement participants and supporters. To begin this inquiry, interviews were conducted with networks of experts from different sustainability-oriented groups. Each of them carries significant influence within their own organization (one of their primary communities of accountability). But they also interact with leaders from other groups, taking the experiences from these relationships back to their home communities. In so doing they are engaging in both religious and cultural production. Tracing these mutual influences it is possible to illustrate how these "coalitions of the unalike" make progress in the quest toward sustainability.[7]

To illustrate how such cultural transference occurs, the political scientist Paul Wapner has argued that environmentalism is a social movement that generates a global, civic politics that is "above the individual and below the state yet across national boundaries" (Wapner [1995] 2004: 125).[8] In order to understand the social changes initiated by environmental non-governmental organizations, he uses a fluid model of cultural production which (drawing on the sociologist Herbert Blumer) he says "interprets activist efforts by noticing and analyzing ... a 'cultural drift,' 'societal mood,' or 'public orientation' felt and expressed by people in diverse ways" (Wapner [1995] 2004: 125). Sustainability movements cross national boundaries and can also be imagined as contributing to a cultural drift or public orientation, and could thus be characterized with a fluid model. Religion scholar Thomas Tweed has proposed a fluid or "hydraulic" model of culture to describe the flows of religious beliefs and practices, which raises the possibility of whether such a parallel could point toward a theoretical convergence that might contribute to a social scientific analysis of the religious dimensions of sustainability. Sustainability discourse has become a venue for the global transmission of a variety of ideas and practices (including religious ones), and these flows beg for more detailed investigation.

Manuel Vasquez is another religion scholar who has noted that "religion has become both a conduit for global flows and a source of the 'scripts' that crisscross various spatial scales" (Vasquez 2008: 158).[9] Vasquez urged careful scrutiny of these flows of practices, institutions, and artifacts, which he rightly notes are tied to global commodities and financial exchange (156). Up to a point, Vasquez's treatment was in accord with Tweed's hydraulic model, but Vasquez cautioned that Tweed's analysis did not adequately attend to power dynamics within and between cultural groups. Vasquez proposed that envisioning these relations as networks helps to recognize the nodes where power dwells and the constrained possibilities that confront the agents and groups who are parts of networks. The use of network theory to describe environmentalism has a history, and like the fluid model of cultural transmission, it may be applied to the sustainability milieu also. For religion is integral to understanding the individual behaviors, social and political institutions, and the heterarchic exchange relations that are imagined as characterizing a sustainable global civilization.

For instance, the sociologist Luther Gerlach published on the character of environmentalist social movements beginning in 1970 (Gerlach & Hine 1970; Gerlach 1971, 2002), noting that the most common organizational structure was neither entirely fluid and amoebic, nor hierarchical and bureaucratic. Gerlach proposed the acronym "SPINs" (Segementary, Polycentric, Integrated Networks) to describe the most common structural features of these social phenomena. Such movements are segmentary because they are comprised of many diverse groups which grow, divide, die, fuse, and so on; polycentric because there are often multiple or competing leaders or centers of such movements; and networked because they form "a loose, reticulate, integrated network with multiple linkages through travelers, overlapping membership, joint activities, common reading matter, and shared ideals and opponents" (Gerlach 2002: 289–90). Gerlach argued that "movement participants are not only linked internally, but with other movements whose participants share attitudes and values" (296). This is evidenced in the relationships highlighted in the case studies presented in this volume, but the evidence gathered here further illustrates that movement participants are sometimes linked in various ways to others who *do not* share the same attitudes and values.

Vasquez rightly cautioned against imagining networks themselves as the primary agents of social transmission, although networks do act as channels that enable place-making activities and identity construction (Vasquez 2008: 168–9). Networked perceptual frameworks are constantly contested even at the *individual* level as agents make inferences and interpret experiences with their adapting cognitive tools (Benford and Snow 2000: 614). These individual agents are particularly important for the spread of sustainability-related values, since leaders of SPIN movements are particularly active in networking with participants from different groups.[10] It is these leaders who build "*personal relationships*" with participants in other groups, acting as "*traveling evangelists*" who carry information, practices, and motivational metaphors across the networks (Gerlach 2002: 296).[11] It is the basic beliefs and core values of social movements, referred to here as religious, that are transmitted across these networks.

The leaders of the particular organizations analyzed in this project are *intentionally facilitating the alignment of disparate values* through precisely the sort of charismatic interpersonal evangelization proposed by Gerlach above. More recent studies by environmental policy experts have focused on similar social phenomena, referring to intentional blending of discreet knowledge domains: "novel analogies in sustainability are those that align two partial domains of knowledge across one of these break points to form a third domain of knowledge, called the *blend*" (Hukkinen 2008: 65). Sustainability, according to environmental policy expert Janne Hukkinen, necessitates the promotion of socially robust knowledge (rather than knowledge that is merely scientifically reliable) for positive policy outcomes. Socially robust knowledge further requires experts capable of promoting cognitive blending of norms from constituencies that are differently situated socially and economically. Such perspectival alignment and cognitive blending processes both lead to the translation of values across different communities of accountability.

COLLECTIVE ACTION FRAMES AND MANUFACTURING MEANING

While social networks facilitate and promote the formation of the moral imagination in particular directions, individual agents within these net-works constantly make inferences about the practices and values that are and ought to be associated with these networks and are thus the primary vectors of social transmission. Groups within networks are socially and politically efficacious to the extent that their constituents frame the material and emotional experiences of their lives with a collective pool of interpre-tive schemata, which "enable individuals to 'locate, perceive, identify, and label' occurrences within their life space and the world at large" (Benford and Snow 2000: 614).[12] Extending this idea, the sociologists Robert Benford and David Snow suggested that movement participants construct *collective action frames* that motivate and legitimate particular activities.

According to sociologists who investigate such frames, social group par-ticipation is a form of active meaning construction through the enlargement of personal identity facilitated by a perceived correspondence between indi-vidual and collective identities. Benford and Snow also suggested, however, that insufficient attention has been given to the processes through which movement participation and identity are linked. Their work on frame-align-ment processes, they believe, has helped to elucidate the link. It is important to recognize that often such collective action frames are contested in the public sphere, with the aim of both sides of the debate to "shape ... ideologi-cal landscapes and societal practices" (Stern *et al.* 1999: 82). But ultimately, as Paul Stern *et al.* contended, "the base for general movement support lies in a conjunction of values, beliefs, and personal norms—feelings of per-sonal obligation that are linked to one's self-expectations" (83). The authors' point is that if participants accept the basic values of a particular movement (endorse their collective action frames), believe that one or more of these values are threatened, and perceive that there are social or political avenues through which personal action can help to minimize the damage to or restore those values, they are more likely to engage in practices to that end. Their findings support arguments for frame alignment and identity trans-formation, but suggest that lumping together the diverse values endorsed by activist and non-activist (but supportive) members of various social movements is unhelpful.[13] In short, they suggested that explicit renderings of the values that particular groups or movements endorse are crucial to discerning their mobilization strategies and their political aims (Stern *et al.* 1999: 91).

The spread of these *blended values* within and across particular groups can be "catching" (for example, as Joel Hunter indicates in Chapter 7). Namely they can spread from evangelizers to those who are in some way primed to receive their messages, whether because of shared values or practices, pre-existing sympathies with particular aims, personal relationships, or social or physical conditions. Gerlach's SPIN networks, as well as the frame-alignment and cognitive blending theories, each have resonances with cognitive anthropological theories that understand the transmission of "cultural facts" as parallel to the transmission of pathogens within populations. Integrating these theoretical models may provide a way to get better data about how values and practices are enacted and spread through social movements. Just as networks should not be imagined as possessing "agency," however, such collective action frames do not exist autonomously, but depend upon individual agents.

The inferences made and values encoded by individuals within particular movements, and then performed in the public sphere, should be the subjects of study. As Atran and his co-authors put it,

> People's mental representations interact with other people's mental representations to the extent that those representations can be *physically transmitted in a public medium* ... These public representations, in turn, are sequenced and channeled by ecological features of the external environment (including the social environment) that constrain psychophysical interactions between individuals.　　　　(Atran *et al.* 2005: 751, emphasis added)

Beginning with philosophical and social scientific explanations of social movements, and moving toward the psychological and cognitive explanations of social transmission within some sub-populations, an interdisciplinary theoretical framework for what motivates participation in some social movements emerges. The analysis has moved from large-scale social movement theory, to network theory (used in both environmental sciences and religious studies), noted how particular nodes (agents) engage in collective action framing and cognitive blending to solidify or challenge existing "powerscapes," and finally looked at the cognitive and subjective forces that influence cultural transmission. This moral anthropology of a "nested individual"[14] is non-reductive: it suggests that cultural phenomena are, as the anthropologist Dan Sperber put it, *ecological* patterns of psychological things, not merely subjective psychological facts. This model does not assume, however, that culture and the networks that comprise it are epiphenomenal or autonomous, with their own energy and capable of imposing particular values onto the minds of citizens.[15] In this, the theoretical framework offered here accords with what Anna Peterson has called a "chastened constructivism," admitting that socially constructed understandings of humans and their habitats impact beliefs and practices, but emphasizing that embodied beings also face biological and ecological constraints (Peterson 2001: 209–12).

To generate qualitative data illuminating what strategies for promoting sustainability seem to have the most significant and lasting effects, this study attempted to map the relationships between leaders in different sectors of sustainability movements, noting instances of overlap in their general approach and the motivational themes, metaphors, and strategies used. What cannot be accurately discerned from the collected data is causation. It cannot prove that one informant "caught" a particular "strain" of the sustainability meme (a particular metaphor, for example) directly from another. If, however, the theoretical framework discussed above has explanatory power, close personal and professional relationships among leaders of groups are important synapses for the exchange of ideas and practices within larger networks of movements and groups. The high-level actors interviewed for this study (detailed in Chapters 7, 8, and 9) are attempting to promote a shift in anthropological understandings by highlighting biological, ecological, and even spiritual interdependence, and through risky engagement with foreign individuals and groups, are opening an honest discussion of values. They often use biophilic or cosmophilic imagery, or use biological and cultural diversity as cognitive tools to facilitate such affectively grounded engagement (see Hukkinen 2008 for more on cognitive tools for sustainability). To the extent that this imagery is religious, those who strategically deploy it in the public sphere are players in "spiritual games." Atran et al. used this phrase to describe the use of language that implies the intentionality and agency of so-called "resources," calling into question their standing as unconscious objects to be utilized for human ends (Atran et al. 2002: 438–9). Spiritual games directly challenge some assumptions of traditional economic game theory—including the notion that humans are the only moral agents playing the game—calling attention to non-economic values that are central to deliberation about what it is that ought to be sustained.

THEORIZING THE RELIGIOUS DIMENSIONS OF SUSTAINABILITY

There are, then, at least three levels (a term used as a heuristic device, not one with normative connotations) where values are recognizable in population subgroups. Values can be (a) related to concepts of self and other through psychological and cognitive processes internal to the individual (the subjective, individual dimension), (b) implicated in specific behaviors of individuals and groups (the performative-community dimension), and (c) recognizable as social patterns of preferences or behaviors (the social dimension). Each of these levels (from internalized ideas and values to personal and interpersonal behaviors to larger patterns of social behavior) may be broken down and examined in more detail. But much work focused on religion and environmental issues has explored the first dimension, individual perceptions and values, assuming that changes in such values lead to ecologically responsible behavior.

Sociologists, on the other hand, have focused on the persistence of the broader social patterns and preferences related to environmental issues, and have also provided empirical evidence relating values and beliefs to behaviors (e.g. Stern et al. 1999). These studies help to provide data that may be helpful to religious studies scholars interested in the gap between values and behaviors, but in most cases such studies say very little about how the triggers of environmentally friendly behaviors are transmitted through culture. As suggested above, such transmission occurs primarily through individual exchange and inference. Individual exchange and inference works most often and efficiently through local networks of persons who are indebted to various, sometimes overlapping, communities of accountability. In most cases there are limitations on these social networks, and also obstacles in the transfer of information between them. A thousand or more years ago, geographic features might facilitate or perhaps inhibit the transmission of goods, peoples, information, tastes, and so on. Today information networks can often bypass geographical constraints by utilizing virtual networks, some of which, such as the internet, are global in scope.

Fine-grained studies conducted by psychologists or thick descriptions from cultural anthropologists within particular communities can help to explore questions raised regarding the first, subjective/individual level mentioned above. Sociologists, ritual studies specialists, and others might probe community practices and performances, helping to provide data that can flesh out level two, the performative-community dimension, where the enaction of values occurs. Others might trace the ways in which social behaviors—including religious ones—form patterns which reflect constraints inherent to the natural and other resources available to particular populations, helping to unpack some of the implications of level three, which refers to large-scale social movements. This project focuses on descriptions and explanations related to levels two and three. The central claims that are developed throughout include: (a) that the emergence of sustainability discourse has historically depended in significant ways on religious groups, persons, and concepts; (b) that highly affective modes of transmitting sustainability discourse, those that are referred to here as religious, have pragmatic value in that they can often initiate, promote, or sustain relationships between persons or constituencies with significantly different worldviews and values; and (c) that there are expert networks that help to transform and transmit particular concepts or narratively embedded ethical ideals across these different constituencies, one of which, embedded within non-governmental organizations, was examined here.

SUMMARY

Themes related to sustainability are transmitted primarily through the interactions of the high-level actors in each of these particular groups and movements, who share their information in an intentional effort to construct large-scale narratives. Therefore, studying the transmission of motivational tropes, metaphors, and language among actors in expert networks in sustainability-oriented movements provides the first data set. Future research unpacking the cultural transmission of sustainability themes should include more extensive and deeper qualitative work among participants in the same organizations and communities, to discern to what extent the information transmitted by these experts influences the perceptions and behaviors of others.

As this study shows, the highly political religious dimensions of sustainability are a persistent part of the global flow of information through various constituencies. As the sources of language used to describe sustainability in the public sphere are revealed (Chapters 4, 5, and 6) they provide some support to Vasquez's contention that powerscapes are important variables in determining the flow of such information. Sustainability discourse in the United States and Europe has affinities for particular metaphorical and imaginative discursive tools, many of which are derived from the natural sciences and religious systems that are either extant in, or romanticized by those in the industrialized world. Even when metaphors and imagery generated by those in the global South are vetted in the international political realm, they are typically related to events sponsored by or heavily invested in by several transnational corporate interests (such as the Johannesburg 2002 and Rio 2012 Earth Summits). Attention to how these themes are translated across oceans and cultures, then, exposes existing nodes of power within international political networks.

Given these dynamic and always political transmissions of ideas, it appears that Vasquez's critiques of Tweed's approach could be addressed if the fluid model was imagined as a more thoroughly organic metaphor. Rather than imagining the fluid model as a set of random and unconstrained flows as in a sea, for example, perhaps it would be better to imagine the model as a riverine system, which is certainly constrained by geographical, geophysical, and spatial boundaries. The river follows the geological features of the landscape just as understandings of sustainability and religion are dependent upon the contours of the particular features of the national or geopolitical "powerscape." Such an organic model of religious transmission may be the functional equivalent of the network model. In addition, it should be remembered that people actively engage in social "engineering," building bridges to other networks often over, or around the particular features of the "powerscape."

Gerlach's network model paired with attentiveness to political power has explanatory power for large-scale social dynamics. The biological metaphor advanced by Sperber and Atran, however, has greater explanatory power when describing how the values and practices that Gerlach analyzes on a societal scale are sustained and transmitted at the individual and community level (Sperber 1985; Atran *et al.* 2002). Vasquez's analysis is a reminder that such biological metaphors run the danger of oversimplifying the contested cultural terrains that people navigate and in which they find meaning. Together, they provide a theoretical landscape for the analysis of the religious dimensions of sustainability, and the political and religious work performed by the concept of sustainability as it facilitates the translation of values across constituencies.

Noting the existence of these expert networks is the first step in identifying the content of several culture-specific learning strategies. In Chapter 10 I speculate about why some of these learning strategies are more persistent than others. With these methodological and theoretical foundations laid, I now turn attention to the ways in which distinct but highly interactive groups participate in the cultivation and spread of the religious dimension of sustainability.

THE EMERGENCE AND DEVELOPMENT OF SUSTAINABILITY

Part II analyzes the first public deployments of the term sustainability, and later its cognate sustainable development. The first uses of these terms were descriptors for resource management regimes intended to prevent the disruption of society. They first came into use in Europe as awareness of the impacts of industrialization grew. Particularly important were the disappearance of undisturbed natural areas and the dawning realization that growing populations and increasingly scarce resources might create problems for the people, governments and groups who controlled them.

As a result, two ideas for the first time became intimately intertwined during the mid to late 1800s. First was the notion of ecological limits, which had been noted and linked with population growth by Thomas Malthus (1766–1834) decades before. Malthus challenged the notion that society (and particularly European civilization) was on a trajectory of improvement and progress. In fact, he argued, if such "progress" continued society might face unpleasant encounters with ecological limits. This realization led to a second, that prudent utilization of resources might allow them to continue to provide for populations into the foreseeable future. The first government-sponsored foresters, then, aimed to find the formulae necessary to ensure that those limits did not create social unrest.[1]

When imported to the United States, such resource management strategies preserved the focus on the maintenance of social control, but religious concepts and beliefs were increasingly used to justify them. This continued through the First World War, when poverty was for the first time recognized as one of the drivers of unsustainable resource use. In the post-war period, as economic recession spread worldwide, it became clear that sustainable resource use was not only or even primarily related to timber production.

The massive soil erosion that compromised the once-impressive agricultural productivity of the central United States clearly illustrated the need for more sweeping and concerted resource management regimes. Soon thereafter, governments mandated experiments with voluntary simplicity, which persisted through the Second World War.

In the post Second World War era, the process of economic globalization began in earnest, and consumption (rather than self-limitation and self-reliance) was imagined as the surest salve for poverty. As the development-oriented strain of sustainability gained a global audience, counter-cultural movements in Europe and particularly the United States illustrated that both sustainability and development were contested concepts. These two terms were rhetorically joined and were deployed by international political bodies and institutionalized religions as a means for increasing quality of life. On the other hand, when such terms were exercised by counter-cultural forces, they illustrated the unsustainability of visions of development offered by governments and their affiliated institutions.

Both of these tributaries to contemporary sustainability movements—those engineered and spread by guardians of the status quo, and those exercised by people who resisted economic globalization and cultural homogenization—grew into global movements in the post-war era. Much of the rhetoric and language used by both sides was explicitly religious. Generally the spiritualized rhetoric used to advertise sustainability and related concepts was drawn (a) from existing religious traditions, (b) from a generic and loosely spiritual metanarrative of sustainability proffered by development institutions, (c) from holistic and often religious interpretations of natural scientific data, or (d) from a growing group of social scientists who advocated the preservation of cultural diversity and accompanying spiritual attachments to the land.

These trends offer a new perspective on the emergence of sustainability discourse. The set of historical lenses used here opens up vistas that highlight the globalization of sustainability discourse, its significant religious dimensions, and its inherently contested nature.

CHAPTER FOUR

THE GENESIS AND GLOBALIZATION OF SUSTAINABILITY

INTRODUCTION

Defining both sustainability and religion broadly (see Chapter 2) allows a closer investigation of a number of historical, intellectual, and policy rivulets that carved their way across the cultural landscape toward larger sustainability streams. This chapter exposes some of the roots of sustainability, which are often mentioned in passing by scholars who investigate sustainability, but are seldom critically analyzed. The conceptual foundations of sustainability and the motivations that root them are heavily spiritualized, and when they have been deployed in public discourse, explicitly or implicitly, they have been drivers of production and consumption behaviors.

Important to this analysis are the values embraced by those who first deployed the terms publicly, and the way these values have been digested and redeployed for, and by leaders of sustainability movements and the general public. Specifically, two foundational ideas related to sustainability—(a) the notion of ecological limits, and (b) the idea of sustained resource use over time—provided conceptual spaces where ecological, economic, and humanistic values were rhetorically and practically joined over the past two hundred years. In many cases, religious and spiritual concepts provided the fertile habitat where the other two concerns could be fruitfully grafted together.

EARLY USES OF COGNATES FOR SUSTAINABILITY

Several scholars attribute the first use of sustainability to the United Nations Conference on the Human Environment held in Stockholm, Sweden in

1972.[1] This makes some sense, since this was the first emergence of a concern for *global* sustainability. But there are much deeper roots to notions of ecological scarcity and limits, the idea of sustainable use of natural resources, and the religious and spiritual attachments to the natural world that supported the emergence of environmental concern in the twentieth century. The word *sustainable* appeared in Middle English (in the late 1200s according to the American Heritage Dictionary) as an adjective that modified a verb or noun, and indicated an ongoing or persistent action or entity.[2] The term *sustainability* was used to refer to wise human use and preservation of natural resources at least as early as 1849, when a German scientist named Faustmann described his attempts to discern what forest rotation would produce the largest yields for the future (Berkes *et al.* 1998: 347). By the middle of the nineteenth century such ideas were widespread in European forest management. Interestingly, many of the core values and goals that are attributed to sustainability today were present, albeit in slightly different manifestations, two hundred years ago.[3]

Even scholars who push the genesis of the term back deeper into the past do not connect it to the present use of the term in any convincing way.[4] Andrés Edwards, to his credit, traces the impetus for sustainability back to the Transcendentalists (such as Emerson and Thoreau), John Muir and the concept of wilderness (Edwards 2005:12), and the emergence of "an awareness of the profound spiritual links between human beings and the natural world" (14–15). Edwards's observation of the "spiritual links" with the non-human world is astute. Although sustainability's first stirrings correlated with an emerging awareness of spiritual links or obligations between human and other-than-human worlds, this strong influence on sustainability discourse has been underappreciated.

Ecological limits and the ethics of scarcity

Ideas about the limits of human habitats and attempts to live within them reach back at least to ancient Greek philosophers (Glacken 1967; see also T. R. Peterson 1997: 7). The Roman Marcus Terentius Varro (116–27 BCE) was perhaps one of the first Westerners to note in print that sheep could easily decimate a landscape if not properly grazed (Glacken 1967: 143), a recognition taken up by John Muir in the nineteenth century as he watched portions of his beloved Sierra Nevada range denuded by later generations of sheep (prompting Muir to brand them with the religiously rich moniker "hoofed locusts").[5] Cultural narratives related to ecological limits persisted from early Western civilization to the roots of environmental movements catalyzed by the activism of Muir and others in the late 1800s.

If environmental movements are, as Hawken (2007a) claimed, one of the primary tributaries of contemporary sustainability discourse, and if Muir and his ken are at the root of environmental movements, then the political interests and social concerns that drive contemporary sustainability movements certainly have ancestors in deeper historical streams. As historian Roderick Nash pointed out, the nature appreciation characteristic of environmental movements began in the cities, prompted by an ethic of scarcity that seeped into European consciousness in the early to mid-1700s as natural resources were overexploited (Nash 2001). During this period ecological limits took on a normative dimension, promoting a shift in human societal norms and spawning the emergence of the intellectual movement Romanticism.

One of the most influential Romantic thinkers, Jean Jacques Rousseau (1712–78) promoted what he called primitivism, a return to dependence on the natural world, while glorifying the native peoples and wild places of the North American continent as exemplars of a "better" way to live.[6] Malthus, whose father was supposedly an acquaintance of Rousseau's, was likewise impressed by the increasing industrialization of Europe, and at the end of the seventeenth century was perhaps the first to connect the idea of ecological limits to population. It was around the same time that Ned Ludd (now a famous anti-technology folk hero) allegedly sabotaged some of the factory machinery that had put him out of work.[7] The wheels of industry were turning faster with each passing year and Ludd and other factory workers were imagined as martyrs (of sorts) of a bygone era when *human* labor (rather than machines) had driven the expansion of markets. Malthus believed this growing mechanization and industrialization would increase human productivity and occupation of resources, triggering a concomitant increase in population. Population increases would ultimately result in unpleasant human encounters with ecological limits, leading in at least some areas to increased competition for resources.

Environmental limits quite literally helped to determine the shape of society as the ethic of scarcity grew more widespread. Early European resource management was not simply a tool for utilizing natural resources; it also contributed to managing citizen populations. For European foresters, science provided for the persistence of the social order by ensuring that social chaos did not ensue from the overexploitation of the land (Worster 1993: 144–5). One of the first North American government-appointed foresters, Gifford Pichot, would draw the same connections between resource management and the social order in the United States.

If the ethic of scarcity motivated the first efforts at conservation on the European continent, then the subsequent celebration of wild places catalyzed the emergence of the "church of the wilderness" in the young United

States.[8] Nash argued that "if, as many suspected, wilderness was the medium through which God spoke most clearly, then America had a distinct moral advantage over Europe, where centuries of civilization had deposited a layer of artificiality over His works" (Nash 2001: 69).

The Transcendentalist philosophers (most notably Ralph Waldo Emerson and Henry David Thoreau) are well known for taking their inspiration from nature, inspiring generations of people to act on behalf of their habitats.[9] Nash noted that John Muir was heavily influenced by the Transcendentalists, particularly Emerson and Thoreau: "For John Muir Transcendentalism was always the essential philosophy for interpreting the value of wilderness" (Nash 2001: 125).[10] It was no coincidence that Muir's founding of the Sierra Club in 1892, the first wilderness preservation organization in the United States, fell so near the announcement by well-known historian Frederick Jackson Turner that the frontier—so instrumental in the formulation of US nationalism and American moral imagination—had officially "closed" (Turner [1893] 1956). Thus, the ethic of scarcity was activated in the United States as well as Europe. When ecological limits were reached or breached, first in Europe and later in North America, preservation and conservation grew into important causes.

Often Muir and his Transcendentalist contemporaries (who are often termed "preservationists") are contrasted with the primarily utilitarian rhetoric of Gifford Pinchot and Theodore Roosevelt (typically called "conservationists" in the literature). Sometimes these "preservationists" have been portrayed as unhelpful because they depend upon moralizing language and emotion-based arguments for keeping certain portions of nature free from human interference. Those on the other side of the debate, however, are no less evangelical in their insistence that utility maximization is a moral good. Bryan Norton noted that both Muir and Pinchot were ideologues because they carried their "preexperiential commitments" with them into the public sphere (Norton 2005: ix). In part Norton is correct—even in their more management-oriented manifestations, arguments that resources should be sustainably utilized were no less dependent on religious and spiritual rhetoric and metaphor than more poetic pronouncements of nature's value.[11] The case of Gifford Pinchot provides a helpful illustration.

The gospel of conservation: the idea of sustainable resource use over time

When the term sustainability was increasingly used in European forest management in the mid-1800s, North America had no schools dedicated to studying forest use and management, no official foresters, and no forestry plan. Gifford Pinchot, the son of a well-to-do and politically savvy family studied forestry in France and imported the idea of sustainable resource use over time to the United States. Thus, what is termed sustainable resource management in the US has genealogical connections with the first resource management programs in Europe. It is this usage, a human-centered perspective linking maximal production to national security and citizen management, eventually translated into a North American context, which would dominate the use of the term into the present.

Gifford Pinchot was largely responsible for both the establishment of the US Forest Service and the emergence of political progressivism. He was thus a pivotal figure in the formulation of the first domestic resource management and economic policies aimed at sustainable resource management and national development (and eventually, *sustainable development*).

In Pinchot's management philosophy the goal of forestry was "to make the forest produce the largest possible amount of whatever crop or service will be the most useful, and keep on producing it for generation after generation of men and trees" (Pinchot 1947: 32). Pinchot's utilitarian calculus included as central variables future generations of humans and trees. Interestingly, protecting the public good from corporate raiders was the foundation of Pinchot's progressive social philosophy, bolstered by his belief that building social equity was a moral duty (Pinchot 1910: 48). In his last work, Pinchot described conservation as centering on three main goals: (1) to wisely use, protect, preserve and renew natural resources; (2) to control the use of natural resources for the common good, and to ensure their equal distribution; and (3) "to see to it that the rights of the people to govern themselves shall not be controlled by great monopolies through their power over natural resources" (Pinchot 1947: 596). "Pinchotism,"[12] as his philosophy has been called, remains highly influential (if implicit) in the United States' resource management philosophy, and was instrumental in the emergence of sustainability movements.[13]

Importantly, though, Pinchot's religious beliefs significantly informed his political ideals and his understanding of how forests should be managed. The spiritual foundations of Pinchot's politics were revealed most clearly in his book *The Fight for Conservation* (1910).[14] The relationship between Pinchot's conservation, politics, and spirituality is exposed in Pinchot's three primary presuppositions. First, Pinchot viewed the conservation of natural resources as the foundation of long-term national success (Pinchot 1910: 4).[15] Second, for Pinchot, achieving the first goal of conservation, national security, was dependent on a prior choice between "unclean money or free men" as the ultimate object of the political system (Pinchot 1910: 92).[16] Third, these moral duties to protect resources for future generations and the common good stem from a deeper commitment to foster the actualization of Christian values in the world. Pinchot was heavily influenced by the social gospel movement, which applied Christian principles to solve social crises created by the industrial revolution (Naylor 2005: 1281). He argued that "among the first duties of every man is to help in bringing the Kingdom of God on earth," and "public spirit is patriotism in action; it is the application of Christianity to the commonwealth ... [it] is the one great antidote to the ills of the Nation" (Pinchot 1910: 95–6). Following the moral imperative to manifest Christian ideals in society would result in the equitable distribution of resources and the sustainability of the nation, since "a man in public life can no more serve both the special interests and the people than he can serve God and Mammon" (Pinchot 1910: 115). Pinchot believed that it was un-Christian greed that drove resource overexploitation, and that those who were guilty of such greediness were working against the common good.[17]

Pinchot's three pillars of sustainable resource use, a long-term perspective, protection of the poor and weak from the predation of moneyed interests, and the invective to serve a higher moral calling, are all instrumental in contemporary discussions of sustainability. As Tarla Rai Peterson noted, "sustainable development was addressed by Gifford Pinchot ... [who] advocated development of resources and prevention of waste for the benefit of the largest possible number of people" (Peterson 1997; see also Pinchot 1910: 42–50). The generic humanism reflected in later definitions of sustainability, for example in the Bruntland Commission report (discussed below), is reminiscent of Pinchot's invocation of (1) a global ethic designed to protect the poor by promoting social equity, (2) the maintenance of economic productivity to preserve national sovereignty and security, and (3) the long-term conservation of environmental products and services.

SOME EARLY FOCI OF GLOBAL SUSTAINABILITY AND ITS RELIGIOUS DIMENSIONS

These two perspectives, the recognition of the importance of ecological limits, and the more managerial model focused on sustainable use of resources over time, contributed significantly to the emergence of environmental and social movements that eventually manifested in a variety of movements loosely related to sustainability in the late twentieth century. Both leaned heavily on religious and spiritual rhetoric and metaphor for support. Unfortunately, important figureheads such as John Muir and Gifford Pinchot are often characterized as being motivated by opposite aims, which tends to accentuate artificial dichotomies in the emergence of environmental consciousness. Muir and his "preservationists" are often described as advocating that wilderness can only be considered truly wild when it is devoid of humans or the footprint of human activity. Pinchot and his "conservationists," on the other hand, are typically portrayed as consequentialist utility maximizers, willing to use (and possibly use up) natural resources so long as the benefits accrue primarily to human users. Although these two personages are offered here as exemplars of different perspectives (awareness of ecological scarcity and limits, and the belief that resources should be conserved for future generations), these perspectives are in fact complementary in contemporary sustainability discourse, not in opposition. Moreover, both of these figureheads deployed religious or spiritual language in direct correlation to the severity of the political fights at stake (Muir, for example, during the fight to prevent the construction of Hetch Hetchy dam [Nash 2001: 167], and Pinchot when he was removed from his office by President Taft).[18] Most importantly, both of these streams of argument are crucial to the ideas behind and practice of twentieth- and twenty-first-century sustainability.

Globalizing the sustainability and development discourse in the twentieth century

The beginnings of the "first wave" of environmentalism emerged at the turn of the twentieth century: from the emergence of scarcity and environmental concern in Europe, the development of Romanticism, the myth of the frontier, the elaboration (in art, music, and national parks) of a new US nationalism in the form of wilderness, the formation of the Sierra Club by John Muir (1892), the creation of the Audubon Society (1905), and finally the growth of a scarcity ethic in the United States around the turn of the twentieth century (Davison 2001).

But alongside these developments, in the first thirty years of the twentieth century, farming technologies improved, increasing food yield per acre and decreasing the number of workers required to produce those yields. During the First World War, the government declared that increased wheat yields would win the war, boosting further production increases (Worster 1977: 60–61). Following the First World War ideas about ecological limits and sustainable use of natural resources persisted in the background. But it was during this politically and socially tumultuous era that the "development" tributary of what later became sustainable development exploded onto the international scene. Worries over basic sustenance and security preoccupied the industrialized world, because it was believed that shortfalls in these areas in less- or un-industrialized places had manifested in very costly military and reconstructive expenditures.

The development expert Gilbert Rist argued that by deploying the idea of *development*, "by defining itself as the precursor of a history common to all, the West could treat colonization as a generous undertaking to 'help' more or less 'backward' societies along the road to civilization" (Rist 1997: 43).[19] With the full inertia of the aftermath of the First World War behind it, development flourished on the newly international world stage as a new "grand narrative" (Rist 1997: 39). For Rist, the concept of development operated as a religious narrative, providing a vision for where the global community was headed, and a normative framework for getting there.

The League of Nations was created at the end of the First World War, just days before the Treaty of Versailles (which officially ended aggression on June 28, 1919) (Rist 1997: 59). The founding document of the League of Nations reinforced the idea that there were "stages of development," which motivated the industrialized world to facilitate the reconstruction of conquered areas to improve standards of living for the "less developed" countries.[20] Just as Christopher Columbus's landing in the New World began the conquest of the Americas in the name of Christianization, "colonization ... now present[ed] itself, thorough the League of Nations, as a 'sacred trust of civilization.' This was not just an innocent form of words, for it placed the final objective [of development] in the realm of religion and the sacred" (Rist 1997: 68; Rist is quoting the League's founding document). This new grand narrative, the "religion" of development, highlighted the all-encompassing vision that the term (and its cognate sustainable development) still offer.[21]

By the 1930s it was clear that massive increases in productive capacity in North America had taken their toll on the soils. This soil crisis, coupled with the economic hangover from the market crash in 1929, prompted a turn to science to discern the causes and mitigate the impacts of the recent environmental crises.[22] The new science of ecology had a rapidly increasing role in the policy formulation process (Worster 1977: 233, 253). The economic downturn of the 1920s and 1930s caused by intensive tilling and farming technologies resulted in unpleasant encounters with ecological limits, and brought the idea of sustainable use into public consciousness once again—this time related (if weakly at first) with notions of development that had incubated in the global North, arguably since colonial times.

The Second World War brought pervasive social and economic changes across Europe and North America.[23] The rhetoric of reducing waste, reusing materials, and recycling products, one of the more common slogans of some contemporary sustainability advocates ("reduce, reuse, recycle"), has a long history.

For instance, my grandparents, who had moved from the "farm country" to the city early in their married lives remembered how to plant again when the US government began its Second World War public relations campaign in support of home-grown "victory gardens." These positive affirmations of voluntary simplification of the middle American lifestyle played a significant role in helping to achieve the productive capacity required to win the war.

There were also, however, more apocalyptic reminders from the federal government that any failure to act according to the new ethic of voluntary simplicity amounted to complicity with the enemy. Several government-produced posters and advertisements indicated that waste helped the enemy, and that certain sacrifices (in terms of use of material goods) was necessary for defeating the enemy. If you were not carpooling, one advertisement said, it was the same as giving Hitler a lift. Perhaps ironically, many contemporary environmental activists suggest something similar—that mindless consumption (especially of oil-based products) is a threat to national security, an aid to the enemies of Western culture in particular, and hastens our demise as a species.[24]

After the Second World War, the wartime productive capacity of the United States and western Europe required additional outlets. The Marshall Plan (1947) was created to help a struggling Europe regain its economic and political footing and simultaneously to provide additional markets for American goods as production shifted from war machines to consumer goods (Rist 1997: 69). In contrast to the war years' demand for reducing material consumption, in the late 1940s and early 1950s the United States' prosperity was tied to the willingness of individuals to amass an increasing volume of consumer goods. *Consuming*—putting money back into the economy—had become a patriotic act. Interestingly then, while the war era helped to provide some of the first experiments with nation-wide voluntary simplicity, wartime growth in industrial output caused a resultant backlash of increased consumerism. This was a watershed moment that significantly contributed to growing sustainability movements. As the first resource management regimes were generated in Europe and the United States by an emerging ethic of scarcity, environmentalism bubbled up in both places as a reaction to the increased exploitation of natural resources, and spread due to the globalization of politics in the wake of the two world wars. The globalization of sustainability and development discourse included concerns for both ecological limits and increased resource efficiency. Moreover, both of these important foundations of sustainability were often tethered to forms of nationalist pride and an ethos that can be (and has been) analyzed as a civil (or national) religion (Bellah 1970: 168–89). During and following the Second World War, this civil religion was especially potent, and an important precursor to sustainability in general and sustainable development in particular.

President Harry Truman's 1949 inauguration address where he outlined his Four Point Plan arguably officially "internationalized" the idea of development (and eventually, its offspring, sustainable development) (Rist 1997: 70–72; Jolly et al. 2004: 50).[25] Development was given a human face, and its spread was aided by its structural similarity to religious discourse (Rist 1997: 77). Rist argued that "the new belief in 'development' had its credibility further strengthened by a naturalist metaphor so long part of the Western collective consciousness" (77).[26] The emerging ideas of development and environmentalism were new ways to frame concern regarding ecological limits and wise use of resources over time. Contemporary sustainability discourse preserved both and added the ingredients of emerging global political and economic bodies.

These political and economic bodies, while they ostensibly had the interests of the world's poorest in mind, have according to many critics actually provided avenues for a more global exploitation of natural resources, a process in which the bulk of the benefits have accrued to an increasingly small cadre of transnational businesses and individuals. The above history relates the sustainability narratives prevalent in North America and western Europe, and thus has not included the voices of those who were (and are) the targets of development efforts. But this history is important precisely because the religious roots of these ideas are so often ignored. While in the literature sustainability is typically treated like a generic humanistic vision, it actually derives from a specific cultural milieu and in many instances from a spiritually grounded ethos. So while sustainable development has certainly helped certain constituencies, it has continually disenfranchised others, a point to which we shall return in the next chapter.

From religious resistance to global faith

By the 1940s, licking their wounds from battles with countries ruled by fascists and emperors, many of the younger generations in northern Europe and the United States were uneasy about both the promise of technological progress and sources of authority (whether political or economic). This youthful unrest, typically associated with the countercultural discontent that bubbled up in the 1950s and came to a head during the 1960s included members of "peace, civil rights, feminist, New Left, and neo-Marxist movements" (Davison 2001: xii). Armin Geertz argued that these movements were facets of a "new primitivism"[27] which grew in part from "the hippie movement" and were based on experience, anti-rationalism, and anti-intellectualism (although I would quibble with Geertz's suggestion that movements grounded in the importance of experience are necessarily anti-rational or intellectual) (A. Geertz 2004: 53). Further, Geertz argued that these movements were directly influenced by the emergence of a closely related tributary of primitivism that grew out of the University of Chicago's History of Religions research program, spearheaded by Mircea Eliade. Geertz argued that Eliade's *Shamanism,* for example (first published in French in 1951), influenced the theosophy movement, the author Jack Kerouac and one of Keroauc's real-life protagonists Gary Snyder, and at least in the US promoted a popular turn to the East and to indigenous traditions as sources of spiritual growth (A. Geertz 2004: 55; also noted by White 1967).[28] Even as these counter-cultural movements grew more aware of development and its impacts on their habitats, the liberal democratic vision of development was given a boost on an international scale when US president John Kennedy proposed to the UN General Assembly (September 25, 1961) that the 1960s should constitute a "Decade of Development" focused on promoting economic growth (Jolly *et al.* 2004: 85).[29]

The countercultural currents in Europe and especially in the United States provided sustainability movements with ties to peace and labor movements, and advertised the idea that development and globalization were not always universal "goods." Related scholarly currents, such as the Chicago school alluded to above, also exposed sustainability movements to other cultures and lifeways. Meanwhile, what Rist called the "global faith" of development was increasingly touted by governments and multinational groups such as the United Nations as the means to alleviate poverty and increase security in a sustainable manner (Rist 1997). Thus, the roots of sustainability and sustainable development reach into both subcultures of resistance as well as institutional, and international political and economic structures. While the spiritual dimensions of civil society's response to sustainable development schemes have been well documented (Wright 1988; Ghai & Vivian 1992; Taylor 1995; Carr 2005; Sumner 2005; Posey & Balick 2006; Wright 2009), less attention has been paid to the spiritual dimensions of international political discourse (although Chapman *et al.* 2000 is a notable exception, and Taylor 2010 has recently begun to fill the gap). Chapter 5 provides additional attention to these spiritual dimensions, focusing on how civil society, multinational political groups, and religious cultural production intersect and contribute to the religious dimensions of sustainability.

CHAPTER FIVE

THE RELIGIOUS DIMENSIONS OF SUSTAINABILITY AT THE NEXUS OF CIVIL SOCIETY AND INTERNATIONAL POLITICS

INTRODUCTION

Religious groups and leaders, as well as spiritual language and metaphors were important to sustainability from its earliest uses, as illustrated in Chapter 4. They variously contributed to three broad types of religious production related to sustainability discourse and practice: (a) the nature-as-sacred religion that occurs within many subcultures of resistance (b) ecological pronouncements from institutionalized religious traditions; and (c) a generic, humanistic civil religion. Each of these has consistently appeared in international political venues attended by civil society actors, and international governance and finance units such as the UN and World Bank. A discussion of major contemporary conferences, publications, declarations, and commissions (in the first section of this chapter) will bring the historical development of sustainability up to the present. With this history, and the increasingly complex web of relationships (between agents, ideas, and practices) in view, it should become clear that the political processes that some scholars (e.g. Light 2002; Light and de-Shalit 2003; Norton 2005) have pointed to as the essential elements of sustainability require inputs from the spiritual dimensions of sustainability for the formulation of sustainable public policy. Analyzing contributions to the religious dimensions of sustainability from institutional religions, political institutions, and religions of resistance at benchmark conferences and events, this chapter concludes by highlighting some contemporary developments at the nexus of civil society and international politics. This approach will also make clear the religious dimensions of secular sustainability groups and movements. Even ostensibly secular international organizations utilize the religious dimensions of sustainability (in the form of spiritualized language, religious metaphor, or discourses of awe and reverence) for their own, often different ends.

For instance, the sections immediately following trace the development of a generic humanism within international political discourse. Although not overtly religious in some cases, this humanism does have significant religious dimensions, especially when projected into a dynamic international political sphere. Religious discourse, then, can act as the tie that binds these varied constituencies (environmentalists, development advocates, conservationists, capitalists, governments, and oppositional subcultures) together in the search for sustainability. Although the inclusion of these religious dimensions may be important for democratic politics, their inclusion does not mean that negotiations will always be positive or fruitful. Indeed, religion may also *prevent* consensus and action at times, but in such cases at least the fundamental value sets that lead to the failure of consensus are explicit, rather than implicit.

GLOBAL ATTENTIVENESS TO LIMITS, THE STOCKHOLM CONFERENCE, AND OTHER INDICATORS OF POSSIBLE DOOM

In the mid-1960s the National Council of Churches (NCC) convened the Faith–Man–Nature Study Group, focused on transforming Christian attitudes toward nature. In 1966 the World Council of Churches (WCC) launched a five-year study program devoted to the impacts of technology on society, including components that attended to environmental effects. The resulting report "accepted the thesis of nature's limits and called for a society that [was] both just and sustainable" (Chapman et al. 2000: 12).[1] Interestingly then, these ecumenical groups were some of the first to use the term sustainable as a shorthand reference for a socially equitable and ecologically responsible global community. In 1967 Pope Paul VI declared his commitment to equitable development, stating that "the new name for peace [is] development" (quoted in Therien 2005: 29). The United Nations first addressed environmental issues directly in 1968 when the Economic and Social Council (ECOSOC) created resolution 1346 (XLV), which recommended that the General Assembly consider convening a United Nations conference dedicated to addressing a "crisis of world wide proportions ... the crisis of the human environment" (Jolly et al. 2004: 125).[2]

This crisis set the stage for the United Nations Conference on the Human Environment in Stockholm (1972), which, in response to the ECOSOC resolution, brought concerns about sustainability to the *global* community by suggesting that un-sustainability was directly correlated with poverty in the developing world.[3] Attendees envisioned development as the only salve for the poverty that made humans vulnerable to environmental fluctuations and encouraged over-exploitation of local resource bases. For example, Principle Eight, endorsed by the commission, stated that "Economic and social development is essential for ensuring a favorable living and working environment for man [sic] and for creating conditions on earth that are necessary for the improvement of the quality of life."[4] Most of the world's problems, the report concluded, were due to "under-development." This was basically the same argument that had sparked international interest in "development" following the world wars. By the time the Stockholm Conference forged the term *sustainable development* to refer to global engineering, the rhetoric underlying the process had changed little since the early twentieth century.

If there was a novel ingredient in the outcome of the Stockholm meeting, it was the idea that while human needs were ultimately paramount, the ecological matrix upon which they depend must be the context in which all good decisions about the shape of development must be made: "Man is both creature and moulder of his environment, which gives him physical sustenance and affords him the opportunity for intellectual, moral, social and spiritual growth."[5] Humans are referred to as "creatures," a word whose origin is rooted in Middle English and which refers to something derived from an act of creation, implying that there is a "creator" behind human existence and their capacity to exact change on their habitats.[6]

The conclusions reached by those at the conference upheld the sovereignty of particular nations to exploit their resources in accordance with their own values. Importantly, even in this early manifestation of sustainability discourse, the unique needs of each nation were recognized: "it will be essential in all cases to consider the systems of values prevailing in each country, and the extent of the applicability of standards which are valid for the most advanced countries but which may be inappropriate and of unwarranted social cost for the developing countries."[7] Although there was a tacit recognition that sustainability might not be a monolithic concept or solution set, participants recommended a "common outlook and ... common principles" to guide the search for sustainability.[8] Perhaps the most important long-term outcome of the Stockholm meeting was the birth of the United Nations Environment Programme (UNEP), headed by conference chairman Maurice Strong and based in Nairobi, Kenya, quite distant from the power centers of the UN. It was as yet unclear whether this new UN arm, or the common principles discussed in Stockholm, would be enough to overcome the increasingly clear evidence that the "global village" was unsustainable. Research was beginning to reveal the outcomes of decades of development and sustainable development work, namely: a widening gap between the

wealthy and the weak or vulnerable, increasingly impactful ecological disasters (in the form of famines, droughts, etc.) due to unsustainable settlement
and population patterns, and the lack of feedbacks which allowed politics to
respond to these interrelated crises. Some researchers had already begun to
quantify or otherwise predict future scenarios based on these trends.

The same year that the Stockholm Conference was convened, Donella
Meadows and her collaborators at the Massachusetts Institute of Technology
(MIT) published their treatise *Limits to Growth* (1972), which was meant
to illustrate to the public and to policy-makers the gravity of these issues.[9]
The researchers used computer models to simulate the trends in population
and consumption of food and non-renewable resources, leading them to the
conclusion that if such trends continued, very real ecological limits would
impose very real suffering on human populations within a hundred or so
years.[10] Although arguably somewhat apocalyptic in tone, it resurrected
what had historically been one of the principal facets of sustainability-related
discourse: the idea of ecological limits.

Other assessments of potentially catastrophic encounters with ecological limits included Garret Hardin's influential essays "The Tragedy of the
Commons" (1968) and "Living on a Lifeboat" (1974), or Paul Ehrlich's now
famous book *The Population Bomb* (1968). A different philosophy was
offered by William Ophuls, who suggested, in his *Ecology and the Politics
of Scarcity* (1977), that only a coercive politics and an accompanying global
scale "green religion" could prevent the deterioration of ecological resources
that resulted from ineffective or absent incentives for conservation (for further discussion see Taylor 2010: 260).

Meadows *et al.*, Hardin, and Ophuls have each had their share of harsh
critics, both for the assumptions underlying their arguments, and their
proposed solutions (i.e. coercive political schemes in Hardin's and Ophuls's
cases). Although such pronouncements of ecological overshoot are now
based in the sciences related to population dynamics and carrying capacity
(Catton 1980), they have strong parallels with Malthusian arguments (see
Chapter 4). Far from disappearing from sustainability discourse as Dresner
has suggested (Dresner 2005: 26–7), they remain important. Religious
language may be (but is not always) evident in such literature, but such
resource-management measures are nearly always considered morally
obligatory.

Gilbert Rist noted that "The birth of the ecological movement coincided
with a period of gloom and creeping doubt in the industrial countries" (Rist
1997: 141). But these predictions of ecological limits and coercive political
measures were not to have the last word. Around the same time came the
first international political declaration that individual and family security

(adequate sustenance, water, shelter, and physical safety) were prerequisites for achieving sustainability.

GLIMMERS OF HOPE FROM THE SOUTH: THE BARBADOS DECLARATIONS AND THE NIEO

The global South in particular continued to emphasize the *social* aspects of development. While the Stockholm gathering highlighted poverty as the primary scourge of peace and equity, it had also prescribed a somewhat invasive idea of growth, facilitated by external development bodies and governments, as its cure. Just prior, in 1971, the WCC convened their "Program to Combat Racism" in Barbados. The attendees, primarily social scientists, were calling attention to what was being called the "Fourth World," populations in already "underdeveloped" (Harry S. Truman's term) nations who were disenfranchised not only by the prevailing international economic and political powers, but also by the governments of their own nations.[11] As the anthropologist Robin Wright put it, these social scientists were advocating

> the notion that indigenous peoples throughout the world are united by their common situation as disenfranchised people, whose existence depends on a moral claim but who challenge the First World to examine its institutions, structures, and values, which have left indigenous peoples powerless and dependent.
> (Wright 1988: 365–90)

In the early 1970s several nations in the developing world proposed a "Declaration on the Establishment of the New International Economic Order" (NIEO). According to a team of UN analysts, "the historic importance of this proposal derives from the fact that it was an authentic Third World initiative, launched at a time of probably the peak bargaining power of the poor countries in the entire postwar period," and was "fundamentally concerned with a radical restructuring of international economic, financial, and political relations" (Jolly *et al.* 2004: 121). Overall, however, "on the most important proposals made by the developing countries, almost nothing was done" (Jolly *et al.* 2004: 23).

At the same time some anthropologists shepherded a growing discipline called *ethnodevelopment*, which provided an analysis of development from the perspective of the global South. Scholars such as Roberto Cardoso de Oliveira ([1964] 1972) and Rodolfo Stavenhagen (1970, 1990) helped to elucidate alternative models of development that highlighted the ways in which access to political and economic power was denied to certain populations despite the emergence of sustainability-related language that advertised inclusive and participatory political arrangements.[12] Disenfranchised by their nation states, some indigenous and traditional peoples began to increasingly rely on non-governmental groups for support. Non-governmental organizations became important mediators between indigenous and local peoples, international political regimes, and multilateral development agencies (Conklin & Graham 1995; Wright 2009). These NGOs, however, were often selective regarding which individuals and communities were targeted for sustainable development, perpetuating the symbolic and political dominance "of certain key figures in the politics, and the imposition of a model that privileged and shaped specific indigenous organizations, while excluding others" (Wright 2009: 204).[13]

A second Barbados Conference was held in 1977, and included in this second conference were several indigenous activists alongside the scholars, marking the extension of their influence into international policy regimes. Overall however, the lack of any concrete results following the Barbados declarations was disappointing for many indigenous peoples and the social scientists who supported their cause. Although there were few results that followed directly from these conferences, the ideas first vetted here and carried forth thereafter by the United Nations Conference on Trade and Development (UNCTAD) did influence the direction of development in a positive direction. The authors of the UN Intellectual History Project quoted Jan Pronk (deputy secretary of UNCTAD and minister of the Netherlands), who related the NIEO and the work of UNCTAD: "UNCTAD … had a major analytical input to international thinking … A little radical, but there would not have been any progress without such a challenge. It was a confrontational attitude on the basis of the Group of 77's New International Economic Order approach" (Emmerij et al. 2001: 53).[14] Moreover, the pressures placed on development organizations and related political and economic institutions were at least in part responsible for these groups' hiring of several anthropologists in an effort to increase their ability to respect and protect the cultures with which they interacted on the ground.

THE BRANDT COMMISSION

Concern about the relationships between the developed and developing world also came from the global North. In 1977 the chair of the World Bank Robert McNamara asked former chancellor of the Federal Republic of Germany Willy Brandt to head a commission that would systematically analyze the main problems with development, particularly in light of the increasing dialogue between the global North and South and the failure of negotiations to systematize the NIEO.[15] According to UN collaborators, the Brandt Commission's recommendations were "ultimately anchored in the great moral imperatives that ... are as valid internationally as they were and are nationally," and appealed "to values more than to rational calculations" (Therien 2005: 33).[16] The Commission published two reports, *North–South: A Program for Survival* (1980), and *Common Crisis: North–South: Co-operation for World Recovery* (1983), both of which advanced Brandt's idea that all nations had a "mutual interest" in generating just and equitable development.

Most of the participants (half from the global North and half from the global South) favored a social-democratic perspective,[17] and while the Commission's ideas may have been somewhat innovative, the payoff was less than hoped for as the Commission's findings were released into a world ripe with political strife.[18] Thus, despite repeated attempts by Third and Fourth World activists and the Brandt Commission to make the case that the prevailing conceptions of environmentally and socially responsible development were not sustainable in most cases, these concerns were transposed into the language of further economic globalization and integration of global markets.

SECURITY AND SUSTAINABILITY

Former Swedish prime minister Olof Palme, chair of the Independent Commission on Disarmament and Security Issues, made deep ripples in the international scene in 1982 by bringing national and global security to the attention of world leaders. The Palme Commission (as it came to be called) was modeled after the Brandt Commission, and focused on: (1) charting a long-term course toward nuclear disarmament; (2) focusing attention on short-term arms control; and (3) stimulating public debate over security issues.[19]

The Report of the Independent Commission on Disarmament and Security Issues, called *Common Security: A Programme for Disarmament* (1982), suggested that the build-up of long-range missiles in eastern Europe, far from ensuring security, actually compromised the security of both Cold War states and the global community. They challenged the long revered language of nuclear deterrence with a doctrine of *mutual interest* in avoiding nuclear conflict. Following the language of "common crisis" offered by Brandt, the Palme Commission declared that addressing the threat of nuclear war was central to *common security* (Wiseman 2005: 46–75). Although largely overlooked by top leaders from the two primary Cold War nations, the Commission's recommendations were adopted and adapted under cover by various high-ranking officials. By the end of the 1980s concepts related to common security had journeyed across the Atlantic, through the Iron Curtain, and back again.[20]

Recall that Pinchot's brand of sustainability (in Chapter 4) included national security as a central concern, but it was thereafter seldom considered related to sustainability until the latter part of the twentieth century. Although the Palme Commission is rarely mentioned as part of the history of sustainability, it is important to the development of sustainability discourse for three reasons. First, security and peace are prerequisites for sustainability. Wars and other armed conflicts are some of the most ecologically and socially devastating activities in which humans engage. Second, the Commission framed such common security (or cooperative security) as pivotal for the global community, citing a profound interdependence, particularly in matters of nuclear warfare. Third, it raised questions about the potential political power of such commissions.[21] What long-term effects have such well-intentioned commissions and declarations had on individuals and their daily practice? To what extent is the general public, whether in the global North or South, informed about the content or intention of such gatherings and publications? Further empirical research is needed to discern their impact.

The influence of one such gathering on sustainability discourse, however, is clear. The definition of *sustainable development* offered by the World Commission on Environment and Development (WCED) remains the most frequently cited and referenced in the global North.

THE WORLD COMMISSION ON ENVIRONMENT AND DEVELOPMENT

In the midst of these global concerns about thermonuclear warfare and unpleasant encounters with Earth's limits, the World Commission on Environment and Development was convened in 1983 by UN Secretary-General Javier Perez de Cuellar.[22] Chairperson Gro Brundtland stated in the foreword of *Our Common Future* (WCED 1987), the publication of the Commission's recommendations, that the WCED was to be a "third and compelling call for political action: after Brandt's *Programme for Survival* and *Common Crisis*, and after Palme's *Common Security*, would come *Our Common Future*" (WCED 1987: x; quoted in Smith 2005: 76–98). Brundtland viewed her charge as one directly in line with the increasingly common

61

recognition that security, social, and ecological problems were linked and moreover, were global in scope.[23]

Building on the foundations laid at Stockholm and in the Palme Commission, the Brundtland report paid special attention to the link between security and sustainability. Chapter 11 of *Our Common Future* is dedicated to fleshing out the links between peace, security, the environment, and development. The report suggested that the danger "of nuclear war, or military conflict of a lesser scale involving weapons of mass destruction, is undoubtedly the gravest. Certain aspects of the issues of peace and security bear directly upon the concept of sustainable development. Indeed, they are central to it" (WCED 1987: 290). It praised the Reagan and Gorbechev administrations (of the United States and the then USSR, respectively) for beginning the end of the Cold War with discussions of warhead reduction. Brundtland and her collaborators, drawing on the Palme Commission's positive statements of common security, stated that

> the level of armaments and the destruction they could bring about bear no relation to the political conflict that triggered the arms competition in the first place. Nations must not become prisoners of their own arms race ... They [nations] must face the common challenge of providing sustainable development.
>
> (WCED 1987: 304)

Finally, the Commission argued in nearly every chapter that more stringent national governing bodies and regulations were required to prevent environmental degradation, and they placed exceptional emphasis on the importance of international governance for preventing problems associated with commons management. Invoking the metaphor of the "wheel of life" (WCED 1987: 262, typically attributed to indigenous cultures), *Our Common Future* noted that common resources were marked by an interdependence not confined by human political boundaries and interests. Thus, larger and more cooperative international governance regimes were needed to protect resources such as oceans, air, Antarctica, and outer space (WCED 1987: 261–87). In many ways, the advocacy of larger-scale management regimes is reminiscent of Hardin's and Ophuls's suggestions that a broader, global scale governance is needed. Brundtland and her colleagues stop short of directly endorsing the sort of coercion (agreed upon or otherwise) advocated by Hardin and Ophuls, but their influence is clear.

Interestingly, the Brundtland Commission report preserved the idea advanced in Stockholm fifteen years earlier that raising standards of living in the developing world was only possible by stretching carrying capacity so that economic growth could continue unabated. As Jim McNeill, Secretary-General of the Brundtland Commission stated, "the maxim for sustainable development is not 'limits to growth'; it is 'the growth of limits' ... many present limits can be expanded, through changes in modes of decision-making, through changes in some domestic and international policies, and through massive investments in human and resource capital" (quoted in Smith 2005: 79).

This was one of the reasons that some critics of the WCED dismissed it as inconsistent, since it defended both economic growth *and* living within the carrying capacity of the planet. For example, historian Donald Worster called sustainability (particularly in its manifestation related to development) a "magic word of consensus" (Worster 1993: 144), which allowed "the capitalist and the socialist, the scientist and the economist, the impoverished masses and the urban elites ... [to] happily march together on a straight and easy path, if they did not ask any potentially divisive questions about where they were going" (144–5).

But upon careful analysis, the Brundtland report did not imply that sacrifices were unnecessary. In its introductory chapter the report dismisses as fantasy any suggestion that there will be no difficult choices: "sustainable development can only be pursued if population size and growth are in harmony with the changing productive potential of the ecosystem ... We do not pretend that the process is easy or straightforward. Painful choices have to be made" (WCED 1987: 9). To be fair to the authors of the report, they believed that significant changes in the distribution of resources, the application of technologies, and social organization were necessary before economic growth could be considered to be equitable and good (WCED 1987: 8). While the search for sustainability is tied to technological improvements that stretch the biosphere's ability to absorb the effects of human activity (WCED 1987: 9), "ultimate limits there are, and sustainability requires that long before these are reached, the world must ensure equitable access to the constrained resource and reorient technological efforts to relieve the pressure" (WCED 1987: 45).

The Brundtland definition of sustainability continues to be the most widely used and visible one.[24] The year after *Our Common Future* was published (1987), the United Nations Educational, Scientific and Cultural Organization (UNESCO) released a work intended for a more popular audience. The title, *Man Belongs to the Earth* (UNESCO 1988) was drawn from a now famous speech ostensibly given by indigenous North American leader Chief Seattle. The work was intended to expand ethical horizons by promoting a spirituality of connection that had become an increasingly frequent accompaniment to sustainability.[25] This publication's implication

63

that humans are indebted to a larger biosphere is especially provocative, particularly given the strong anthropocentric tone of *Our Common Future*. For example, the Brundtland report concluded the introduction with the statement that "First and foremost, this Commission has been concerned with people—of all countries and walks of life. And it is to people that we address our report" (WCED 1987: 23). *Man Belongs to the Earth* (1988), however, clearly invokes a conception of humans' place in the natural order that implies a greater dependence on the ecological matrix within which humans persist. Later meetings retained influences from both the more anthropocentric tone of Brundtland and the more biocentric sentiment of the UNESCO report, although the human-centered approach continues to dominate sustainability discourse.

BEYOND BRUNDTLAND: THE ROAD TO RIO

The same year that the Brundtland Commission completed *Our Common Future* (and two years prior to the UNESCO publication), His Royal Highness Prince Phillip (the husband of the United Kingdom's monarch Queen Elizabeth II),[26] leader of the World Wildlife Fund (WWF), invited six of the world's religious leaders to Assisi, with their stated goals being to discuss:

- how the environmental crisis is a mental and ethical crisis due, in part, to powerful, predominantly Western and Christian world-views that encourage materialistic, dualistic, anthropocentric, and utilitarian concepts of nature;[27]
- that environmental organizations and politicians are victims of the same economic and technological thinking that provoked the crisis;
- that alternative world-views and ethics must be respected to counter current dominant thinking; and
- that the world's religions constitute enormous human and spiritual potentials.   (Jensen 1999: 494)

This early meeting of environmental and religious minds had two important offspring. First, according to some, it inspired some at the 1993 Parliament of Religions, under the leadership of Hans Kung, to propose the Declaration Toward a Global Ethic (Golliher 1999; Jensen 1999: 446). Second, in 1995, HRH Prince Phillip, the World Wildlife Fund (WWF) and a larger number of religious leaders (representing eleven "world religions" this time) met in the UK to revise their previous commitments. It was during this second meeting that the Alliance of Religions and Conservation (ARC) was formed under the leadership of Martin Palmer (Jensen 1999: 494). ARC is one of the few non-governmental conservation organizations that have maintained long-standing working relationships with the WWF, the World Bank, and the United Nations, all of which have their own working definitions of sustainability (see Chapter 8 for more details about ARC).

Between 1987, when the Brundtland Commission released its findings, and the 1992 United Nations Conference on Environment and Development (UNCED) in Rio, two other important events helped to solidify the importance of religion and spirituality to the quest for sustainability. The first came in 1990 when over thirty well-known scientists composed "An Open Letter to the Religious Community," an invitation for people of faith to join with scientific leaders to find common cause in the protection of the Earth. The scientists noted two primary reasons for issuing their call: (1) religious leaders had long been a significant force leading change toward peace, human rights, and social justice; and (2) the scientists reported that many of them "had profound experiences of awe and reverence before the universe" (Chapman *et al.* 2000: 14), and that "efforts to safeguard and cherish the environment need to be infused with a vision of the sacred" (Chapman *et al.* 2000: 13). The second significant moment came when these combined constituencies, following a conference in 1992, released their "Declaration of the Mission to Washington of the Joint Appeal by Religion and Science for the Environment," which argued that religious and scientific leaders had an obligation, in the face of the impending environmental crisis, to work together toward the common good:

> Insofar as our peril arises from a neglect of moral values, human pride, arrogance, inattention, greed, improvidence, and a penchant for the short term over the long, religion has an essential role to play. Insofar as our peril arises from our ignorance of the intricate interconnectedness of nature, science has an essential role to play. (Quoted in Chapman *et al.* 2000: 15–16)

The importance of global interconnectedness and moral values to the sustainability ferment was important in these northern, institutionalized venues (that is, within the established world religions and the scientific establishment). In 1988 when Mikhail Gorbachev assumed the role of prime minister in the USSR, there was added optimism about the global future which helped to preserve the idea of sustainable development. After the fall of the Berlin Wall in 1989 this optimistic momentum was seized upon and translated into the UNCED, a significant step in creating global awareness of environmental and social problems.

The Brundlandt report had concluded by suggesting that the UN sponsor "an international Conference ... to review progress and promote follow-up arrangements that will be needed ... to set benchmarks and to maintain human progress" (WCED 1987: 343). The 1992 UNCED was the response to this call. The Conference drew together over one hundred heads of state and thousands of other delegates from all over the world and was the largest such gathering up to that time (Rist 1997: 188), indicating the high profile concern garnered by environmental and social problems (Baker 2006: 55).

In preparation for the upcoming UNCED (sponsored by the United Nations, and attended by representatives of the "establishment") a "World Conference of Indigenous Peoples on Territory, Environment and Development" was held the week prior to the UNCED at Kari Oca, a site on the outskirts of Rio (the site of the conference perhaps symbolically highlighting the marginalization of indigenous voices in the development dialogue). Invoking the metaphor of "Mother Earth" or "Pacha Mama," the indigenous peoples drew attention to their own blending of knowledge and spirituality. They claimed that they were "knowers of nature" and that their "resistance, [their] strength comes from a spiritual relationship with nature" (Hart 2005: 1764). One indigenous activist noted that they had "come to share with the world and the United Nations our way of thinking, our visions, our way of life, an alternative. We do not speak of the 'environment'; we speak of the spiritual and physical world in which we live" (quoted from Valerio Grefa, Ecuador, in Hart 2005: 1763).

For Grefa and others, the Joint Appeal from scientists and religious leaders (discussed above) was important, but endorsed a rift in epistemological approaches (between science and religion) not approved by indigenous peoples. Tadadaho of the Haudenosaunee Nation echoed Grefa's sentiments, "We need to seek a balance between the spiritual and the political. There should not be separation of spirituality from political or social life. Americans have two houses, one for government and one for prayer. Our people keep them together" (Hart 2005: 1763).[28] This "People's Summit," as it is often called, drew some 20,000 additional people to Rio. This group, philosophically, intellectually, and geographically separated from the UN sponsored Earth Summit, highlighted a different set of issues, including food production and alternative economic and environmental positions (Rist 1997: 188, 191). Thus, the idea of sustainability, and its major benchmarks, have been attended and promoted by both institutional and elite sectors of society as well as resistance-oriented subcultures of civil society.

Although its overall contribution to the quest for sustainability is still contested, the Earth Summit did result in five important outcomes:

1. the approval of the Rio Declaration, which included twenty-seven prin-
    ciples of sustainable development (Rist 1997: 189; Baker 2006: 55);[29]
2. the approval of Agenda 21, a document of over 800 pages which pro-
    vided sets of guidelines for implementing sustainable development with
    particular attention to local communities;[30]
3. the creation of the United Nations Framework Convention on Climate
    Change (UNFCCC), which drew on the findings of the International
    Panel on Climate Change (IPCC);[31]
4. the Convention on Biodiversity (CBD), which endorsed the value of
    indigenous ecological knowledge, and stated that sovereign nations
    should have rights to the biological resources of their territory;[32]
5. the Declaration on Forest Principles, which created broad frameworks
    and recommendations for sustainable use of forest resources.

In addition, in a directly religious overture at the 1992 Earth Summit, chairman Maurice Strong and several other delegates endorsed what they called
the "Earth Charter." Promoted on the international stage largely by religion
scholars, the Earth Charter invokes a global ethic grounded in a moral
anthropology of kinship with other humans and non-human entities that is
in many ways religious (Rockefeller 2005; Taylor 2010: 184–7). Beyond the
endorsement of social justice and equity and the incorporation of environmental concerns into the goals of political bodies such as the UN, the 2002
Earth Summit in Johannesburg, South Africa[33] saw evidence for the possible
emergence of what some believe may be a sort of global civic earth religion
(Taylor 2004a).[34] During the opening ceremony, participants were treated to
a performance that depicted the common emergence of humanity in Africa,
and suggested that humanity's past, and also its future, must be bounded
by the limits of a finite world. It is worth quoting Taylor's recounting of the
event:

> In this musical theater, a child was found wondering what hap-
> pened to the forests and to the animals. In response, in prose
> and song, a cosmogony compatible both with evolution and
> Gaia spirituality was articulated. The earth was conceived of as a
> beneficent person while at the same time, the emergence of com-
> plex life on earth was depicted in a way suggesting an evolution-
> ary unfolding.   (Taylor 2004a: 1003)

Taylor argued, "It may be that such a religion, in which the evolutionary
story, embedded in the broader Universe Story, fosters a reverence for life
and diverse practices to protect and restore its diverse forms, will play a

major role in the religious future of humanity" (Taylor 2004a: 1004; see also 2010). That remains to be seen, but this evolutionary story has certainly played a role in the rhetoric of sustainable development.

Outcomes, in most cases, have been more modest than participants at Rio and Johannesburg hoped.[35] For now, it is important to note that sustainability rapidly developed from being relevant primarily to individual behaviors,[36] to being relevant to national sovereignty and health,[37] and finally to the global community[38] in a short period of time. Sustainability as an overall goal is now taken for granted in many venues and organizations, and an ecologically grounded spirituality is an increasingly frequent complement to the discourse of sustainable development. These religious narratives of interdependence undergird both global subcultures of resistance, and the American and European mainstream. According to some, a new sustainability ethic is implied by the metanarrative of sustainability. As the anthropologist Darrell Posey put it, "on the level of international policy-making, the emergence of a new paradigm encapsulated by a global ethic centers on the terms *sustainability* and *sustainable development*" (Posey 1999: 446).[39]

CONTEMPORARY CONTRIBUTIONS TO THE RELIGIOUS DIMENSION OF SUSTAINABILITY FROM INSTITUTIONALIZED RELIGIONS, POLITICAL INSTITUTIONS, AND SUBCULTURES OF RESISTANCE

John Smith of the Alliance of Religions and Conservation (ARC) "always considered spirituality a sort of fourth dimension of sustainability," and was at one time at work on a dissertation on that topic (interview May 29, 2008).[40] Smith is a "devout" atheist and socialist who nonetheless believes that developing a sustainable and just culture is impossible without religious people and communities. Despite his atheism he believes that his work cultivates the sort of mindfulness that is an exercise in spiritual formation. So do many others who work within the broad arena of sustainability.[41]

Smith and other NGO leaders suggest that, whether religious in the traditional sense or not, they are doing religious work by intentionally facilitating new forms of exchange, promoting interpersonal and community cohesion, and focusing the desire of communities of people. Some of the common themes with religious dimensions in the literature related to sustainability have become clear already: the idea that humans are deeply interconnected to other biological, ecological, or cosmological wholes, and the importance of individual and ecological limits. Normative concepts are typically embedded in narratives (Hauerwas 1981, esp. 1–87; MacIntyre 1989; Johnson 1993; Lakoff and Johnson 1999), particularly when they are translated for those outside the community to which those norms are native. Comparing and contrasting some of the ways in which sustainability tropes have been utilized by institutional religions, international political bodies, as well as subcultures of resistance will begin to demonstrate the breadth of uses to which such tropes can be put.

Institutional religions and international politics

While many scholars have noted that political resistance movements typically consider attentiveness to traditional land tenure and use to be particularly important, and have attended to the religious motivations for such resistance (Taylor 1995: 334–54; Peterson 1997; Wright 1998; Darlington 2005: 1629–30; Mburu 2005: 957–61;), less academic attention has been paid to the participation of religious groups in international political decision-making or development agencies.[42] Religious ideas, particularly invocations of interdependence and the importance of interpersonal empathy, did not evolve independently within subcultures of resistance and among structures of political and economic power. Rather, at several points they cross-pollinated, creating new manifestations of old religious ideas, and sometimes entirely new narratives.[43]

The Committee of Religious NGOs, those who characterize their work as religious, spiritual, or ethical, have been accredited and actively involved in United Nations proceedings since its infancy (Neff 2007; Pigem 2007).[44] But the interest of national and international political bodies in religious belief and practice has increased since the turn of the millennium, in part because religious fundamentalisms have been reinvigorated in North America, Africa, the Middle East, and South Asia (among other places). While most of western Europe has in the past century steered a course toward increasing secularism, traditional religious groups continue to control large proportions of land, capital, and political influence. For instance, former Prime Minister of Great Britain Tony Blair recently founded a non-profit group called the Tony Blair Faith Foundation dedicated to "proving that collaboration among those of different religious faiths can help address some of the world's most pressing social problems" (Elliot 2008).[45] In this, Blair joins former Soviet Union president Mikail Gorbachev, founder of a group called "Green Cross," which promotes environmental justice along with a sort of green global ethic.[46]

Since the Joint Appeal from religious leaders and scientists in 1990, religious scholars and practitioners have often worked with scientific leaders to promote acknowledgement of the importance of religious narratives in the search for sustainability. The United Nations Environment Programme generates several press statements each year detailing the engagement of religious groups and leaders with their projects. UN Secretary-General Ban Ki-moon recently argued that the UN should play a crucial role in promoting cultural diversity and dialogue, and noted that religion and its free exercise were fundamental to achieving the cultural respect that is a prerequisite for such dialogue.[47] At the United Nations' inception in 1945 forty-two faith-based organizations were accredited, while today the number stands at over four hundred religious non-governmental organizations (Neff 2007, quoting Ban Ki-moon). Not only are religious groups reaching out to international political institutions and development organizations, but these political bodies and development organizations are reaching back, inviting faith groups to exercise their political will, their economic muscle, and their collective conscience to achieve a more sustainable and just global community.

In an address to evangelical Christians, Secretary-General Ban Ki-moon quoted Isaiah 58:10 to great applause, reminding his audience that service to the poor stands at the center of the Christian vocation.[48] Ban also acknowledged that while the UN must necessarily strive to stand outside any particular religious tradition, in a very real sense the UN is itself "an instrument of faith ... inspired by what unites, not by what divides, the great religions of the world" (Ban 2007). He went on to note that the key motivation for participating in the quest for a better, more sustainable world was often religious:

> If you ask the people who work for the United Nations what motivates them—whether they are building peace in Timor-Leste, fighting human trafficking in Eastern Europe, or battling AIDS in Africa—many reply in a language of faith. They see what they do as a mission, not a job. [49]   (Ban 2007)

This focus on "what unites us" illustrates why a global civil earth religion might be a frequent accompaniment to UN development and sustainability discourse. Invoking emotively tied stories that are understood as somehow spiritual or religious is an easy way to stimulate cross-cultural moral sensibilities. As Scott Thomas has argued, the global resurgence of religion and its importance to global politics was stimulated by and integrally related to criticisms of modernity, also often one of the targets of sustainability discourse (Thomas 2005). Sustainability then, as its history has been traced here, is deeply related to and dependent upon the global resurgence of religion in international politics—the emergence of sustainability and the resurgence of religion may be viewed as complementary trends.

The Forum on Religion and Ecology (FORE), spearheaded by religion scholars Mary Evelyn Tucker and John Grim (who in 2007 moved from Bucknell University to the Yale School of Forestry—founded by sustainability ancestor Gifford Pinchot), has been instrumental in disseminating this "good news" about the increasing collaboration of religious groups and scientific and political elites. The UNEP press releases are collated and sent out by the Forum on a monthly basis.

Oppositional subcultures and sustainability

The interpersonal empathy involved in developing moral concern for other living creatures, and the ecosystems of which they are a part, is an often-cited and important piece of the moral milieu of subcultures of resistance. These subcultures generally see their primary task as opposing, or hampering the "progress" endorsed by multilateral development organizations (such as the World Bank) and international political regimes (such as the United Nations). Nonetheless, they frequently use parallel if not nearly identical motivational tropes, and also intentionally cultivate relationships with those outside of their particular communities of accountability for strategic reasons. Making explicit these two sets of stories, subcultural and mainstream, may help them to find common ground for the common pursuit of sustainable living.

Highlighting resistance as the core meaning of sustainability, Jennifer Sumner argued that sustainability is best defined as the creation of a set of structures and processes that invigorate and grow the civil commons.[50] At the heart of the civil commons she imagines "the three building blocks of sustainability: counter-hegemony, dialogue, and life values" (Sumner 2005: 112). For Sumner, sustainability is defined as an alternative vision that challenges (a) business as usual, (b) existing social structures, and (c) prevailing economic wisdom. More than that, however, Sumner suggests that the search for sustainability is rooted in our affinity with the deep inter-relatedness of the world, and aims to repair damaged relationships with the ecological matrix cultures depend upon:

> empathetic ways of knowing need to be woven into a new understanding of sustainability if we are to survive as a species ... they can help foster the kind of relationship with the environment that stresses the interconnectedness of all things. Ultimately, we must come [presumably at a cultural scale] to know what the Buddha said in his first sermon: Everything depends in its origination on everything else at once and in unison.   (Sumner 2005: 102)

What Sumner envisions as "building" the civil commons is essentially an exercise in recognizing the commonalities among various subcultures of resistance to the prevailing socio-politico-economic powers.[51] Paul Hawken, immersed for over thirty years in the sustainability milieu, terms this complex cross-fertilization of groups "intertwingling," a new set of partnerships facilitated by technologies and social relations that compress time and space, bringing the world ever closer (Hawken 2007a: 5). Social and ecological resistance movements, as noted above, find common cause in cultural streams like the sustainability milieu, but their collaboration predates the contemporary popularity of sustainability (see Garè 1998).

For example, in the United States, many environmentalist subcultures look to Native Americans as possessing inherently "environmental" ethical perspectives, and as the first real "resistance" to the colonizing forces that continue to expand the reach of globalization. Native American resistance, moreover, enjoyed a revitalization in the late 1960s and 1970s when indigenous rights emerged for the first time into the consciousness of international political bodies as human rights violations committed in the name of development became increasingly common.[52] In the US for example, in 1969, some two hundred Native Americans and supporters occupied the island of Alcatraz for over a year, calling themselves the "Indians of All Tribes," to protest treatment of Native Americans (Deloria 1992). In 1973, a standoff at Wounded Knee led by American Indian Movement (AIM) activists resulted in some violence, and the arrest of many Lakota and other Native Americans protesting governmental insensitivity to native land rights.[53] Many Native Americans have taken these events and weaved them into a new narrative of resistance connected to traditional lifeways (see for example Hand 1998; Vilaca & Wright 2009). It is clear that such episodes impact both Native American communities and other subcultural constituencies in the US, particularly those concerned with cultural preservation and diversity.

Sarah Pike, for example, in her excellent treatment of New Age and Neopagan subcultures, noted that both groups, beginning in the 1960s and 1970s, drew on Native American traditions to motivate alternative ways of relating to other humans and non-humans:

> The desire to share in native peoples' perceived harmony with nature become a common theme of the 1960s counterculture and in 1970s Neopaganism and New Age communities … New Agers acted to fill this need (for sacred spaces) by resacralizing the landscape with a combination of indigenous myths and stories of UFOs and ancient lost civilizations. (Pike 2004)

In addition, Bron Taylor has highlighted the coalitions formed by environmentalists and Native American groups, for instance in protest of the construction of large telescopes on the summit of Mt Graham, a sacred place for many Apache (Taylor 1997).

These and other subcultures of resistance, although they differ in their basic tenets and foci, tend to exhibit some similarities. Taylor has argued for example that these groups "generally view the animistic, pantheistic, and/or panentheistic spiritualities of indigenous peoples, or certain religions originating in Asia, as offering positive environmental values superior to those found in large-scale, centralized, monotheistic societies" (Taylor 2005d: 603). Grassroots social movements, even if not catalyzed by ecological concerns, tend to recognize that the forces they resist, typically governance by outside elites and disruption of traditional land tenure, are intimately related to deterioration of habitats and quality of life. Taylor suggested that *"renewing sustainable lifeways is the overall objective of popular ecological resistance movements, and this depends on the restoration of the commons"* (Taylor 1995: 334–54, italics his). Extending the analysis beyond ecological movements to grassroots social and political resistance, Taylor concluded that many of these subcultures embrace a spirituality of connection which focuses on relationships between human beings, and between humans and the non-human worlds.

Of course, many questions have been raised about the "authenticity" of such cultural recombination and borrowing, particularly with regard to New Age and Neopagan appropriations of indigenous ritual (see Harner 1990; Krech III 1999; Chidester 2005b). What is clear, however, is that they help some people to navigate the complex worlds they find themselves a part of, and also impact popular culture. Thus, as the religion scholar David Chidester has argued (2005a), even authentically fake religions, those that are obviously the product of social bricolage and appropriation, are expressive of personal values, motivate particular behaviors, and are therefore doing real religious work. The intention here is to provide a descriptive analysis of these trends, not to adjudicate whether or not they are instances of authentic religion. They are, though, performing real religious work.

The above trends are highlighted to illustrate that some key ideas related to social movements exhibit a remarkable capacity to slide across subgroup boundaries, and can occasionally even be transmitted between subcultures of resistance and mainstream social and political groups. Within varied sustainability-oriented social movements, I suggest that the notion of interconnectedness and interpersonal encounter has been disseminated through a broad cross-section of grassroots resistance movements as well as within mainstream institutions.

One of the most important avenues by which contemporary cultures learn about and define this interconnectedness is through the natural sciences. While science is not truly multicultural in its Western manifestations (Harding 1998), its methodology has been adopted by natural scientists across the globe. In Chapter 6 I examine the contributions of the natural and social sciences to the religious dimensions of sustainability. First, however, some reflections on the globalization of sustainability discourse and how sustainability is shaped by the nexus of civil society and international politics.

THE AMBIVALENCE OF SUSTAINABILITY

As illustrated here, sustainability and sustainable development have always had significant normative dimensions, promoting certain ethical standards or modes of public behavior as more moral than others. Generally the most convincing criticisms of sustainable development are related to the normative dimensions of these social movements, specifically critiques that question the utility of pursuing sustainable development through the top–down promotion of a globally acceptable ethic. Such critics suggest that a common ethic, even if coupled with improvements in efficiency, technology transfer, and the promotion of more effective communication cannot untie the tricky knot of power relations among humans and their diverse social, political, and ecological systems. Locally relevant values and knowledge are crucially important and should not, according to these critics, be diffused into a common ethic.

Other critics believe that sustainability can only succeed if nature is infused with some sort of intrinsic value, or if humans are able to embrace a new worldview. For example, reflecting on that "magic word of consensus, 'sustainability'" (1993: 144), Worster suggested that there are three primary problems with the concept of sustainable development: (1) it suggests that the natural world exists primarily for human use; (2) even when humans acknowledge some limits on that use, there is an assumption that the carrying capacity of local or larger systems is easily determinable; and (3) such assumptions rest on the "unexamined acceptance of the traditional world-view of progressive, secular materialism ... We are led to believe that sustainability can be achieved with those institutions and their values intact" (Worster 1993: 153–4). Worster goes on to invoke the idea of intrinsic value, arguing that "the living heritage of evolution has an intrinsic value that we have not created but only inherited and enjoyed" (154–5).

Aidan Davison (2001) has provocatively agreed with Worster that the optimistic assessments provided by definitions of sustainable development offered hope only in the form of recycled slogans from the modern era cloaked in ecological veneer. In documents like the Brundtland report, the hard edge of sustainable development, which requires sustained economic growth, "is wrapped ... in the softer, alluring vision that sustainable development is gathering humanity together as one cooperative, caring community" (Davison 2001: 31). Contrary to such optimistic assessments from international commissions or agencies, Davison opposed "such sanguine assessments with the argument that the appearance of either consensus or intellectual clarity in sustainable development discourses is superficial and deceptive" (2001: 37). Further, in Davison's estimation, the appropriation of the term by instruments of the dominant culture certainly does not "indicate that ecological awareness has been smuggled into the core deliberations of the technological society. It indicates the exact opposite—namely, that the interests of the technological society have been smuggled into ecological awareness" (38). The deployment of the term sustainability has its shadow side, and the term and its spiritual accompaniments can be wielded by corporate and government entities to perpetuate existing power structures or to marginalize particular groups. This is one of the fears that opponents of a global ethic frequently noted during my fieldwork (detailed in Part III).

Although some, particularly those who worked for international religious and interfaith NGOs, expressed worries about global ethics, such ideas are often articulated at the international level by religious scholars and anthropologists, ostensibly people who endorse biocultural diversity and who are sensitive about the imposition of Western values and practices on marginalized peoples. In part then, fears about such a global ethics might be overstated (see Chapter 8 for more detailed discussion of this topic), but the pitfalls of universal ethics deserve further discussion and dissection. For any vision of a sustainable global village that is sufficiently broad enough to encompass practitioners and representatives of particular religious traditions as well as international politicos and secular humanists is essentially itself a form of religious cultural production. Many of these constituencies, however, have very different understandings of their missions, goals, and their approaches to working toward sustainability. Too often such differences are glossed over in order to highlight an imagined consensus.

Although there are significant differences between how religious advocates and secular conservation organizations approach sustainability, they also exhibit some common understandings of the causes of connected ecological and social crises. For example, one common belief is that these crises are at bottom *spiritual* crises, and that religion thus has a crucial role to play in correcting them. Leaders of all of the groups analyzed in Part III cited Lynn White's now famous essay "The Historical Roots of Our Ecologic

Crisis" (1967) as one of the principal motivators for the "greening of religions." For example, White's essay is cited in the foreword to every volume of the Harvard Series on World Religions and Ecology (conceived and supervised by the religion scholars Mary Evelyn Tucker and John Grim), seminal Christian creation care texts (Schaeffer 1970; Wilkinson 1980), as well as in a joint publication by the World Bank and the World Wildlife Fund (Dudley *et al.* 2005). One of White's most important points was that the Judeo–Christian "dominion" theme in the book of Genesis exhibited an elective affinity for certain technological advances in Europe in the Middle Ages, contributing to a culture that overexploited natural resources. Importantly for his religious respondents, White determined that since the cause of the ecological crisis was so clearly religious, the solution must be also. International groups are starting to agree that environmental issues cannot be solved without religious intervention. In collaboration with the World Bank and ARC, WWF argued in print that,

> what has often been lacking in conventional conservation approaches is the regard and respect for *all* values of an area of land or sea—including both tangible and intangible values. While cultural values are sometimes considered when creating protected areas, spiritual and religious values are seldom taken into account by conservationists, yet an understanding of these issues is often critical to successful management.
>
> (Dudley *et al.* 2005: 39)

Saving more in-depth explorations of these ideas for later chapters, I hope here to point out only that these widely divergent groups engage with each other relatively frequently and often use similar language. This overlapping language often takes the form of religious metaphor or story, foregrounds concern for marginal peoples and the freedom to retain particular cultural lifeways, and invokes descriptions of deep biological or cosmological interconnectedness. The public discussion of "basic principles" by United Nations' Secretary-General Ban Ki-moon provides a good example. Among these principles are "justice, conscience, and most important, consciousness. Consciousness of the community of humanity and all living things, and consciousness of our sacred duty to them" (Ban 2007).[54]

Over the past century, environmentalism (Palmer & Finlay 2003; Dunlap 2004; Dudley *et al.* 2005), development (Rist 1997), capitalism (Loy 2000: 15–28; Harvey 2005), and social and ecological resistance to capitalism (Taylor 1995; Sumner 2005) have all been described as religions or at least as having significant religious dimensions. In the global North sustainability movements, which in various ways manifest all these other religion-resembling phenomena, also manufacture a religious narrative whose roots lie in specific readings of the natural sciences, data from the social sciences, as well as existing religious and spiritual practices and traditions. In other words, the language used to describe what sustainability *is* typically derives from one of these three sources. The preceding chapter focuses on the latter, the contributions to sustainability from existing religious traditions and practices. Chapter 6 focuses on the contributions of natural and social scientists to the religious dimensions of sustainability.

CHAPTER SIX

THE CONTRIBUTIONS OF NATURAL AND SOCIAL SCIENCES TO THE RELIGIOUS DIMENSIONS OF SUSTAINABILITY

INTRODUCTION

The detonation of the first atomic weapons manifested in a simulacrum of a life form: a tall, straight mushroom. Mushrooms typically grow out of dead and decaying matter, given life through the death of another (or tens of thousands of others). Like the mushroom-shaped cloud, an elegant irony accompanied the splitting of the atom: the perception and feeling of a deep connection to nature which many bomb scientists reported while laboring on one of the most destructive tools ever devised. Physicists and life scientists have contributed to sustainability movements a sense of awe and reverence derived from their professional work.

Such perceptions and beliefs are typically grounded in an understanding of biological or cosmological relationality, and are typically communicated to others with language drawn from science, although often stretched beyond its accepted scientific usage. The suggestion that the cosmos is "evolving," for example, is an application of a biological term to a particular (and in some cases normative) depiction of astrophysical spacetime. Such affectively oriented language gleaned from scientists has been deployed within the sustainability milieu by many people to describe the central themes of sustainability discourse: interconnectedness, awareness of limits, and interpersonal empathy or risk. While biophilic affinities (those couched in language derived from the life sciences and directed at biological entities) extend to the carbon-based world, some scientists imagine human well-being against the backdrop of a larger cosmological narrative and argue that humans must develop "cosmophilic" affinities.

At least within the Western scientific tradition, the first seeds for these blossoming affinities were planted around the turn of the twentieth century as several physicists (such as Ernest Rutherford and Max Planck) conducted experiments that opened the door to a new sort of physical science later known as quantum mechanics. In 1935 Albert Einstein, Boris Podolsky, and Nathan Rosen published a three-page article in *Physical Review* (now commonly referred to as the EPR paper) on a thought-experiment designed to test whether the new quantum mechanical picture of reality could be considered complete.[1] Their work ushered in two research programs that are relevant to the idea of sustainability. First, somewhat indirectly, Einstein's work in physics, and his letters (beginning in 1939) exhorting US president Franklin Roosevelt to begin work on nuclear weaponry, set the stage for early work on atomic fission, and thus, the first atomic bombs. Second, the notion of "quantum entanglement," the focus of the EPR experiment, blossomed into an interpretive metaphor that exhibited elective affinity for other holistic interpretive frames such as systems science (Laszlo 2001: 175–9), the Gaia hypothesis (Capra 2002: 6, 29), and later narratives such as Thomas Berry and Brian Swimme's *Universe Story* (Swimme and Berry 1994).

The affinities for deep relationality found among physicists have parallels among life scientists. Certainly the roots of ideas related to biodiversity are present in the writings of Charles Darwin (Taylor 2010: 30–31), Gilbert White (Worster 1977: 3–14), John Burroughs (Worster 1977: 14–23; Taylor 2010: 69–71), and other life scientists who experienced a sense of awe and wonder in nature in their research and personal life. In addition, naturalists such as John Muir, Ralph Waldo Emerson, and Henry David Thoreau had voiced such ideas before the turn of the twentieth century (see Taylor 2010, chapter 3 for a detailed analysis). One of the primary contributions of Edward O. Wilson and other conservation biologists in the twentieth century was the generation of memorable terms such as *biodiversity* and *biophilia* for use in the fight for conservation and for sustainability (Wilson 1984; Takacs 1996). These manufactured terms were also pre-dated by holistic interpretations of the physical sciences that endorsed an evolutionary perspective on the emergence of morality but placed it within a larger, cosmological story. Several physicists and concepts from various subfields of physics influenced the ways that people conceived of sustainability and its on-the-ground implementation, although these tributaries are not as frequently highlighted as the contributions from the life sciences.

Through a study of certain ideas from the life sciences and the physical sciences that have influenced the sustainability discourse, specifically the ideas that ecosystems, the planet itself, or even the cosmos are deeply interconnected and "organismic" entities, it is clear that sustainability advocates strategically deploy scientific concepts, language and metaphors to advance their arguments and to "market" them to others. Although science is generally conceived (at least in the industrialized West) as the central pillar around which secular society constructs its moral imagination, the cosmologies and implicit ethical imperatives presented in sustainability-related sciences at least run parallel to, and in many cases intersect more explicitly religious interpretations of such phenomena.[2]

Sustainability is deployed in the public sphere in different ways by various constituencies, and they all use science (or pseudo-science) to buttress their own conceptions of sustainability. As rhetorical analysts Killingsworth and Palmer noted, "the connection between science and the environmental reform movements—a match directly encouraged by authors like Thomas Berry and implied in the perspective of deep ecology—has become the most problematical and the most important link in the evolution of environmental politics in America" (Killingsworth & Palmer 1992: 48).[3] It will be illustrative to show how scientific ideas and data are gathered by scientists, displayed for the public eye, digested and politicized in the democratic arena, and then redeployed in the context of sustainability.

THE SEARCH FOR A "BRIDGING SCIENCE"

Twentieth-century scientists such as Aldo Leopold (Meine 2005), Rachel Carson (Sideris & Moore 2008; Taylor 2010), E. O. Wilson (Wilson 1998, 2006), and Stephen Kellert (Kellert & Wilson 1993, Kellert & Farnham 2002) have all evidenced a sense of the sacredness of evolutionary unfolding or have advanced strongly normative ideas about how humans can sustainably interact with the ecological matrix upon which they depend. They have thus contributed to the cache of religious metaphors available for advocacy. Scientists such as James Lovelock added leavening to the metanarrative of sustainability with his now well-known Gaia hypothesis (Lovelock 1979). According to Lovelock, the earth could be imagined as a self-regulating super-organism. Much to his surprise, Gaia theory became standard fare among many of the aforementioned New Age and Neopagan communities searching for new metaphors to guide their search for human meaning (Monaghan 2005).

Killingsworth and Palmer's aim was to investigate the rhetorical function of such ideas. To categorize their public deployments they postulated a continuum of perspectives on how humans value nature: from "Nature as Object" (on one extreme) to "Nature as Spirit" (the other extreme).

80

Their novel twist was the suggestion that the continuum is in the process of bending into a horseshoe, the ends moving gradually toward each other as contemporary science fosters the emergence of "holistic ecology," *a bridging science* capable of integrating these two former extremes. Of course, those on the "Nature as Object" portion of the "horseshoe" are often reticent to cede authority to what Killingsworth and Palmer referred to as deep and social ecologists.[4] But the authors were hopeful that such resistance might be overcome by greater acceptance of this bridging science. Their discussion of possibilities for such a science included "Nascent theories ... such as the Gaia hypothesis ... and holistic versions of general systems theory," which they lamented were still "consigned to the margins of the accepted canon of knowledge" (Killingsworth & Palmer 1992: 16).

Two decades removed from Killingsworth and Palmer's work, the Gaia hypothesis remains a controversial theory. Its premises, however, have certainly been woven into mainstream venues, such as the invocation of "Mother Earth" tropes in international political venues for the UN (see Taylor 2004a; Hart 2005) and the personification of the earth's systems in many climate change discussions (Monaghan 2005). Indeed, Lovelock actually considered his Gaia hypothesis to be a metaphor that might help to "market" the concepts of systems science to a broader audience (see for example Lovelock 2005: 683–5). The ability of such ideas to slide between mainstream and non-mainstream science and public awareness is an illustration of how the sustainability milieu functions as a marketplace for concepts and practice. The medium of exchange often takes a naturalistic form that, at least on the surface, resonates with traditional science, and posits an "earthen consciousness" that intuitively appeals to deep ecologists and their intellectual kin. The expanded consciousness often associated with deep ecology was directly influenced by religious teachings (Weber 1999; Henning 2002; Jacobsen 2005) and similar concepts have also been championed by scholars who offer non-supernaturalistic "religions of nature" (see for example Crosby 2002).

If the Gaia hypothesis has remained on the margins of interpretive science, systems science has enjoyed immense success in both scientific and political arenas. The interdisciplinary work *Panarchy* (Gunderson & Holling 2002), for example, and the increasing prevalence of adaptive management in resource management regimes signals the widespread acceptance of systems science. In practice, it is often difficult to overcome the political and bureaucratic obstacles that impede quality adaptive management schemes, but such ideas are becoming more common in on-the-ground scientific restoration and conservation.[5] In some cases they are explicitly related to sustainable use, or restoration of resources (for their religious dimensions see for example H. T. Odum's [2007] chapter "Energetic Basis of Religion," or William Jordan III's work [2003]).

While Killingsworth and Palmer hoped that the Gaia hypothesis or a holistic form of ecology might eventually tie off the horseshoe, there is one set of social movements where systems science, the Gaia hypothesis, adaptive management, hierarchy theory, and holistic language repeatedly bubble up (sometimes tethered together, sometimes not): sustainability movements. Sustainability advocates frequently reference these scientifically informed concepts to promote tangible social, political, or economic shifts. To be successful, however, the adaptive and iterative community dialogue that some advocates propose requires some common vocabularies for negotiation.

FROM BIODIVERSITY TO BIOPHILIA

One of the specific common terms used across disciplines and constituencies in contemporary sustainability discourse is "biodiversity." Biodiversity is, like sustainability and religion, a malleable and emotively charged term, one deployed for particular purposes (Takacs 1996). The term was coined and developed by conservation biologists, and thus contains some of the normative flavor of that professional field. But its use has flourished beyond its early confines.

The idea of biodiversity

Conservation biology, as a field of academic study, emerged in the mid-1980s as a synthetic discipline aimed at integrating biological science and social and political advocacy—an explicitly normative science (Norton 1986, 2003).[6] Biologist Michael Soulè and others founded the Society for Conservation Biology in 1986 and shortly thereafter launched the journal *Conservation Biology*, moving the field toward the mainstream. It is interesting to note, however, that the first two editors of the journal (Soulè and Reed Noss) had ties to radical environmental groups and sympathies with the philosophy of deep ecology, both of which have affinities for nature religions (Taylor 2005a). Soulè also developed a close relationship with Arne Naess, the philosophical father of deep ecology, and has openly stated that his professional activity is related to his Buddhist meditative practice.[7]

Conservation biologists have been the primary champions of the use of the term biodiversity since its popularization. And while many (perhaps most) conservation biologists would be uncomfortable discussing the spiritual implications of deep ecology, religious ideas influenced some of the most important people in the field. If conservation biology was developed with the help of many who had affinities with countercultural movements and nature-based spiritualities, the term biodiversity itself was in large part developed by those in the scientific mainstream.

David Takacs (1996) traced the concept back to scientists such as Aldo Leopold, Charles Elton, and Rachel Carson. While they did not use the term biodiversity, they employed similar concepts such as "natural variety, flora and fauna, wildlife, fellow creatures, wilderness, or simply nature" (Takacs 1996: 11). Norman Myers, and Paul and Anne Ehrlich, who published books detailing the quickening of species loss, all believed that these disappearing species possessed intrinsic value, and the Ehrlichs suggested that their argument for preserving biological diversity was at bottom a religious one (Takacs 1996: 35). The first popular appearance of the shortened term "biodiversity" (from biological diversity) probably came in 1986, at the National Forum on BioDiversity, sponsored by the National Academy of Sciences (NAS) and the Smithsonian Institution.[8] From the beginning, biodiversity was envisioned by the organizing biologists as a tactical term designed to influence governmental and public perception of the loss of species and habitats. Participant Dan Janzen stated that the Forum "was an explicit political event ... designed to make Congress aware of this complexity of species we're losing. And the word [biodiversity] was coined ... [and] punched into that system at that point deliberately" (Takacs 1996: 37).

In short, conservation biologists' promotion of biodiversity was a way to market the idea of ecological limits (or carrying capacity) in a way that was explicitly normative. As Takacs put it:

> Battles over biological resources rage ... in every remote corner of the Earth. These battles ... set at odds the perceived needs of humans and those of many millions of other species, and of the natural processes that nourish them and us. Scientists who love the natural world forged the term *biodiversity* as a weapon to be wielded in these battles. (Takacs 1996: 3)

This highly affective language describes the value of biodiversity as not just scientific or utilitarian, but rather something profoundly connected to human flourishing. It is a good example of motivational tropes which are performing religious work.

For many, biodiversity is the defining feature of sustainability, and the other dimensions (the economic and social) are subsumed under the quest to maintain biodiversity (see Lovejoy in Patten 2000).[9] In many cases biodiversity discourse is blended with themes of deep interdependence and a generic form of nature reverence. The environmental scientist Tim O'Riordan, for example, used highly emotive and, I would argue, religious language in describing the importance of biodiversity: "The future of bio-diversity signifies the future of humankind ... By being cognizant, and by being morally alive, humanity can save its own body and soul" (O'Riordan 2002: 13). As Takacs noted in his book, this language is not so unusual. Later in the same work O'Riordan returned to the theme of deep relationality: "Not to protect biodiversity means not to protect humanity from its com-munion with the planet. As we lose biodiversity, so we lose our individual and collective souls. To use biodiversity as a barometer for our ethos, and as waymarks for our pathways towards sustainability, is our best course" (O'Riordan 2002: 26).

The love of diversity

The spiritualized language increasingly used by scientists to describe the reasons individuals and governments ought to care for biological diversity indicated the maturation of the idea of biodiversity toward an affectively oriented affinity for living things. In 1984 Edward O. Wilson spawned a research program that explained, in terms of biological and genetic mecha-nisms, the reasons that biodiversity might be imagined as somehow related to human "souls." Wilson popularized *biophilia*, the idea that living organ-isms possess a genetically based affinity for other living things, which he believed should evoke a deep awe and concomitant respect for nature, and a new foundation for ethics based on the adaptive advantages of ecosystem preservation (Wilson 1984).[10] The project was driven, ultimately, by the quickening of species loss, but Wilson suggested that there was a deeper reason to care about the disappearance of all species (not just the charismatic ones). Quoting Aldo Leopold's "land ethic" as the foundation for a respectful approach to nature, Wilson's collaborator Stephen Kellert stated plainly that "Biological diversity and the ecological processes that make it possible are the crucibles in which our species' physical, mental, and spiritual being have been forged" (Kellert 1993a: 26), and argued that a fundamental shift in human consciousness was necessary.

This shift in consciousness (what Leopold would have called the develop-ment of an "ecological conscience" [Leopold 1949: 207–10]) was character-ized lucidly by Scott McVay in Kellert and Wilson's *The Biophilia Hypothesis* (1993). Alluding to Melville's masterpiece *Moby Dick*, McVay recalled a scene where the protagonist, Ishmael, was tethered to one of his mates as the mate removed the precious blubber from a kill.[11] Ishmael pondered the implications of the rope between them, and realized that his mate's fate would be his own: "this situation of mine was the precise situation of every mortal that breathes ... he, one way or other, has this *Siamese connexion [sic] with a plurality of other mortals*" (McVay 1993: 5, italics in original).

McVay, also a scientist, related several instances of what might be called biophilic "conversion" moments where people are quite suddenly struck by the "humanness" of other animals, the realization that their emotional lives are every bit as rich as ours.[12] For example, he recalled an intelligent acquaintance that remained skeptical of reports about drowning swimmers who were rescued by porpoises. One day McVay met her skepticism with an offer to accompany him to his lab, which contained a tidal pool and a female porpoise. McVay's acquaintance agreed, and once there entered the water and assumed "the dead man's float." McVay's recollection of the incident is worth retelling:

> From behind, the porpoise swam onto the woman's back and clasped its flippers firmly under her arms and began to propel her around the pool with powerful tail flukes. At first she resisted. She was unused to letting go or losing control. She noticed, however, that she could see and breathe. The weight and vertical stroking of the flukes lifted her head clear of the water as the two—joined by a belly-to-back Siamese connexion—made a circuit of the pool to the gasps of the onlookers. She "let go." She told me she relaxed as deeply and as fully as she ever had. The porpoise made two complete circuits of the pool and then shot straight up in the air, releasing the woman gently and precisely on her knees on the cement lip of the pool. She said softly, "I understand".
>
> (McVay 1993: 7)

By "letting go" of her assumptions about other-than-human animals, she formed an emotively grounded connection with the dolphin. The swimmer's expression of "understanding" did not simply indicate that she understood how dolphins saved swimmers. She was conveying a deeper lesson taken from a profound and affectively rich encounter with another being.

An edited volume by Stephen Kellert and Timothy Farnham (2002) further explored the spiritual aspects of biophilia, with biologists, ecologists, and religious scholars weighing in on how biophilia can give rise to an ethics of kinship. Their preface stated that "we see our own salvation in the preservation of the health, integrity, and beauty of creation" (Kellert & Farnham 2002: xiv). According to Kellert and Farnham, an ethic of right relationship with the non-human world, the recognition of human interdependence with other creatures, and the cultivation of sustainable lifeways can only come by building bridges between science and religion. If the scientific concept of biodiversity recognizes the richness of life, the idea of biophilia suggests that humans form an affective bond with this interdependent web. This idea that humans can and should have affinity for other living organisms is central to many sustainability movements.

The putative importance of biological diversity made its way into the Brundtland report, the most well-known work elucidating the idea of sustainable development. The maintenance of "biological" and "genetic" diversity are both referred to as crucial for achieving sustainable development for a variety of reasons, including potential contributions to human welfare, ecosystem services (WCED 1987: 147–8), and the "ethical cultural, aesthetic, and purely scientific reasons for conserving wild beings" (WCED 1987: 13). The Commission concluded chapter 6 on "Species and Ecosystems" with the admonition that "Our failure to [save species and their ecosystems] will not be forgiven by future generations" (WCED 1987: 166). It is worth noting the close parallel with E. O. Wilson's claim in *Biophilia* that "the one process now going on that will take millions of years to correct is the loss of genetic and species diversity by the destruction of natural habitats. This is the folly our descendants are least likely to forgive us" (Wilson 1984, quoted in McVay 1993: 4).

These themes of interconnectedness and interpersonal relationship, couched in religion-resembling language and grounded in scientific evolutionary narratives, are common among life scientists engaged in sustainability discourse. Biophilia grants an additional layer of affective power to the already rich idea of biodiversity. For Wilson, Kellert, and others, the human affinity for life is an adaptive evolutionary trait and the basis for environmental ethics. It will be clear in Chapters 7 through 9 that many of these ideas were recounted by those who contributed to the ethnographic portion of this research. These ideas and metaphors, illustrative of a deep human affinity for the natural world, however, have also been spliced onto broader cosmological narratives, facilitating the further emergence of an affectively rich spirituality grounded in "cosmophilia."

FROM BIOPHILIA TO COSMOPHILIA

Spurred by the metaphysical speculations of famous scientists such as Albert Einstein, David Bohm, Fritjof Capra, and Richard Feynman, by the middle of the twentieth century physicists were also articulating awe and reverence inspired by their work, and were thus contributing to the still nascent metanarrative of sustainability. Killingsworth and Palmer argued that the completion of the atomic bomb was the crowning moment for the "Nature as Object" end of their values continuum: "Their [science, government, and industry's] greatest glory came in alliance with one another, potently symbolized in the Manhattan Project and the continued development of the scientific–military–industrial complex after World War II" (Killingsworth & Palmer 1991: 15). But these successes were facilitated by men whose motives were not so much military as human.

Awe, reverence and the path to destruction

The environmental historian Mark Fiege connected bomb scientists' experiences with nature, which in many cases moved them to pursue science as a profession, to those of some of the life scientists discussed above: "the experiences of children such as Oppenheimer, Meitner, and Rabi [all Manhattan Project scientists] mirrored events in Rachel Carson's girlhood" (Fiege 2007: 585). Later, Fiege compared Carson's upbringing to that of noted physicist and public intellectual Richard Feynman: "Nature study with loving parents, wonder experienced in local landscapes, scientific careers, the championing of unmediated contact between children and the physical world: Carson and Feynman shared much" (Fiege 2007: 587).

Fiege noted that many of these scientists' best ideas materialized or were vetted on long walks in natural settings. J. Robert Oppenheimer (the project director) maintained a ranch in the mountains of New Mexico, and many of the European scientists working on the project were mountaineers.[13] Fiege argued that "Physicists, chemists, and mathematicians studied atoms out of profound curiosity, and when they detected the inner workings of the tiny particles, they experienced awe, amazement, delight, and transcendence" (Fiege 2007: 581). Of course, such awe and reverence did not prevent them from building a new type of bomb that caused mass death wherever it was unleashed. But Fiege, comparing Oppenheimer to Aldo Leopold this time, argued that when Oppenheimer realized the destructive capacity of the bomb, and understood that humanity's only hope

> lay in the binding obligations of the world community, [Oppenheimer] was closer to Leopold than either of them could have known. Oppenheimer and other atomic scientists could find inspiration in a mountain. But somewhere on a lonely, windswept, vertiginous slope, they also learned, in their own way, to think like one.[14]
> (Fiege 2007: 602)

This reference to Leopold's "conversion" moment, often referred to as a paradigmatic example of an ecocentric ethic, suggested that Oppenheimer and others like him were beginning to perceive the outlines of a broader, more cosmocentric ethic.

Like the first views of the Earth from space, the detonation of the first atomic bombs brought a deeper level of consciousness to the global community. It was abundantly clear for the first time in recorded history that *Homo faber* had manufactured a tool that could cause its own extinction. The sustainability of the species was for the first time questioned by large portions of the global population. Some early invocations of ideas related to global sustainability were vetted in international commissions such as the Palme Commission (1982) (Wiseman 2005). Interestingly, early activist energy dedicated to preventing thermonuclear war later shifted toward environmental movements.

A web of hidden connections

If the manufacture of the atomic bomb facilitated the integration of scientific, governmental, and industrial sectors, its detonation acted as an alarm, alerting the global community to the possibility of its destruction. There were several cultural responses, and some focused on positive steps that could be made in the wake of nuclear despair. Greenpeace, inspired by Quaker concepts of non-violence, was birthed by nuclear insecurity and concern over ecological degradation (Hawken 2007b: 196; Wapner 1996). Others, such as Joanna Macy, began their activist careers envisioning positive responses to fears about nuclear wars and winters. In the late 1970s Macy began conducting what she called "Despair and Empowerment Workshops" designed to help people cope with and vent the emotional strain caused by the escalating Cold War arms race (see Macy 1983).[15]

In the late 1980s, as the Cold War warmed, many peace and nuclear disarmament activists turned their energies toward increasingly dire predictions of environmental degradation. Macy, along with activist John Seed, created explicitly environmental rituals such as their "Councils of All Beings," where participants meditated on the non-human creatures around them, identified with them, and spoke for them in a healing circle where all beings (especially those with no political voice) were recognized and heard (Seed, *et al.* 1988).[16] Seed's now famous metaphor that "I am the rainforest, recently come into consciousness, defending myself" suggested that his direct action in defense of the rainforest was in fact *self-defense* (Seed 1983, 2000).[17] Bryan Norton told me that Seed's idea was probably the single most helpful notion to come from deep ecology, and was an important corrective to science's tendency to project environmental problems and solutions as somehow "out there" rather than intimately intertwined with the choices people make individually and culturally (interview January 3, 2008).

It was in this rich cultural loam of the late 1970s and1980s that the ideas birthed in quantum mechanics over a half century earlier began to exert influence in environmental circles. Many of those who brought such ideas from science to the sustainability milieu, such as physicists David Bohm and Fritjof Capra, characterized them in spiritual terms, using metaphors of deep interconnectivity.

Two of the fathers of quantum theory, Niels Bohr and David Bohm, disagreed about how to interpret quantum mechanical mathematical formalism. Bohr emphasized that there was an inherent *ontological* uncertainty implied by the mathematical formalism of quantum mechanics. That is, there was genuine causal indeterminacy at the quantum level. Einstein, and later Bohm, contended that the uncertainty Bohr noted was really an *epistemological* uncertainty—although the physicists' tools were not yet sensitive enough to "see" them, there must be one or more "hidden variables" working to produce the results that appeared to be underdetermined.[18] One popular way to account for these hidden variables was to invoke the idea of quantum entanglement, where the "hidden explanatory factor" was imagined to be the radical inseparability of physical reality: a "wholism" whose recognition, it was often imagined, could spark a new sort of moral imagination in humans.[19] By the late 1970s Bohm had published with well-known theologians John Cobb and David Ray Griffin, discussing the theological implications of such wholism (Cobb & Griffin 1977; Griffin 1988).[20]

Other physicists were writing about the implications of what they were calling the "new physics," and in print combining physical descriptions of reality with religious and/or mystical traditions. Fritjof Capra, for example, in the foreword to *The Tao of Physics* (Capra [1975] 1984) argued that the lopsided scientific imagination of the West was giving way to a crisis of "social, ecological, moral and spiritual dimensions" (Capra [1975] 1984: xvi).[21] Like many others, he traced his understanding of systemic holism to profound experiences in nature and experimentation with entheogens.[22] During one of his entheogen-fueled experiences, Capra reported that he "suddenly became aware of my whole environment as being engaged in a gigantic cosmic dance" (xix). Capra elaborated: "I 'saw' the atoms of the elements and those of my body participating in this cosmic dance of energy; I felt its rhythm and 'heard' its sound" (xix).

Bohm agreed with Capra that "fragmentation" of thought prevented humans from having a coherent worldview, and suggested that "a proper world view ... is generally one of the basic factors that is essential for harmony in the individual and in society as a whole" (Bohm [1980] 2002: xiii). For Bohm, this proper worldview was wholistic: "relativity and quantum theory agree, in that they both imply the need to look on the world as an *undivided whole*, in which all parts of the universe, including the observer and his instruments, merge and unite in one totality" (13, italics in the original).

What makes Capra and Bohm interesting is that they not only interpreted quantum mechanics ontologically (that is, as suggesting that the world *really is* an interconnected, unified whole), but also normatively. While both of them are physicists, they subsume their understanding of physics into a larger interpretive framework that includes biological, cognitive, social, and religious dimensions.

Capra later noted, in *The Hidden Connections: Integrating the Biological, Cognitive, and Social Dimensions of Life Into a Science of Sustainability*, that he realized in the 1980s that the "new physics" was not an ideal "paradigm and source of metaphors" for the conceptual shifts that had manifested throughout the physical and life sciences, and in social movements, since the 1960s (Capra 2002: xvi). Instead, in this book, Capra used "sustainability" and "systems science" as the guiding paradigms, for these terms better captured the thrust of these associated cultural movements. Capra, then, was using *sustainability* for a strategic purpose, deploying the term in publication because he believed it to have greater descriptive power and public impact. These are just a few of the myriad examples of the ways in which science has been used to promote sustainability.

Scientific discourse acts in two ways in the construction of the metanarrative of sustainability. First, it offers empirical evidence about the ways the world works. Second, it points to potentially adaptive ways of gaining knowledge, speaking about that knowledge, and arranging social interactions around that knowledge. Moreover, in the instances discussed above (which only hint at the depth and richness of such discussions), spiritual ideas and ideals are used both to interpret physical reality, and to translate these interpretations to others. The two ideas that most commonly emerge from holistic interpretations of science are the foundational interconnectedness of the living world and the cosmos, and the notion that a new "paradigm," or new "consciousness" of human affinity for the unfolding universe, "a cosmophilia" is emerging.

NATURAL SCIENCES AND THE NARRATIVE OF SUSTAINABILITY

Biodiversity, biophilia, and invocations of what I have called cosmophilia imply the sacredness of evolutionary processes and have been influential within sustainability discourse. The ideas that humans have a deep and affectively oriented affinity for living things or the entire cosmos are increasingly discussed in contemporary scholarship, the popular realm, and the policy arena. Just as oppositional subcultures exchange ideas and metaphors rather freely, within the sustainability milieu ideas such as biophilia and cosmophilia may arise independently (within the life sciences and physical sciences, respectively), but these ideas are then exchanged across the boundaries of these disciplines with ease. Moreover, they exert influence on other academic disciplines relevant to sustainability, such as environmental ethics.

For example, environmental philosopher J. Baird Callicott attempted to tag quantum mechanics as a source for environmental ethics. His primary goal was to solve what he called the "most recalcitrant problem for environmental ethics," the creation of a coherent theory of the intrinsic value of nature (Callicott 1985: 257). Drawing on Capra and Paul Shepard (a human ecologist influential in the deep ecology movement), Callicott argued that "If quantum theory and ecology both imply in structurally similar ways in both the physical and organic domains of nature the continuity of self and nature, and if the self is intrinsically valuable, then nature is intrinsically valuable" (275).[23] Note here the parallel between Callicott's philosophical position and the credo popularized by John Seed (discussed above) that he *is* the rainforest defending itself.[24]

Although Seed is not an academic, the others mentioned above are, so I should be clear that these concepts do not belong only to academics (whether of the scientific or philosophical variety). Ideas about ecological and cosmological interdependence and heightened human consciousness have also been circulating for some time within popular venues. For example, the popular documentary film *What the Bleep Do We Know?* (WTBDWK) (2004) was billed as "Exploring the worlds of Quantum Physics, Neurology, and Molecular Biology in relation to the spheres of Spirituality, Metaphysics and Polish weddings."[25] The film featured interviews with several mystics, neuroscientists, and religious leaders who suggested that the human mind can literally shape the world around it because it is an internally related and integral *part* of that world. An emotively grounded interconnectedness with the cosmos is the central theme of the film. A follow up six-disk special release called *Down the Rabbit Hole*, and an ongoing series of books, study groups, and a newsletter ("The Bleeping Herald") attest to the popular impact of such themes.

Some scientists promote the idea of "quantum consciousness" as portrayed in *WTBDWK* (Capra, for example), while other grassroots programs promoting sustainability perpetuate ideas drawn from life scientists such as Aldo Leopold and Rachel Carson, physicists such as Capra and Brian Swimme, and ideas such as Lovelock's Gaia hypothesis and Wilson and Kellert's biophilia hypothesis.[26] In all of these cases, "cosmophilic" ideas are used strategically to influence the development of a wider moral imagination, one that envisions humans as integrally related to a process of cosmological evolution.

For instance, to preview the discussion in Chapter 9, the Northwest Earth Institute (NWEI) promotes a series of "discussion groups" for communities that include publications from all of the above scientists. What began as a husband and wife team promoting sustainable lifestyle choices in the Pacific Northwest has blossomed into a grassroots movement that over several years has included over 120,000 participants. The *Exploring Deep Ecology* discussion module is advertised with a quote from deep ecologists Bill Devall and George Sessions: "The work we call cultivating ecological consciousness involves becoming aware of the actuality of rocks, wolves, trees, and rivers— the cultivation of the insight that everything is connected" (NWEI 2001a: I-1). Brian Swimme discusses the cosmological "Epic of Evolution": "Within the evolutionary point of view, you realize—holy todelo!—the mind itself is just an expression of the powers of the universe" (IV-10). These ideas are not mere academic mantle-pieces; they have become fodder for the public imagination.

The idea of biophilia, in these cases, is too narrow: the affinities of living things are imagined to reach beyond the carbon-based world, manifesting in cosmophilia. Even when the language of sustainability advocacy is not explicitly religious, in many cases it reflects core values and deep beliefs of particular individuals, communities, or groups, and when deployed in the public sphere it is performing religious work. Ideas about interconnectedness and "alternative" ethics or anthropologies have been raised and popularized by both life scientists and physical scientists, often using religious language and metaphors. Moreover, it is usually through such religious language that these scientific concepts are interpreted for the public. Particularly in these circles, where science is explicitly connected with sustainability, scientists promote an approach to envisioning the environment that is distinctly normative. To the extent that these scientists are treading on normative territory, and are connecting their own existence and moral sensibilities not only to living things, but also to affinities with broader cosmological evolutionary narratives and "forces," a "cosmophilia," they are contributing to the religious metanarrative of sustainability.

SOCIAL SCIENCES AND SUSTAINABILITY

The social sciences have also contributed to the crucial human dimension of this emerging metanarrative of sustainability. Anthropologists and later religious scholars analyzed cultures whose lifeways were envisioned as "alternatives" to Western culture, while some economists began to propose "alternative" models of exchange. To the extent that they use language of deep relationality and interconnectedness, and promote differing social arrangements and exchange, they are doing religious work. Moreover, these models are frequently referenced by scholars and activists outside of the social sciences as important to sustainability.

Traditional ecological knowledge and sustainability

Louise Fortmann, professor of sustainable development at UC Berkeley, suggested that appropriate development schemes always included input about the ways that the targets of development conceive of and classify their worlds—what she called "other peoples' science."[27] In most cases today, such science is referred to as traditional ecological knowledge (TEK). As an illustration, consider the anthropologist Darrell Posey, who recalled that during his fieldwork in the Xingu River region in Brazil's Amazon basin he had disposed of a large quantity of tapir meat after discovering an infestation of maggots. When they returned, his native hosts were livid. Posey was evidently unaware that the maggots' saliva contained an enzyme that cured the meat, preserving it for later consumption. It was common practice for these tribal peoples, but for Posey it was a foreign concept. Several scholars have attempted to take seriously the knowledge systems of indigenous and other marginalized peoples, and in recent decades such examples of native wisdom have been utilized by natural and social scientists for political aims, specifically to generate more equitable and sustainable development (see for example Wright 1988, 2007). Posey was long a vocal champion of indigenous knowledge and rights, but his research also obscured important nuances. The anthropologist Eugene Parker, whose academic interests intersected geographically and culturally with Posey's, contended that Posey's claims about the *apete* (managed forest islands) signaled not only a misunderstanding of the indigenous experience but also indicated Posey's intentional disregard of the native peoples' own explanatory categories. Posey's claims, Parker argued, were "a remarkable house of cards" (Parker 1993: 722). Posey's life and work exemplify in a microcosm the complex and contested ways in which indigenous and traditional ecological knowledge has been disseminated, popularized, used, and abused, especially in Western academic circles.

Humans have always "managed" their habitats to some extent, and some recent studies demonstrated how traditional peoples have historically actively managed ecosystems. But intellectual and scholarly attention to the ways in which particular groups interact with their habitats did not emerge until the late 1800s, when systematic classifications of flora and fauna were developed. Indeed, European colonialist encounters with tribal peoples led to the first organized collection and cataloging of exotic plants and their traditional uses. The first modern botanical gardens and zoos were intentionally designed to display foreign species for public enjoyment. This was, perhaps, the first inkling in the Western world of what could be called ethnoscience. Interests in exotic species and cultures influenced the emergence of European scientific societies, including the Royal Society of Science, and by the end of the 1800s ethnobotany had emerged as an area of academic interest, and anthropologists such as Franz Boas and his student Frank Speck had begun the work of characterizing indigenous classification systems. By the middle of the twentieth century Harold Conklin had composed the first dissertation on ethnoecology, Richard Schultes had begun his monumental work cataloguing the plant knowledge of indigenous cultures in the Americas, and within decades specialized degrees emerged in related areas.

In most cases investigations focused on culturally or medicinally important species, or on elucidating folk taxonomies. For instance, the anthropologist Marvin Harris (1966) noted that cattle management on the Indian subcontinent was related to specific aspects of the Indian worldview, which had been shaped primarily by the experience of living in a resource-scarce environment. Roy Rappaport's analysis (1967) of the Tsembaga peoples' ritual pig slaughter in Papua New Guinea and Gerardo Reichel-Dolmatoff's work with the Tukano peoples of Amazonia (1976) also helped to illustrate the complexities of indigenous resource management. Such studies, along with others, helped to make the argument that traditional resource management was both holistic and sustainable.

It is important to note, though, that not all scholars have maintained that indigenous or traditional resource management is more sustainable than the typical Western management regimes. For instance, the paleontologist Paul Martin argued, in what has become widely known as the overkill hypothesis, that human hunters caused the disappearance of megafauna across the Americas (Martin 2005). Similarly, in a study focused on Native North American populations, the anthropologist Shepard Krech (1999) asserted that these populations were not in any meaningful sense "conservationists," and like other humans had occasionally overexploited their resource base.

The anthropologist and specialist on Native North Americans Sam Gill (1987) has also proposed that the popular eco-friendly concept of "Mother Earth" attributed to indigenous peoples was a Western motif adopted by Native North Americans in the 1900s. As expected, such portraits of indigenous peoples have been contested by some native scholars. The Lakota scholar of religion Vine Deloria has targeted the so-called overkill hypothesis and Krech's treatment of the ecological Indian as erroneous (Deloria 1997, 2000).

The picture, then, is complex. In much of the world, sustainable, local management activities are not explicitly related to Western understandings of conservation or sustainability, but rather are typically related to pragmatic concerns and to the good of a community. But clearly locally adapted management practices can in some cases offer valuable contributions to long-term and large-scale planning for sustainability.

From the late twentieth century, ecological, political, and social movements began to utilize the work of social scientists studying traditional resource management as a part of advocacy campaigns. Academics were also becoming activists and were disseminating their theories to broader constituencies.

For example, the ecologist Fikret Berkes suggested that traditional ecological knowledge was the embodiment of a lifestyle that was the product of extended residence in particular places, and could be combined with postmodern science to achieve "sustainability" (Berkes 1999: 154–5). Environmental philosopher J. Baird Callicott argued (1994) that "postmodern science" epitomized by the "new physics" and the "new ecology" could create a consilience of Western and indigenous knowledges, resulting in a more productive search for sustainability. Callicott advocated a new, multiethnic environmental ethic: "an international environmental ethic firmly grounded in ecology and buttressed by the new physics will complement, rather than clash with, the environmental ethics implicit in the world's many indigenous traditions of thought" (Callicott 1994: 209–10). While Callicott's vision, where "the contemporary custodians of traditional and indigenous non-Western systems of ideas can be cocreators of a new master narrative for the rainbow race of the global village" sounds intuitively appealing, actual political and social structures may be needed to support such large-scale narratives (Callicott 1994: 192). For example, such literature recommends as a starting place methodological pluralism and a more political access for those who advance such plural epistemologies. In many cases, however, the use and abuse of such language and ideas in international politics has contributed to what some anthropologists consider to be a persistent paternalism toward indigenous or otherwise marginal cultures (Wright 2009).

One specific effort to publicize this problematic paternalism and to move toward acknowledgment of indigenous perspectives is the United Nations Declaration on the Rights of Indigenous Peoples.[28] This document, like most international declarations, is non-binding. Nonetheless it provides a pointed critique of Western colonialist cultures' destruction of indigenous cultures, and advocates the protection of intellectual and natural resources, defense of traditional practices, identity markers, and land tenure. These are "the minimum standards for the survival, dignity and well-being of the indigenous peoples of the world" (Article 43).

Traditional or neo-traditional lifeways (that is, those that are based on observation, experience, and extensive local knowledge), including the beliefs and practices that help populations to negotiate these lifeways, are neither metaphysically irrational nor merely simplistic, erroneous renderings of how the world "really works."[29] According to those who extol the virtues of indigenous and traditional cultures, their persistence illustrates the accuracy of their understanding of the embodied, situated worlds in which they participate. Darrell Posey suggested that Western scientific management regimes are over time growing closer to older, traditional forms of management:

> Many people in industrialized countries are ... trying to re-integrate the concept of "sacred balance" into a practical ethic of land, biodiversity, and environment. This movement takes its inspiration from Leopold's ideas of "land ethic" and "environmental citizenship" ... Indigenous, traditional and local communities ... express their profound concerns in cultural and spiritual terms precisely because they recognize its deep-rootedness. (Posey 2004: 204)

Posey explicitly drew on Black Elk's Lakota teachings, David Suzuki's book *The Sacred Balance* (Suzuki 1997), indigenous narratives, and publications from international political bodies. This exemplifies the cross-fertilization of these varied constituencies and the common language used by them, but also illustrates some of the remnant romanticization of indigenous peoples that is often promoted in the public sphere.

Traditional social-ecological systems can be helpful without this tendency to romanticize the beliefs and practices of cultural others. As Berkes *et al.* have argued, "adaptive management in modern society could be seen as ... a sort of rediscovery of principles applied in traditional social-ecological systems. It is a search for a sustainable relationship with life-supporting ecosystems, a social and institutional response to resource scarcity and management failure" (Berkes *et al.* 1998: 358). They are suggesting that some traditional social-ecological systems are instructive not because the people possessed some inherently sustainable ethic or worldview, but rather because their social structures were more sensitive to perturbations in the ecological system. Berkes and his collaborators believe this is a valuable lesson for rethinking how to structure socio-political systems within the industrialized world.

Berkes and his collaborators sum up how natural sciences, social sciences, and values are tied together and placed within an ecological matrix, providing a nice segue into the discussion of economics as it relates to sustainability:

> [J]ust as physics moved in other [less reductionistic] directions ... (e.g. Capra, 1982), so too has biology (e.g. Kauffman, 1993) and economics (e.g. Anderson, Arrow and Pines, 1988) ... The critiques of reductionistic biology or, for example, neoclassical economics, are now becoming dated. Those bodies of scholarship are being superseded by true innovative integration of economics and ecology.   (Holling 1998: 344–5)

Exchange relations and the metanarrative of sustainability

After the tragic events of September 11, 2001, US president G. W. Bush reported to a special Joint Session of Congress that "freedom itself was under attack."[30] In this speech, the freedom that the US represented was explicitly related to economic activity. Economic sanctions were created to cripple existing terror networks,[31] and Americans were encouraged to go about their business, especially with regard to their typical purchasing and consumption patterns.[32] In the same speech, Bush pleaded for "your [Americans'] continued participation and confidence in the American economy. Terrorists attacked a symbol of American prosperity. They did not touch its source ... We will come together to take active steps that strengthen America's economy, and put our people back to work."

Chapter 4 highlighted other examples of economic arguments used to promote capitalism and consumption following the two world wars. Capitalism, in its present form, however, has a peculiar attribute that makes it a repeated target for sustainability advocates. Neoclassical economics always assumes some level of substitutability of resources and goods (Sumner 2005: 87).[33] Since at least the 1970s several scholars and activists have argued that the present form of capitalism has historically been one of the primary engines of ecological degradation and social injustice. For example, Gary Gardner of the Worldwatch Institute argued that market capitalism represents a threat to *all* world religions, and that religious attitudes are the necessary counterbalance that could prevent humans from fouling their nests (Gardner 2002: 9). Economists Thomas Prugh, Robert Costanza, and Herman Daly put it more forcefully, arguing that capitalism is

> fatally blind to the critical issues of the scale of the global economy and the maldistribution of the world's wealth, denies ethical obligations to community welfare, shifts all possible costs to others (including the public), seeks to co-opt the political process by means of moneyed interest groups and otherwise erodes and corrupts the public sphere, and encourages the global homogenization of culture.   (Prugh *et al.* 2000: 71)

There have typically been three sorts of economically grounded responses to traditional neoclassical arguments that markets can generate justice and facilitate increased cultural resilience. First, some scholars have argued that localized diversification rather than growth in sheer size of markets can provide similar or equivalent economic stimulus for increasing levels of human well-being (see for example Mander and Goldsmith 1996).[34] Second, economists such as Herman Daly, drawing on the idea that growth is not always good, have offered instead a provocative vision of a "steady-state" economy (Daly [1973] 1980, 1996). Finally, others have suggested that capitalism is skewed at least in part because it clings to GNP as a standard of a "successful" economy. Examples of alternatives to GNP include the standard imposed by the nation of Bhutan, which uses a "happiness" index for assessing the performance of the economy (see Anielski 2007: 137–45).[35] Nobel Prize winner Amartya Sen ([1999] 2000) has likewise argued that the success of development projects ought to be measured not by the increase in production or exchange but in the degrees of freedom provided to the citizenry. These alternatives are of central importance within sustainability circles, highlighting the limits to economic activity and pathways toward increased technological efficiency.

Perhaps the most well-known use of economic logic to highlight ecological limits in the twentieth century was *Limits to Growth* (Meadows *et al.* 1972), a report commissioned and promoted by a group of elite scientists, businesspeople, and government agents from around the world. Partly in response to this report, the editors of the well-known journal *The Ecologist* penned their *Blueprint for Survival* the same year, reviewing ecological and social problems and providing some suggestions for moving toward a sustainable society (Goldsmith *et al.* 1972: 1). They hoped to promote "a new philosophy of life" which might bring on "the dawn of a new age in which Man *(sic)* will learn to live with the rest of nature rather than against it" (vi). Their citation and assessment of one of the Bishop of Kingston's lectures is interesting, particularly in the context of economics. In this particular speech, the Bishop[36] provides a new set of "commandments" about human responsibility for maintaining God's "household":[37]

> You shall not take the name of the Lord … in vain by calling on his name but ignoring his natural law. In other words, there must be a fusion between our religion and the rest of our culture, since there is no valid distinction between the laws of God and Nature, and Man must live by them no less than any other creature. Such a belief must be central to the philosophy of the stable society, and must permeate all our thinking. Indeed, it is the only one that is properly scientific, and science must address itself much more vigorously to the problems of cooperating with the rest of nature, rather than seeking to control it.   (Goldsmith *et al.* 1972: 165)

In this remarkable passage, the journal editors did not intend to promote Christianity. Rather, they used religion in a broader sense to refer to core values and deep beliefs, and to claim that "good" social science accounts for such values, rather than pretending to remain value-neutral. Moreover, religion has been a key element in recognizing that economies make sense only within ecological boundaries. Herman Daly has argued that "we need a new central organizing principle—a fundamental ethic that will guide our actions in a way more in harmony with both basic religious insight and the scientifically verifiable limits of the natural world. This ethic is suggested by the terms 'sustainability.' 'sufficiency.' 'equity.' 'efficiency'" (Daly 1996: 218). Like the Bishop, Daly provided an "eleventh commandment": "Thou shalt not allow unlimited inequality in the distribution of private property" (206).[38]

The economic future, at least according to many economists, does not depend on endlessly growing the global economy, and may be better served by fostering more localized exchange relations and technology transfers. The scholars above are talking about a "new" way of envisioning our exchange relations. Certainly economic globalization brings significant benefits in the form of health care, raised standards of living, and arguably social equality and justice. But it has also spawned emerging fundamentalisms (abroad as well as in North America and northern Europe), and increased intolerance and violence (both state-sponsored and reactionary). But there remains hope, as Tom O'Riordan puts it, that "If the world political, religious and economic leaders combine the centrality of wealth, health, stability and security with sustainability, then there is a chance that the outcome of the unforgettable events of 11 September will generate a profoundly transformative legacy" (O'Riordan 2002: 27).

Toward a constructive social scientific research program

Like the rest of the ecological matrix upon which they depend, humans are variable and unique. Human cognitive capacities, while undoubtedly following genetic predispositions and general developmental patterns, represent processing capacities unique to particular places and modes of life. This diversity is in large part what makes life interesting but it can be inconvenient for politics. Even in political programs labeled with terms related to "sustainability" or "sustainable development" people have different understandings of what those words mean, and differing perceptions of end goals. It is this dizzying variety that prompted Bryan Norton to propose a new "constructive" social science research program, one concerned with developing "a new kind of integrative social science, a social science that will find its role as mission-oriented science within an adaptive management process" (Norton 2005: 291). In this new research program, social values are empirically confirmed (or falsified) through interdisciplinary assessment of their contributions to societal resilience. While Norton recognizes that pluralism inevitably leads to "a range of values from consumptive to transformative to spiritual," affectively held values are relevant only *within* particular communities of accountability (Norton 2005: 373). For Norton, operationalizing the definition of sustainability requires that a particular community specify its most important values within an open and adaptive process (432).

This process-oriented model is indeed helpful for viewing policy making as a series of "reflective" and "action" phases, where public discussion on community mores (the reflective phase) lays the groundwork for experimental action, which leads to revisitation of community goals. While Norton's model is valuable, his contention that religious or spiritual language should not be utilized in public deliberation between communities to describe policy goals is problematic.[39] First, these religious values can in some cases be instructive for people outside of a particular community, and engagement with outsiders may help to inform that community's own values.[40] As the cases in Chapters 7 through 9 demonstrate, core values within communities are intentionally "marketed" outside their social boundaries for the purpose of forging partnerships and educating others about community values.

Second, fencing religious values out of public deliberation not only truncates creative decision-making applicable to the people it affects, but also raises an artificial boundary within an already difficult process. To suggest that religious values are not translatable across cultures, or to argue that they make the political process too laborious and slow is to place only limited trust in democratic capabilities. As Norton said, "In the end, I guess, we all face a choice: We must decide whether we are first and foremost environmentalists or first and foremost democrats ... For my part, given these alternatives, I choose democracy" (Norton 2005: 251). But if, as anthropologists and others are aware, most of the world's population does not draw significant boundaries between religious and political life, then democratic processes, especially those coupled with sustainable development schemes designed to help marginalized peoples across the globe, *must* allow reflection and public debate on religious values to produce viable, sustainable public policy.[41] Some of those who tell their stories in the following chapters indicate that they engaged in deliberation with cultural or ethical others precisely *because* of their religious beliefs and values, not in spite of them. This challenges Norton's claim that such commitments to risky partnerships (commitments to negotiate with others outside of your own community) have nothing to do with "*the particular beliefs and values of the participants*" (Norton 2005: 285). In fact, in some cases they are directly related, and hiding this from public eyes may hamper the process of public debate.

In part, Norton is using a definition of religion that is Protestant in spirit if not in name. That is, Norton endorsed the idea that religion is a private affair confined to the home and the home community. Religious values, however, support both the flourishing of individuals and communities, and negotiate relationships with others. Recognizing the close relationship between cultural diversity, religion, and environmental well-being is essential to the creation of just policy regimes. Perhaps the integrative, constructive, and mission-driven social science that Norton envisions could benefit from more epistemological inputs, a sort of comparative epistemology. But many of these alternative epistemologies are grounded in spiritual knowledge.

Noted ecologists Berkes, Colding, and Folke note that in sustainable development

> we know ... that there are *multiple epistemologies* [involved], different ethical positions with respect to the environment, and different cultural traditions in the perception of ecosystems and resources. To extend our consideration of the range of resource management alternatives requires an openness to different epistemologies and cultural traditions, and the worldview behind them. [42]   (Berkes *et al.* 2002: 427)

There is a close relationship between knowledge and power, and this relationship becomes especially crucial in intercultural encounters facilitated by sustainable development schemes. As Michael Redclift put it, "the consideration of epistemology in sustainable development carries important implications for our analysis, since it strikes at the cultural roots of quite different traditions of knowledge" (in Ghai & Vivian 1992: 33). This relationship between power and knowledge can in some cases, particularly when framed within the context of religion, stall or even dismantle negotiations altogether. But according to Redclift and others, core values, life practices, and the myths that grow from and inform them should at least be acknowledged and vetted for public scrutiny rather than dismissed as subjective matters outside the realm of interpersonal and community conversation.

One crucial gap in the implementation of sustainable development lies between the values-laden politics of those peoples who find themselves the targets of development and the ostensibly value-neutral utilitarian politics of contemporary Western liberal democracy and its accompaniment, a peculiar form of market capitalism (Deloria 1992: 202–53; Torgerson 1999: 120; Prugh et al. 2000: 67–87; Wright 2009). Such democratic political structures carry their own sets of foundational values, whether they are made explicit or not.[43] To his credit, Norton believes that adaptive management, which lies at the heart of sustainability, is a value-laden science. But while Norton's model allows vetting of many sorts of social values in the public sphere, it leaves religious language locked within particular communities. Some political scientists argue that these value commitments (as well as a host of others) should be made public if a democratic system is to operate effectively (Gilroy & Bowersox 2002). These value sets should be debated in public, with the full input of local populations.

Without direct attention to the resource decisions made by people on the community scale and the local-level power relations that facilitate and constrain them, sustainability on a broad scale is unlikely to develop (Ghai and Vivian 1992: 29). In many cases, particularly in the global South, such community decisions are heavily influenced by religious life.

LOOKING FORWARD TO THE CASES

Three significant streams of religious metaphor and language—from existing religious practice (i.e. world religions, nature religions, and international civic religion, discussed in Chapter 5), the natural sciences, and the social sciences (discussed above)—have as implicit common foci the idea of interdependence, the recognition of ecological and individual limits, and an ethic of interpersonal empathy, where democratic processes and development prospects depend on genuine attempts to "hear" the stories of cultural "others." In most cases the priorities of these various constituencies are woven together using religious language, often translated through non-governmental organizations that facilitate interactions between them. These groups are able to communicate across these boundaries (grassroots/ international, and secular/religious) using the linguistic and metaphorical content of the religious dimensions of sustainability.

The following chapters explore such religious production through cases, beginning with non-governmental organizations that are more obviously religious (in the traditional sense of the word, in Chapter 7), moving toward those that are interfaith or non-denominational (Chapter 8), and secular (Chapter 9).[44]

PART III

THE ETHNOGRAPHIC DATA AND SUSTAINABILITY CASES

The previous sections have explored new perspectives on defining sustainability and religion, offered a theoretical approach for exploring the religious dimensions of social movements, and explored the history and popularization of sustainability and its cognates. In particular, Part II illustrated the significant religious dimensions of sustainability-oriented social movements, and the sources of the language used to popularize and provide moral force to them. Part III illustrates, (a) why expanded definitions of the key terms are important, and (b) the ways in which the values articulated by those who first used the term sustainability have been variously endorsed and challenged by different constituencies.

The ethnographic work detailed here is in some sense a pilot study, focusing specifically on a targeted network of high-level actors in sustainability-oriented non-governmental organizations. It could be expanded to include more cases and more informants. In-depth interviews conducted with these thought leaders was informed by a small-scale mixed methods study conducted in 2005 detailing perceptions of nature's sacredness among secular sustainability advocates in Gainesville, Florida, and by nearly a decade of participation with and observation of sustainability activists and advocates.[1]

The in-depth interviews were designed to first gain a better understanding of how participants understood and utilized the term *sustainability* in their own professional and personal lives. Second, they were asked about the sources of their own "environmental conscience" (to use Aldo Leopold's term). I was interested in the temporal variable—whether such a conscience emerged in childhood, or whether it was related to other, later personal or communal experiences. In addition, participants were asked about the scale of their ecological conscience—whether it was related primarily to commitments to family, or other, broader communities of accountability. Finally, I was interested in the extent to which they had (or had not) partnered with other individuals or groups with significantly different value sets on issues related to sustainability. This last set of questions was designed to attend to which sustainability-oriented narratives and themes were most "catching" and transmissible, and which were most frequently exercised in interpersonal encounters.

Most of the informants agreed on several points. First, that core values and beliefs are important for political deliberation, and can be crucial in negotiating with others who have dissimilar values. Second, nearly all of them detailed profound experiences in nature or emergent sensitivity to social injustice or inequity as formative for their ecological conscience. Finally, many of them also expressed their intention to abjure a *definition* or a formalized *approach* to sustainability in favor of prolonged, deliberative participation with ethical others—what I have referred to here as an ethic of personal risk. Learning the fundamental values and beliefs that motivate others, it seems, is one crucial ingredient in achieving sustainable partnerships between people and groups with differing values sets.

The cases that follow, and the interviews that further buttress the arguments posed thus far in the book, are merely a starting point. The hope is that they inspire further empirical work among different constituencies to discern what those individuals and groups mean when *they* use the term sustainability. In the end, a better understanding of what drives people to participate in the formation of the interpersonal and intergroup relationships that provide the fertile ground for sustainable societies may aid in the promotion of this culturally adaptive meme.

CHAPTER SEVEN

WALKING TOGETHER SEPARATELY: EVANGELICAL CREATION CARE

INTRODUCTION

Northland Church's morning service started right on time as the three movie theater screens across the back of the stage lit up with thousands of stars. With the heavens speeding by on the screens, at least a dozen singers cried out repeatedly "Lord of all creation ... the universe declares your majesty!" In the midst of the stars, several names for God appeared in series (Jehovah, Elohim, Yahweh, and others, finally concluding with "LORD" in all capitals). The song went on to recall the immensity of the universe together with the unity of the Creator God and the cosmos, concluding with God's admonishment to Job "Where were you when I laid the foundation of the earth?"[1] A "cosmocentric" perspective, one that takes the cosmos itself as the unit of moral considerability, was at least implied in the imagery and words. This sort of language is increasingly common, although its use by evangelicals should be clearly differentiated from the sort of cosmophilia endorsed by many scientists and scholars in Chapter 6.[2] Such an expanded sense of moral obligation may be rare among evangelical Christians, but some high profile evangelical leaders are attempting to create a large-scale shift in values among conservative Christians in the United States.

This chapter focuses specifically on the emergence of environmental advocacy among evangelical Christians in the United States, the political structures they have formed around this development, the partnerships they have brokered with others outside their faith tradition, and their local and national impacts. This constituency was selected as an example of explicitly religious organizations and groups because of their political importance and their high-profile advocacy of environmental care. In addition, they provide an interesting counterpoint to the usual focus in nature-themed scholarship on mainstream liberal Christian groups. While the idea that there is some common "Judeo-Christian" historical consciousness is outdated, the claim has frequently been made that the United States is a "Christian nation."[3] If Christians generally are a powerful lobby and a prevalent source of the American moral imagination, evangelical Christians, as the largest single religious group in the United States (26 per cent of the adult population), wield significant political, economic, and social power.[4] While some have become frustrated by the apparent political savvy of these constituencies, many do not acknowledge the thoughtful brokering of partnerships with other religious and secular groups that underlies their political and social stamina.

Although the term evangelical is often used rather loosely, I refer to these Christians as "evangelicals" primarily because that is their term for self-identification. George Marsden suggests that contemporary evangelicalism includes "any Christians traditional enough to affirm the basic beliefs of the old nineteenth-century evangelical consensus," which include:

> (1) the Reformation doctrine of the final authority of the Bible; (2) the real historical character of God's saving work recorded in Scripture; (3) salvation to eternal life based on the redemptive work of Christ; (4) the importance of evangelism and missions; and (5) the importance of a spiritually transformed life.
> (Marsden 1991: 1-2)

According to this broad definition the informants in this chapter are evangelical. As with any other religious denomination, however, there is wide variance within these boundaries. Marsden noted that evangelicalism and fundamentalism are essentially religious "*movements*," and their identity cannot be neatly confirmed by definitional fiat (Marsden 1991: 3, italics his).[5] Ecologist and evangelical Calvin DeWitt used a more expansive definition stating that *evangelicalism* exists within nearly all Christian denominations, including Catholicism (DeWitt 2006: 572). Paralleling Marsden's definition to some extent, DeWitt characterized evangelicalism as a belief in the Bible as the authoritative source for understanding how to live on earth, and the belief that the "good news" of salvation must be actively proclaimed.[6] Generally, evangelicals are distrustful of both secular and ecclesiastical authority, which has arguably hampered their engagement with the natural sciences.[7] But their knowledge of and dialogue with the natural sciences are increasing, and the individuals encountered in the course of this research often cited scientists as central to their understanding of environmental issues.

The evangelicals discussed here are atypical and controversial figures, often criticized by those within their own faith communities for earnestly engaging with the broader secular society. Certainly the evangelicals who attend the 12,000 member Northland Church in Orlando, Florida and representatives of the Evangelical Environmental Network (EEN) are very different from those who identify themselves as evangelicals and resist mountaintop removal in Appalachia, or those who consider themselves evangelical but generally resist participation in politics. The peculiar network discussed here is changing how evangelicals relate to the broader culture, and transforming evangelical culture by cultivating some socially progressive policies within a theologically conservative constituency. These are non-traditional, non-denominational evangelical leaders who take it as part of their religious vocation to cultivate partnerships with people and groups outside their evangelical communities.

Importantly however, evangelicals have been careful to set themselves apart from other religious responses to the environment, and especially from secular environmentalism—the way they put it, they are "walking together separately."[8] The partnerships they form often fail to achieve any lasting results. But when the partnerships *do* work, they are significant and lasting, in part because the participants are clear about the sources and shape of their core values. Rather than use these religious values as bargaining chips, however, these evangelicals use them as socio-political markers to help those within their communities and outsiders better understand the sets of rules by which they intend to negotiate. Analysis of these strategic relationships debunks stereotypes of conservative evangelicals which suggest that they ignore scientific facts, are naive to political manipulations, and culturally insular. To better grasp the ethical foundations of evangelical environmentalism, it is helpful to understand the genesis of this religious social movement.

THE GENESIS OF EVANGELICAL ENVIRONMENTALISM: FROM ENVIRONMENTAL STEWARDSHIP TO CREATION CARE

The history presented here illustrates that ecological issues are a growing concern among evangelicals, but that does not mean that they are a concern for all evangelicals.[9] The collaborators drawn upon here, however, represent a high-profile group of leaders who are changing the public face of evangelicalism in the United States, and the stories they tell about the sources of their advocacy are thus relevant. All evangelical respondents mentioned a relatively short list of people as responsible for the emergence of evangelical environmentalism, including Jim Ball, Richard Cizik, and Calvin DeWitt.[10] Before a more thorough analysis of their core theology, however, some historical background may be helpful.

Lynn White and the greening of evangelicalism

Evangelical environmental advocacy emerged, with popular awareness of ecological degradation generally, in the late 1960s and early 1970s. To date most academic treatments of evangelical environmentalism trace the intellectual roots of the "greening" of the world's religions back to historian Lynn White's argument (1967) that the dominion theme in Genesis, through an elective affinity for particularly invasive technologies, caused the current ecological crisis (see Schaeffer 1970; Wilkinson 1980: 104; Larsen 2001: 39–85; DeWitt 2006: 577). Impelled by White to demonstrate that the Christian tradition could be a vibrant, living religion relevant to contemporary problems, several Christians began rifling through their traditions searching for glimmers of green. Evangelicals were no exception.

The first extended evangelical response to White came with theologian Francis Schaeffer's *Pollution and the Death of Man* in 1970, which provided much of the theological foundation for what later became known as evangelical environmentalism, or creation care. Schaeffer answered Lynn White's charge by arguing that a *perversion* of the Christian message was responsible for environmental disasters. Schaeffer argued that humans were divinely appointed rulers over creation, charged with maintaining harmonious relationships between humans and nature. Christianity, properly understood, could provide the transcendent grounding that could combat what Schaefer perceived as widespread cultural anxiety and depravity.

According to Schaeffer, Charles Darwin had toward the end of his life expressed a profound existential anxiety derived from his realization that "nature, including man, is based only on the impersonal plus time plus chance" (Schaeffer 1970: 11). Schaeffer interpreted Darwin to mean that he could no longer find beauty in nature because he could discern in it no divine spark. A parallel inability to find joy in nature, Schaeffer believed, had become widespread by the late 1960s even manifesting in popular music such as The Doors' song "Strange Days," from which Schaeffer took the inspiration and title for his first chapter (12).[11]

For Schaeffer, the basic tenets of an ecologically responsible Christianity included the following key concepts: (a) nature was valuable *in itself* because it was made by God (1970: 47); (b) humans and the whole creation are *equal in their origin* being created by God (48); (c) Christ's incarnation indicates that the physical world will be redeemed; and (d) humans, created in the image of God, must exercise a wiser sort of "dominion" over the "lower" orders of nature (50, 69–77).[12] These foundational ideas became central to later enunciations of evangelical creation care.

By the late 1970s, other concerned evangelical academics had organized a forum, the first official gathering dedicated to implementing a practical evangelical response to White's challenge and the church's perceived inaction. The forum was launched in 1977 by the Calvin College Center for Christian Scholarship, which focused its initial year on "Christian Stewardship and Natural Resources" (Wilkinson 1980: vii; DeWitt 2006: 579). The fellows selected by the College to participate were Peter DeVos (professor of philosophy), Calvin DeWitt (professor of environmental studies), Eugene Dykema (professor of economics), Vernon Ehlers (professor of physics) and Loren Wilkinson (professor of english). They published the results of their work as *Earthkeeping: Christian Stewardship of Natural Resources* (Wilkinson 1980).[13] This book extended the theological foundations laid by Schaeffer, providing a more detailed analysis of ecological degradation, land use, population, and technology, and effectively introduced the idea of Christian *stewardship* as an evangelical environmental theme.

THE FURTHER DEVELOPMENT OF BIBLICAL FOUNDATIONS
FOR EVANGELICAL ENVIRONMENTALISM

The authors of *Earthkeeping* emphasized that Lynn White's thesis was central to the development of ecological evangelicalism: "It is our thesis that White is, with a few important exceptions, correct in his analysis of the effect of Christianity on views of nature" (Wilkinson 1980: 104). Among the most important exceptions for the Calvin fellows was that it was *Christendom*, not Christianity which was to blame for the ecological crisis: "What White and others have pointed to as the destructive influence of Christianity is, in fact, the destructive influence of pre-Christian ideas, imperfectly transformed by the gospel, and too often mistaken for the gospel itself" (Wilkinson 1980: 104). The fellows thus echoed the argument advanced by Schaeffer (1970) that it was not Christianity, but a *perversion* of Christianity that was responsible for the environmental crisis.

It has been particularly important to evangelicals to distance themselves from Christendom (which they believe is tainted by pre-Christian influences), and from environmental*ism*, which in conversation and in evangelical literature is often equated with a religious reverence for nature itself.[14] As Wilkinson and his colleagues put it,

> All Christians immediately disassociate themselves from such
> views of the relationship between God and nature [the identifica-
> tion of God with nature], for if there is one thing about biblical
> religion which is abundantly clear, it is that God is the maker
> of the world, and thus he is completely apart from it. He does
> not depend on it, but it depends utterly and completely on him.[15]
> (Wilkinson 1980: 205)

Thus, while the human is considered an exception within the animal world,
continuity with nature is emphasized:

> What the words and the whole account [the Genesis account of
> creation in the Hebrew Bible] suggest, then, is what contempo-
> rary biologists and ecologists have been trying hard to tell us:
> whatever else they are, humans are also *earth*; they share their
> nature with its soil, its plants, its animals. (Wilkinson 1980: 208)

The authors of *Earthkeeping* argued that nature tends toward stability, and
that, whether voluntarily or involuntarily, the ecosphere would eventually
cause human population and consumption to stabilize. Christianity also,
they agreed, promoted the idea of harmony between humans and the creation entrusted to them, and thus "a task arising from the Christian gospel
is to bring about such stability, and to do it through means other than starvation and warfare" (Wilkinson 1980: 44). In a remarkably astute analysis
they suggested that inadequate food distribution, population growth, and
unfettered market capitalism all contributed to social inequity, a symptom
of a "fallen" society.[16]

This creation-centered theology remains the foundation of creation care
efforts today. DeWitt, in two public lectures in April 2008, recited nearly ver-
batim the interpretation of the Hebrew words *abad* (to work) and *shamar* (to
keep) provided in the volume authored by the Calvin fellows. These terms
are used in the Genesis creation story to describe human responsibilities
toward creation. DeWitt argued (as had Wilkinson and his collaborators)
that these Hebrew terms connote humans' call to *serve* and *preserve* God's
garden (or creation), to exercise their dominion in a non-coercive partnership with non-human nature (interview with DeWitt, April 8, 2008; see also
Wilkinson 1980: 209).

In recent decades, when climate change grew into a focal point of activism
and international politics, it was frequently suggested that natural disasters
were on the rise, and that human suffering caused by climate change would
likely increase. The poor, many evangelical leaders realized, would bear the

brunt of the impacts of climate change.[17] As a result, this creation-centered theology pioneered by the Calvin fellows grew more complex, adding a biblically grounded concern for "our neighbors" to the notion that humans were God's beneficent gardeners. Thus, while the first creation care publications focused on the relationships between humans, God, and nature, later theological reflection focused on Jesus's imperative to care for "the least of these" (a notion drawn from Matthew 25:40, where Jesus suggests that caring for the poor, sick, and hungry is equivalent to caring for Jesus).

The Evangelical Environmental Network

By 1980, a small evangelical magazine called *Firmament* (published by Bob Carling) had emerged to promote the spread of evangelical environmentalism, while DeWitt and others formed the new Au Sable Institute of Environmental Studies.[18] The Institute offered university-level coursework and fieldwork opportunities in environmental studies. Students remained enrolled at their home institution, but could transfer credits from Au Sable for courses that integrated the natural sciences and their methodologies with theological instruction.

The mission of the Institute was to challenge the two perceived shortcomings of Christianity in the public sphere. First it was designed to combat the fragmentation of knowledge by conceiving of environmental studies as an integrative discipline dedicated to "integration of knowledge of the Creation [science] with biblical principles."[19] Second, it was meant to correct the behavior of humans, including evangelicals, who "corporately and individually, [had] become destroyers of creation" (DeWitt 2006: 584). Between 1980 and 1985 eighteen institutions had agreed to accept college-level credits from Au Sable, and twelve professors participated in Au Sable's programs (DeWitt 2006: 579).[20] Over the next decade the Au Sable Institute and other evangelical responses to the environment grew, prompting David Larsen to characterize this increasingly prevalent stream of evangelical theology as "the AuSable theology" (Larsen 2001: 203–20). The outlines of what was to become the AuSable theology were sketched out in *Earthkeeping* (Wilkinson 1980), a biblically centered vision that attended to instructions from the "Book of Nature."

The Au Sable Institute organized an international consultation on evangelical eco-theology in 1992, and at this meeting the International Evangelical Environmental Network (IEEN) was created (interview with DeWitt, April 8, 2008; DeWitt 2006: 579) with the impassioned claim that Christians "must dare to proclaim the full truth about the environmental crisis in the face of powerful persons, pressures and institutions which profit from concealing the truth" (quote from the summarizing report, quoted in DeWitt 2006: 580).

Led by Jim Ball, a graduate of Drew Theological Seminary, the Evangelical Environmental Network (EEN) (according to DeWitt, a US-based derivative of the IEEN) held their first meeting the following year and captured the phrase "creation care" from the title of a small-distribution magazine (formerly *Firmament*) dedicated to evangelical environmental stewardship.[21] According to their website, the EEN's work centers simply on "worshipping God, loving His people, and caring for His creation."[22] Ball and others immediately set to work on the "Evangelical Declaration on the Care of Creation," which was signed by dozens of high-profile academics and pastoral and lay leaders.[23] The Declaration brought a rush of attention to Ball and the EEN, who had helped to engineer the declaration and promoted it among high-profile evangelical leaders. The EEN, the Au Sable Institute, and other evangelical organizations continue to actively participate in ecological justice campaigns, particularly those related to climate change.

By 2005 the Au Sable Institute's influence had grown with more than sixty participating colleges and seventy professors. As the largest single religious group in the United States, evangelicals exercise significant sway in the political realm especially with regard to environmental legislation, and the EEN and the Au Sable Institute help to encourage the recognition and wise use of this power.[24]

Northland Church, Longwood, Florida

In the 1960s, alternative, contemporary Christian worship services were being held at the Circle Church in Chicago, Illinois.[25] Other churches, patterned on their vibrant, simple worship services, began to spring up in other parts of the country, including in Clearwater, Florida. Two members of the Clearwater Circle Church, Lyle and Marge Nelson, were transferred to Orlando, Florida. They started a Circle Church in Orlando, and eventually, in 1972, the Nelsons and nine others established Northland Church[26] (on the north side of Orlando), meeting in two different elementary school gymnasiums over their first ten years.

By 1984, the congregation had grown to 500 people, and it became clear that a more permanent facility was needed. As the congregation's leaders searched for a structure, a rift emerged within the congregation between those who wished to remain loyal to the founding principles of the Circle Church (small congregation size, no ownership of buildings or other structures), and those who did not wish to remain constrained by a small congregation. The latter group purchased a defunct roller skating rink and in 1985 pastor Joel Hunter joined them as pastor. The renovations on the building were completed in 1988, and between 1985 and 1997 the congregation grew to more than five thousand people. In 2007, construction was completed on their new 160,000 square foot, forty-two million dollar facility next door to the old skating rink. The church and the distribution of its message had grown immensely. More importantly for this project, Joel Hunter, as a Board member for the National Association of Evangelicals (NAE) and the EEN, has since 2005 become one of the most important evangelical voices for creation care.

While evangelical policy advocacy in the past decade has focused most visibly on opposing termination of pregnancies and restricting the legal definition of marriage to the union of a man and a woman, there is another constituency emerging among evangelicals that eschews some of the fundamentalist leanings of more conservative evangelicals. This increasingly vocal group has been reinvesting political energy into issues that are directly concerned with ministering to the poor (both at home and abroad) and on protecting creation. They believe that it is through the convergence of resource shortages and wars that more people will inevitably perish. Thus, ethical pronouncements focused on policing marriage boundaries and life and death issues have for some morphed into a more globally aware ethic of accountability to the poor. Contrary to the perception that evangelicals shy away from scientific knowledge, many of these leaders have intentionally formed working alliances with scientists to increase their own political acumen and weight in the international policy sphere.

GOD DOESN'T SPEAK WITH FORKED TONGUE:
EVANGELICAL LEADERS AND SCIENTIFIC KNOWLEDGE

Joel Hunter, the pastor of Northland Church, admitted that many Americans believe that evangelicals are opposed to science, and try to inject religion into politics. It was a charge that he was well prepared to answer:

> They're lumping together … actually theologically, they're called fundamentalists—and fundamentalists do eschew learning and science, and you know, things of the mind … They've got a battle going on with the world … things of the world. The much larger constituency are evangelicals who absolutely see no …

contradiction between science and scripture. They do not believe that God speaks with forked tongue. You know, He used one tongue to create scripture and another tongue to create science.
(Interview March 31, 2008)

Dr Hunter and other evangelicals interviewed during this research agreed on two things: (a) science was crucially important for understanding our world and for working toward environmentally responsible and sustainable behaviors, and (b) "scientism," the valorization of science as the ultimate arbiter of truth, was misplaced faith in a social construction (although an admittedly valuable one). Even though they shared some commonalities, there was a range of positions on the importance of science to moral reasoning.

For example, Raymond Randall, volunteer head of the "Creation, I Care" committee at Dr Hunter's Northland Church, suggested that "It's when we elevate it [science] to the primary thing, that's when we run into a problem. Both sides [in the debate over climate change] think they've got the 'truth' and we're not getting anywhere" (interview March 30, 2008). In one conversation, Randall cited Dr Hunter's position on the relationship between science and faith. If there is a discrepancy between science and scripture the appropriate response, according to both men, is to look at the disagreement systematically, noting that either scripture has been misinterpreted or that the scientific data is flawed (interview March 30, 2008). Thus far the ethic of personal risk has been offered in rather broad and theoretical terms (in the first chapters). Some idea of how it relates to the theological commitments discussed here may be illustrative.

After a series of talks, Raymond Randall declined to participate as the director of a non-profit volunteer network sponsored by Interfaith Power and Light (IPL) (a religiously inspired alternative energy organization, see Chapter 8 for more details). Some staff members of IPL believed the refusal stemmed from his desire to avoid openly endorsing the science that illustrates that climate change is anthropogenic (from interview with Sally Bingham, July 6, 2008).[27] Randall, however, suggested that his reticence actually stemmed from the motivations cited by IPL for changing energy use and other behaviors. In Randall's view, IPL endorses the idea that shifts in the Earth's climatic patterns have been caused by humans, and thus works to utilize the political weight of faith communities to correct the crisis. In contrast, for Randall, scientific evidence that humans are responsible for climate change does not inform his participation in creation care. Randall works against climate change because he believes that he is being obedient to God's wishes, not because he is concerned about the ecological consequences of human-induced climate change. For Randall, it is the source of

116

motivation that differs: IPL's motivation is this-worldly, while his own motivation is transcendent. Because they are an interfaith group, IPL cannot use explicitly Christian theological language as the centerpiece of their public argument. For some the distinction may be minor, but for evangelicals, it is a particularly important one. As Joel Hunter put it, "The issue to evangelical Christians isn't global warming; the issue is whether or not we will exercise a moral and biblical obedience to a direct command of God (Genesis 2:15)" (Hunter 2007).[28]

Although the perception was that Randall was uncomfortable with science, in his understanding the science was irrelevant to his behavior—whether climate change was anthropogenic or not he was obeying a biblical mandate by acting to steward the Earth by reducing human impacts on the environment.[29] But he underlined the importance of the core values that provided the motivation for action: "If you look at 'climate change,' 'sustainability,' and 'creation care,' the monikers given [to the sets of social movements referred to here as sustainability movements] by the environmental movement, the business movement, and the church [respectively], the actions taken are largely the same" (interview May 30, 2008). He noted that reducing energy consumption, increasing water efficiency, and reducing solid waste were common elements between these approaches. But "it's the motivation that's different," he told me: "In the environmental movement it's 'We're gonna save the world ... our world is ending'; in the business movement it's, 'Hey, you know what, at least for the time being, we can probably capture market share—make a little more money'; in the church it's 'being more biblically obedient'" (interview May 30, 2008).

This is an excellent example of why it may be important to include debate about core values and deep beliefs in cooperative enterprises, even when interpreting scientific evidence, for it is clear that the lenses through which such scientific data is viewed make a difference. Despite differing values, it is possible that diverse constituencies could work together toward common policy goals. But a practical convergence of values may never emerge if the values underlying practical actions keep different parties from working together to begin with.[30]

Dr Hunter volunteered his understanding of the relationship between religion and science (March 30, 2008):

> We believe that if there seems to be a disagreement between science and scripture, it's because either we've misinterpreted scripture, or, science hasn't caught up yet ... There was a time, for example, when science thought virgin birth was ludicrous, now there's a whole field of study called parthenogenesis.[31]

While almost certainly not attempting to rob the virgin birth of Jesus of its supernatural importance, Hunter is, at least in this instance, indicating that a non-interventionist perspective on divine action could be as theologically satisfying as a more fundamentalist perspective which conceives of God's action working against natural laws in many cases.

Randall's and Hunter's accounts of the relationship between religion and science were nearly identical, which provides evidence that ideas and interpretive frameworks can be transmitted between actors engaged in similar networks. Importantly, these ideas and interpretive frameworks are also translated and transmitted to those outside the evangelical community. For example, evangelicals have formed alliances with the scientific community, and through these alliances, Hunter cultivated a relationship with E. O. Wilson.[32] Hunter told me he once asked Wilson, "So, why are you guys teaming up with evangelicals?" According to Hunter, Wilson replied,

> Are you kidding? If you took all of the humanist organizations in the United States ... all of these [secular] organizations, took all of their membership, we'd add up to maybe 5,000 people—that's half of your church! You've got 30 million members in the NAE! Why would we not know that we need you to encompass this [response to the environmental crisis].
> (Interview with Hunter, March 30, 2008)

Hunter called these partnerships "little confederations, little alliances," but he was forthcoming about the big tactical advantage provided by these little alliances: "The curious thing about this is that the scientists, a lot of them, are just secular humanists, I mean they're not believers. But they've got the information *we* need, because evangelicals don't have the science. But we've got the base that they need" (interview March 30, 2008). Whether or not the political advantages that accrue to both sides are made explicit, they are important in motivating the formation and maintenance of such partnerships.

RIGHT RELATIONSHIP: HUMAN PARTNERING FROM A COSMOCENTRIC PERSPECTIVE

At a Sunday service at Northside Church Dr Hunter held aloft his grandmother's Bible, well-worn and tattered, and told the congregation of somewhere around 12,000 (with others tuning in through simultaneous webcast) with tears in his eyes that sometimes he simply opened the Bible at random, pointed to a verse, and meditated on what that particular passage had to teach him that day. It was a way of putting trust in God, believing that God's word would be relevant to whatever struggle he was facing at that time. Reflecting on this trust in the Lord, Dr Hunter said "You can't change others, but you can let God change you" (March 30, 2008). He told this story in the context of discussing interpersonal relationships: God wants humans to have healthy, loving relationships because God *is* a relationship (a Trinitarian one). Relationship, at least according to the lessons gleaned by Dr Hunter from his grandmother's Bible, means engaging with others with an open heart without the expectation that the other will change to suit your needs or desires, but with the hope that you can nonetheless have a positive relationship together. "Righteousness," Dr Hunter emphasized, "is about meeting the demands of relationships" (March 30, 2008). This is the evangelical Christian manifestation of one of the central themes in sustainability discourse, the ethic of interpersonal empathy, or risk.

Recognizing the interdependence of life is another one of the key common elements typically found in sustainability advocacy, and it is evident in these evangelical circles in the recognition that the entire created world has a common ancestry (it ultimately derives from God) and ideally exists in a state of *shalom*, or right relationship.[33] At the "Let There Be Light" Creation Care Conference (C3) held at Northland Church, a panel consisting of Dr Hunter, Rabbi Steven Engel, and Imam Muhammad Musri discussed the importance of maintaining a right relationship with all of creation. Engel invoked the "spaceship earth"[34] metaphor, and using terminology that permeates the sustainability movement, stated that "we are all related" (February 21, 2008).

Here is one significant difference between this evangelical constituency situated within the sustainability milieu and constituents of the environmentalist milieu: environmentalist understandings of "common ancestry" are linked to evolutionary emergence; the evangelical interpretation suggests that all creatures and indeed the whole world were created by, and are thus dependent upon, God. These evangelicals do not perceive a conflict between science and their theology. All of those discussed here accept some of the tenets of evolutionary theory, although typically not in the way it is typically understood by scientists. In that, however, they are no different from the mainstream citizenry of the US (nearly 50 per cent of whom are skeptical of science in some way). Only 5 per cent of scientists, versus 47 per cent of the general public believe that humans were created in their present form several thousand years ago. Ultimately, nearly half of the general population is at least skeptical of Darwinism (Holden 2006: 769).

At the C3 at Northland Church, Richard Cizik, who at the time was the vice president for governmental affairs for the NAE, implored those gathered to raise their standards for providing moral leadership in the crusade against human-induced climate change and environmental destruction.[35] He called on the gathered group of ministers and lay leaders to cultivate "transformational relationships," those which raise the ethical standards and aspirations of both the leader, and the followers.[36] Cizik is undoubtedly one of these transformational leaders, was one of the most significant figures to give creation care political teeth, and according to DeWitt was one of the first to "inject" the popular evangelical community with the environmental message (interview April 8, 2008).[37] According to Cizik, many members of Congress now consider evangelical leaders the "go-to" people for climate change issues—they have become political "insiders" (C3, February 21, 2008). They are perceived as the most educated on the issues, and most aware of the moral implications of policy decisions.

Leaders like Hunter and Cizik are making decisions from a religious standpoint, directly connecting (in the private and public spheres) their activism with a Christian moral framework. They are intentionally brokering tactical partnerships with the expressed aim of generating large-scale change in the formulation of public policy, the management of exchange relations (they favor more just economic arrangements), and the inclusion of spiritual and religious values in the public sphere. These leaders are generating ripple effects among their followers.

For instance, Dan Hardaway, a member of Hunter's Northland Church, reflected on how his faith leaders had encouraged him to make small behavior changes, which in turn affected the quality of his relationships with others. Hardaway was moved enough by his changing relationships to post a thoughtful testimonial on the "Creation, I Care" website:

> I felt like for the first time, as I have taken some very minor steps, I was engaging people who I sought to reach. Now instead of just articulating my differences, I am making progress in loving them. I've even become vigilant about rinsing out the recyclables. We are buying more efficient light bulbs and even bought a blanket for my hot water heater. Christ is still returning, and I'm not a tree hugger, but the environment is becoming an area of concern.[38]

Alexei Laushkin, program assistant at the EEN, considers his faith centrally relevant to the cultivation of relationships with those outside his evangelical community because he believes it is important for evangelicals to be witnesses for Christ with their entire lives, not just on one or two politically hot topics. Religious values, in this case, make a significant difference in the amount, manner, and quality of engagement in politics and the public sphere. Laushkin put it this way:

> If religious groups are going to be religious groups *in* society ...
> then they have to not necessarily be tied in to a particular ideol-
> ogy. If they're going to speak to transcendent values, they have to
> speak about these transcendent values in all parts of life ... and
> developing those relationships and making those arguments, you
> know, in the public square in a way that doesn't turn people off
> with our language, but helps people understand who we are and
> where we're coming from ... in a constructive fashion.
>
> (Interview May 13, 2008)

If religion and sustainability are both fundamentally about relating to ethnic, cultural, or ethical "others," then these evangelicals are participating in sustainable relationships when they invoke the evangelical calling to pay particular attention to the needs of marginalized others, those whose politi-cal voices are muted, or whose physical opportunities are limited. At the C3 event, Cizik invoked a question well-known in Christian circles, "Who is my neighbor?"[39] Drawing on the biblical tale of Daniel, Cizik noted that there are politicians in Washington "who sacrifice the Empire for their friends," specifically their oil and gas producing friends (his language). Such skewed domestic priorities affect the global social and political scene. In the end, therefore, according to Cizik, the answer to the question "Who is my neigh-bor?" must include "the Indians whose lives are being taken away by the ris-ing seas!" (C3, February 21, 2008). The way Cizik framed it, evangelicalism must include the recognition of divinely imposed limits on our own opu-lence for the sake of the greater good and a sense of "biblical outrage" at the realization that it is consumer markets, and not devotion to God, that drive American culture. As Joel Hunter wryly put it (quoting Saint Augustine), "He who has a lot of goods has someone else's goods" (February 21, 2008).[40] To characterize this expanded evangelical moral sensibility, Cizik concluded with the reflection that "We [evangelical leaders] have to have a cosmocen-tric worldview—not an anthropocentric worldview" (February 21 2008).

PATRON SAINTS OF ECOLOGY: MODELING BEING (A BETTER) HUMAN

The sort of cosmocentrism invoked by Cizik is of a particular type, how-ever. Some academics, according to DeWitt, attempt to trace evangelical environmentalism to leaders such as noted Catholic priest Thomas Berry and related scholars and writers. As DeWitt made clear, the sort of cosmo-centrism espoused by Berry (who called himself a *geologian*), or parallel, Process-oriented models of divinity, are off-putting to most evangelicals.[41]

DeWitt specifically cited suggestions made by Berry that Christians ought to "put the Bible on the shelf for twenty years," or that God was an "emergent property" of cosmological evolution. Mary Evelyn Tucker and John Grim and a number of other scholars who have shaped the emerging field known as Religion and Ecology are long-standing proponents of Berry's thought, and in many cases have used it to frame what they perceive to be a common quest of the world's religions toward sustainability. The notion that evangelical environmental stewardship follows Berry's views, however, is offensive to some evangelicals, and according to DeWitt, amounts to "hubris" (interview April 8, 2008).

DeWitt, Hunter, Cizik, and others have consciously and carefully begun to provide some color to a different sort of cosmocentric worldview for the evangelical masses through the construction of positive myths and stories that re-imagine the place of the human within the natural matrix, a dependent creature in a "good" world.[42] For example, DeWitt argued in his speeches at the C3 and at the University of Florida (April 2008) that "economy" should be redefined to recognize that the creation (ecology) is the foundation of the economy.[43] Blending scientific classifications with theological concepts DeWitt characterized Jesus as the king of the plant kingdom, the animal kingdom, and the mineral kingdom, and as a teacher who mostly taught on "field trips" (February 21, 2008). This blending of evangelicalism and science, however, was nothing new. As noted above, evangelicals have long cultivated relationships with scientists as a means to increase their political access.

The "Climate Forum 2002" at Oxford (UK), for example, a meeting of scientists, policy-makers, and Christian leaders, was designed to achieve the goal, according to participant Cal DeWitt, of getting "American evangelicals and scientists to see if we could *penetrate* the evangelical community" (interview April 8, 2008).[44] A follow up meeting was held in December 2006 at Melhana Plantation in southern Georgia, resulting in a resolution released on January 17, 2007 called "An Urgent Call to Action."[45] The combined group declared that in their dialogue they "happily discovered far more concordance than any of us had expected, quickly moving beyond dialogue to a shared sense of moral purpose. Important initiatives were already underway on both sides, and when compared they were found to be broadly overlapping." Beyond this encouraging convergence of aims, the group expressed significant non-anthropocentric sentiment when they argued protecting biological diversity was a "profound moral imperative" that serves "the interests of all humanity as well as the value of the non-human world."

These environmentally and socially engaged evangelicals have actively worked to separate themselves from, and combat the negative public perceptions of the extreme religious right, who claimed responsibility for G. W. Bush's victory in the US presidential race of 2004. Joel Hunter's books *Right Wing, Wrong Bird* (2006) and *A New Kind of Conservative* (2008) tried to correct the mistaken conflation of evangelicals with their fundamentalist Christian cousins and spelled out more clearly what it means to witness for Christ in the twenty-first century. Hunter (and creation care advocates) focus on "the least of these," the poorest peoples in the world who stand to bear most of the increasing biological, emotional, and cultural costs of climate change. These evangelicals see their vocation as a new sort of lived witness, often acknowledging their moral stances on beginning and end of life issues, but focusing their activist and political energies toward advocacy for the poor in marginalized countries, and for a culture change in the US. As Laushkin imagined his role and that of other evangelicals within sustainability movements,

> What we're doing is part of that broader movement [toward sustainability], but each broader movement in American society brings their own perspective to the table, and those perspectives can look quite different to [other] constituency groups ... We [evangelicals] are more conservative overall ... We see our [his and other creation care leaders'] role ... as being messengers to the conservative part of society.   (Interview May 13, 2008)

But this "good news" for conservatives is not just transmitted among the evangelical leadership, and cosmocentric discourse is not used only to broker partnerships outside the evangelical community. These strategic partnerships and expanded ethical perspectives are also encouraged at the local level, and derive from the grassroots. For example, Tri Robinson, pastor of the Vineyard Church in Boise, Idaho attributed his Christian concern for the environment to an outdoor experience at the age of sixteen. He recalled "standing on the side of a mountain in California, wondering who God was." Robinson said that God spoke to him on that mountain, and eventually guided him into the ministry. Although an outdoor peak experience had been deeply formative for him, he did not bring advocacy for the natural world into his ministry for some time (address February 21, 2008).[46]

Boise is surrounded by some of the wildest country in the US, and environmental sentiment runs strong there (whether it is of the more preservationist variety or the deep appreciation for nature that may arise from hunting, fishing, and other outdoor activities). Robinson and his congregants had participated in restoration and other conservation activities, but never under the auspices of the church. After some deep reflection and prayer, and decades removed from the voice on the mountain, Robinson, a former ecology major and high school biology teacher, discerned that God required him to bring the message of environmental stewardship from that mountainside into the pulpit.

At that time, Robinson performed three services on Sundays to accommodate all of his worshippers, and on the day he started his earth ministry all three sermons were concerned with creation care. With tears in his eyes at the C3 gathering, Robinson recalled that it was the only time in his ministry that he had ever received three standing ovations in a row at his services. These environmentally oriented sermons gave rise to more, and a cosmocentric perspective combined with biblical concern for "the least of these" translated into social activism in Boise. The Vineyard Church has since started an organic garden where members grew over 31,000 pounds of food in 2010, all of it donated directly to the homeless. A free medical clinic has also materialized on site. "It has changed our church," Robinson said, "people are touching the heart of God in new ways" (February 21, 2008; see also www.vineyardboise.org/garden/, accessed August 12, 2011).

Joel Hunter closed the C3 event with an admonishment to the gathered church and lay leaders that they had both a Christian and a democratic duty to speak their values directly into the policy formation process. His conclusion was forceful, if blunt: "If you follow Jesus, you don't destroy the earth. Personal change literally saves lives" (February 21, 2008).

Personal transformation is particularly important for evangelicals, who also value the individual liberties that accompany capitalism and democracy.[47] But such transformation is not *merely* individual, it always occurs within particular communities of accountability whose faith commitments are entangled with politics and economics in complex ways. Such communities often imagine that their faith-based socio-political reasoning sets them apart from complete identification with what evangelicals perceive to be the dominant secular culture. Although the largest population of Christians in the US, evangelicals envision themselves as out of step with the mores of the masses. Laushkin noted the clash between consumerism (what he perceives to be the focus of American culture generally) and what he imagines the Christian vocation should be, namely a focus on family and community. He further related consumerism to other unhealthy, but uncritically accepted behaviors that permeate our culture. "There are people in LA that drive two hours a day to work," Laushkin told me with mild disbelief. He continued, "From whatever perspective you use, whatever ideology you ascribe to, you're not going to say, 'that's how we were meant to live.'" In a more pensive tone, he then asked, "When was the last time you enjoyed a sunset, you know? It was given to us every day, for our enjoyment" (interview May 13, 2008).[48]

Stories about what is important, specific visions of the "good life," about participation with "others," and about providing transformational leadership are growing into guiding metaphors for the evolving evangelical creation care movement, which itself is a particular theocentric approach that has significant philosophical, ethical, and practical overlap with other facets of sustainability movements.

NORTHLAND CHURCH AND A MESSAGE DISTRIBUTED

Many of these evangelical leaders intentionally cultivate partnerships that involve some level of risk, recognizing that openness to pluralism is a necessary starting point of social, political, and economic negotiation. But many evangelicals reject forms of pluralism that promote moral relativism. Most of those encountered in this fieldwork, for example, would feel uncomfortable admitting that their understanding of God, the Creation, and the order of the cosmos was only one among many views and not in any way "true" or privileged. But one need not endorse metaphysical pluralism in order to recognize that Western cultures are becoming more diverse. These newly developed partnerships involve acceptance of and transparent participation with others, whether at the community, state, national, or international levels. The use of terms such as "cosmocentric" or "theocentric"[49] to describe their theological position, and to advocate for the extension of moral concern to non-human lives and ecosystems, recalls for evangelicals the intertwined past and destiny of human and non-human systems. It also focuses attention on the deep relations that bind the world together. Consciousness of these webs of connections are more than a metaphor for some green evangelicals: they are a blueprint.

Northland Church is a "church distributed," with one mother church (Longwood, FL), three smaller churches in Oviedo, Dora, and West Oaks, Florida, and an additional 1200–1500 smaller groups of people joining in via the internet for each Sunday's message. One of the "core values" listed in every Sunday's program is to "reconnect by building relationships." Joel Hunter's rationale for the Church Distributed best describes the impetus for the message:

> God designed us to work in partnership. Multi-agent partnerships are distributed systems. In fact, most of nature— and most of technology—are distributed systems. On a macrolevel, every ecosystem is a distributed system because each one has interdependent and widely varied components. If even one component

of the functional unit we call an ecosystem fails, then everything in that system is affected. On the micro level, the smallest entities of the universe all have interrelated connections. When an elementary particle, the photon, is stimulated, an immediate response can be detected in a photon eight miles away. There is no doubt that the universe is connected. Survival in ever-changing environments requires interaction with others. Integration of differences is a key to a hardy life—even in the plant world. [50]

(Hunter 2007)

In a sort of biomimicry, Hunter suggests that Northland Church is organized according to the most successful features of the natural world, namely distributed (and thus resilient) systems that have deeply interdependent partnerships.

These groups are doing religious work by forging new individual and community identities (re-centered on ministry to the poor), focusing desire (re-aiming the political energies of congregations), and facilitating a more mindful sort of exchange (by encouraging responsible trade through purchasing). The importance of this last point should not be overlooked when Northland Church and no doubt other comparable congregations gather approximately $250,000.00 in tithes and offerings each week.

THE AMBIVALENCE OF THE EVANGELICAL LABEL, THE TENSIONS OF LITERALISM, AND THE PARADOX OF BELIEF

Interestingly, although these evangelicals are atypical in some ways, in others most of the informants were similar to mainstream evangelicals. For instance, they claimed to be biblical literalists although some of them hold beliefs that are technically speaking irreconcilable. This suggests that easy labels such as "evangelical" ought to be used with caution, for the reality is often more nuanced than the label. To unpack the ambivalence of such labels, it is first important to highlight the biblical foundations of evangelical creation care, which include (a) a theology that declares the creation good, (b) the belief that Jesus' physical resurrection illustrates the inclusion of the whole created world in future culmination of the kingdom of God, and (c) the idea that assenting to the first two creates obligations for humans who are called to rule over the world. Each of these ideas, on its own, would probably not give most evangelicals pause. But increasing numbers are resonating with interpretations of the Bible that integrate these ideas, those pioneered by people such as Richard Cizik and Jim Ball and popularized by preachers such as Joel Hunter. Are the theological foundations of evangelical environ-mentalism, however, generalizable to mainstream Christian constituencies?

Some central features of evangelicalism are unlikely to be widely adopted within mainstream liberal Protestant denominations, let alone other religious groups. Belief in the literal truth of the Christian Bible, for example, is an increasingly rare attribute among mainstream Protestants, and it may grow more so as the tenets of evolutionary theory are better understood and communicated to the general public. Even so, this does not mean that biblical literalists will necessarily grow more liberal in their understanding and interpretation of Christianity. It is possible that literalism will die out. But an alternative scenario is also possible, in which there is no general decline in the number of believers in the literal truth of the Bible, but rather substantial changes in interpretive methods that continue to find creative (and sometimes paradoxical) ways that science and biblical literalist theology can coexist. As CI's Ben Campbell put it, "The trick is in the interpretation of the Bible" (interview July 29, 2008).[51]

To illustrate, Joel Hunter's suggestion that parthenogenesis may be a plausible explanation for how Jesus could have been born without a father provides an implicit endorsement of a naturalistic explanation for an event that, if explained naturally, could compromise the foundation of Christianity. Such apparent paradox is not uncommon in Christianity, and conflicting concepts are found in several of the world's other religious systems also. Campbell's own recollection of conversations about how evangelical Christians wrestle with the theory of evolution is worth recounting. "The Bible," he said, "is full of a lot of things." The stories (as he called them) contained within are non-chronological. Campbell continued,

> We falsely believe the Bible as though it's a twentieth-century, straight narrative, not recognizing some Middle Eastern approaches to storytelling ... If I [taking on the perspective of the authors of the Genesis narrative] were talking to a fairly primitive society, and trying to explain to them the process by which the world was created, and the fact that God was involved, how would I do it? Would I talk about something that's 40 billion years old? ... [No,] I would frame it in a timeframe that *they'd* understand. I would show a similar trajectory of God's involvement, and a *process*. Which if you read the two Genesis narratives, it [the story] follows that [patterns of divine action in history]. More or less. Our concepts of what we think about in scientific terms, it follows that [suggesting that the Genesis account can be interpreted as parallel to scientific theories of the evolution of the cosmos].

127

> Seven days?[52] Well, I don't have to believe *that* [seven-day crea-
> tion] to believe that God created the world.

For Campbell, if evangelicals drive people away from the biblical message by, for example, demanding that the creation story refers to a literal seven-day creation, they are not fulfilling their Christian vocation. Yet Campbell and the other evangelicals still contend that they take the Bible to be literal truth. Such paradox does not, however, prevent these Christians from finding in these stories moral guidance.

Campbell's attitude illustrates, as do Randall's and Hunter's nearly identical suggestions that God does not speak with forked tongue, that the interpretation of the Bible may change over time, although the content may be presumed to be unchanging and literally true. Four out of the five targeted evangelical high-level actors who participated in in-depth interviews named at least one scientist as a personal inspiration for their creation care advocacy (three cited E. O. Wilson, and two of them cited several others). Other more recent joint declarations by evangelicals and scientists have helped to push large proportions of the evangelical population to reconsider their understanding of science. The most common attitude toward science among this interesting group of progressive evangelicals assumes that science is an important and reliable way of gaining knowledge about the world, but that it has very little to say about the content of faith and its moral jurisdiction. Science and religion are, to use the phrase coined by noted biologist Stephen Jay Gould, non-overlapping magesteria (NOMA).[53] The Protestant understanding of authentic religion as a private and emotional affair is obvious among these evangelicals, who suggest that faith provides the most satisfying explanations at the personal level of understanding, even while acknowledging that science in most cases accurately describes the material world. For some like Randall, attributing environmental activism to obedience to the biblical message rather than to analysis of scientific data makes a stronger case for fighting climate change, for the scientific method is an ongoing process of confirmation and falsification and not the discovery of an objectively real world. If activism flows from commitment to transcendent principles it essentially dodges tough questions about which scientific data is more credible. Although technically speaking some literalist interpretations of the Bible could not coexist with key features of evolutionary theory, including the notion of macroevolution or the emergence of living material from previously inanimate matter, in reality some people resonate with and consider these conflicting perspectives morally relevant.

The perception that it is only evangelicals and fundamentalists who misunderstand science and lobby against its use in the public sphere may be incorrect. While large proportions of the general public believe nature can provide moral guidance and spiritual inspiration (see Proctor 2006), about half of the general public (far more than the number of evangelicals in the population) does not connect such reverence for nature with evolutionary science in any personally meaningful way, believing that humans were created in their present form around ten thousand years ago (Holden 2006: 769).[54] Evangelical Christians, like many in the general population, are selective and often contradictory in their endorsement of religious and evolutionary ideas. It seems uncertain, therefore, whether a greater acceptance of evolutionary theory would automatically lead to more environmentally benign attitudes, or a reduction in the general number of evangelical Christians.

In any case, although evangelicals have often suggested there is a biological continuity between humans and the rest of creation, their understandings of evolutionary science still typically retain an ontological distinction between human and non-human nature. Created in the image of God, humans are called to exercise a beneficent sort of dominion, often referred to as stewardship. The idea that non-human nature is worthy of respect and possibly even reverence can coexist with strong human exceptionalism provided it is framed within a *theocentric* perspective, one that imagines all value as residing in or deriving from the divine. If a transcendent creator declared the whole creation good and deemed humans rulers of it, then any strong anthropocentrism may be masked by references to a divinely ordained cosmological order. The elevated place of humans above the rest of creation suggests that evangelical creation care is unlikely, even over the very long term, to develop affinities with dark green spiritualities although they clearly continue to make important contributions to the sustainability milieu.[55]

One seeming contradiction that surfaced as I investigated evangelical creation care was the ontological distinction presently noted between humans and non-human creation. Wilkinson and the Calvin College fellows begin with the argument that "We simply cannot escape from our embeddedness in nature or nature's embeddedness in us" (Wilkinson 1980: 3), and that "whatever else they are, humans are also *earth*; they share their nature with its soil, its plants, its animals" (208). Yet the authors later note that *complete* identification of humans with creation is problematic:

> such an understanding implies that persons cannot exist apart from their bodies. Yet it seems to be the clear teaching of the New Testament that those who have died, and whose bodies decay, nevertheless continue to exist until the day of resurrection, when they will be clothed with "spiritual bodies." Thus this portrayal

129

> of mind and soul as dependent upon the body would seem to be
> incorrect.   (Wilkinson 1980: 230)

The relationship between humans and the rest of nature is summed up with an allusion to and play upon the idea of the hypostatic union, the idea that Jesus is simultaneously fully human and fully divine: "Humans are fully dust, and fully soul; they are soulish dust" (Wilkinson 1980: 230).[56] This evangelical perspective, then, preserves a thoroughgoing human exceptionalism even with impassioned pleas for humans to remember that they are part of and dependent upon their ecological matrix.

At least in its early manifestations, evangelical environmentalism endorsed a view of Darwinian science that did not necessarily match empirical data. For example, in a statement that strongly resonated with the Gaia hypothesis (offered by biologist James Lovelock), Wilkinson argued that "In the ability to sustain itself over a long period of time, an ecosystem is like an individual organism" (Wilkinson 1980: 13). Further, this capacity for self-regulation, it was suggested, had a built-in tendency toward justice and equity, for the follow-up argument deployed by Wilkinson and his collaborators imagines that "starving animals are rare in nature" (13). In such cases, Christians are reading the plot of the "peaceable kingdom," wherein all creations dwell together in harmony, into a real-life Darwinian drama characterized by predation, death, and often starvation and suffering (see the strong critique of most eco-theology by Sideris 2003).[57] Their acceptance of evolutionary science may be incomplete, but this has not prevented their embrace of some values central to the sustainability milieu. Although generally anthropocentric in tone (or at best theocentric with a strong human exceptionalism), evangelical advocates of creation care are strong allies, at least in terms of political impacts, in social movements toward sustainability.

FURTHER REFLECTIONS ON THE TRANSMISSION OF A RELIGIOUS "VIRUS"

Every Sunday at Northland Church Dr Hunter delivers his message to at least 12,000 people, both present in Longwood and through the internet.[58] From hundreds of members in 1985 (when Hunter took over as pastor), the church grew so quickly that groups of members began to meet in their own communities, tuning in through the internet. Aside from the main congregation that now meets in the 160,000 square foot mother church each week, each of the three "satellite" churches now has its own junior pastors, youth groups, singles groups, committees (and so on), and all gather to hear pastor Joel each Sunday, although anyone can watch the services.[59] The "distributed church" began as a practical solution to overcrowding but has become a religious community philosophy:

> This is not another church-growth strategy or some let's-play-nice-together ecumenical effort. It is a connecting strategy that results in spiritual maturity. Christians must intentionally combine in more effective ways to go into the world to present the Gospel and support each other. (Hunter 2007)

The distributed church seeks new relationships, cultivates new territory there, and spreads rhizomically. Likewise, the ideas, practices, and values associated with creation care and larger sustainability movements spread through evangelical Christian communities and beyond, carrying with them novel forms encouraged by each encounter. As Joel Hunter said at the Climate Change Conference at Northland in February 2008: "This day is about being equipped for leaders to take this message back to their constituency group. We can make this movement *viral* this way!" His implication was that the church was an effective medium of communication for many who would not otherwise think of making environmentally and socially responsible consumer choices. The church could help "infect" others with similar sets of social and practical norms.

Hunter's friendships (and in some cases formal partnerships) with Jim Ball (executive director of the EEN), Richard Cizik (vice president for governmental affairs for the NAE), and Sally Bingham (Interfaith Power and Light, see Chapter 8 for more details), to name a few, help to shape his moral sensibilities and enhance the strength of his networks. His participation in UN-sponsored peace-building processes (for example in Doha in 2007) has provided an international venue for these agglomerated values. Finally, he brings this rich international experience back to Longwood, Florida, and attempts to promote the "greening" of a very large and affluent set of Christians (who have their own networks of Christian friends). The network of leaders discussed above, as will become evident in later chapters, is embedded in even larger networks of participants in global sustainability movements. It is not solely the charismatic leaders of such movements who concoct and distribute these big ideas, nor is it the cultures or organizations themselves that inject ideas into the minds of a passive citizenry. There are "expert networks" (such as the ones described here) that exchange ideas across community borders. Further, there are grassroots programs and organizations that imitate and reinterpret the values exchanged at the level of experts, and in turn generate feedback to experts who re-examine, reformulate, and repackage their own values and those they carry into broader communities of accountability. For example, after Joel Hunter signed the Evangelical Declaration on Climate Change, he requested a full audit of the ecological footprint and energy usage of the sizeable Northland Church. Raymond Randall spearheaded the formation of a committee that generated the audit based on the values outlined by the community leader (which in turn derived from interaction with scientists, lay leaders, and other evangelicals). The audit helped to generate educational material that can be shared with other congregations in an attempt to spread this new form of Christian service in the name of creation. Hunter has used this audit within his expert networks as a concrete example of how he and his church are making positive changes, and Northland has also created educational materials to walk other congregations through their own energy and land use audits.

Note the similarity between what is occurring amongst leaders of the evangelical Christian movement and other religious leaders (such as Sally Bingham, and Mary Evelyn Tucker and John Grim in Chapter 8) to the free exchange of conceptual tools and metaphors between oppositional subcultures detailed in Chapters 3 and especially 5.

The relatively rapid and successful spread of the creation care theme across a broad segment of evangelical Christians, and its popularity in the US media, is an example of the rapid cultural transmission of a social movement. The leaders interviewed here are participating in the ongoing construction of a set of positive myths that reframe the evangelical identity in terms of ecological and social justice, and thus they contribute in their own unique manner to the metanarrative of sustainability.

CHAPTER EIGHT

STORIES OF PARTNERSHIP: INTERFAITH EFFORTS TOWARD SUSTAINABILITY

ALLOWING A THOUSAND FLOWERS TO BLOOM

Fazlun Khalid, founder and director of the Islamic Foundation for Ecology and Environmental Sciences (IFEES) said that building a sustainable world was impossible unless the planet's cultural diversity was considered one of its strengths, rather than something to be overcome with a diluted, global ethic. For Khalid, varied extant ecological and social crises can only be fruitfully addressed by preserving a diversity of perspectives, actions, and partnerships. Quoting Mao Tse-tung, Khalid said, "I'm for allowing a thousand flowers to bloom! Let people work, make their own solutions from their own beings and their own places ... *Solutions* and *places* and *beings* are different" (interview May 29, 2008). In this, Khalid agreed with Martin Palmer, his former employer and the Secretary General of the Alliance of Religions and Conservation (ARC). Addressing the necessity of plural approaches to achieving sustainability, Palmer suggested that any unity of purpose or perspective in sustainability was a fantasy (echoing Davison's earlier point):

> It's just not how humanity works. Christianity's been trying to unify everyone for the past 2000 years, communism for the past 200 years, capitalism for the past 100 years. It doesn't work. Why don't we just go with what we know *does* work: pluralism and diversity? [These] can often lead to conflict, but *that's an issue of defining what we're saying!* (Interview May 27, 2008)

Palmer's insight is precisely what I have highlighted throughout: sustainability requires clear statements of the goals and deep-seated values of various stakeholders for effective problem solving. "Defining what we are saying" in the case of sustainability depends upon careful elucidation of core values and deep beliefs, whether explicitly religious or not. In short, the search for sustainability and the partnerships that make it possible depend not just on pluralism, but an empathetic form of deliberation that highlights stakeholders' core values. As Palmer put it, "Pluralism says: 'what is that you bring to the table that's distinctive, and can I work with that? What do I have to give up?' It's engaging with what fires people. What vision they have" (interview May 27, 2008).

Chapter 7 noted that some evangelical witness for the environment is grounded in biblical stories, tactically complex in the formation of partnerships, and intent on ensuring that evangelical goals are not conflated with other environmental activists and their motives whose foundations are not biblical. The focus there was on groups within a particular religious tradition. This chapter examines interfaith organizations whose primary purpose has been to bridge the gaps between different religious groups and between religious groups and a variety of secular institutions charged with environmental responsibilities. The focus is on the strategies that interfaith advocates and groups use to facilitate and maintain partnerships across faith traditions, and to translate these traditions into terms that resonate with secular groups.

Pluralism requires negotiation across boundaries, whether such boundaries are personal, communal, or organizational. To illustrate, this chapter highlights ARC, and Interfaith Power and Light (IPL), and includes input gathered from high-level leaders in these organizations.

IPL, ARC, AND INTERFAITH APPROACHES TO BUILDING SUSTAINABILITY

To better understand how these groups work together toward sustainability it will be helpful to detail the emergence of the two groups that are the focus here. ARC was created through a mandate from a high-ranking international figure, while IPL began at the local level in one activist's attic. Nonetheless, they share some of the same priorities and strategies.

Let there be light!: the emergence of Interfaith Power and Light

Sally Bingham, founder and director of IPL, recalled that she began her journey toward combating climate change when she was invited to participate as a trustee for the National Defense Fund (NDF), an environmental legal defense group. Her "awakening," as she called it, came in 1985 as she listened month after month to the NDF scientists' detailed descriptions of over-fishing, water pollution, deforestation, coral reef decimation, and by the middle of the 1980s, climate change. At the time she was a member of the Church of Heavenly Rest in New York City.[1] The more Bingham learned, the more emotionally depressed she grew about what was happening to the earth's ecosystems, and the more insistent she became with the clergy in her church. She pestered them, asking "How can [you] stand there and talk about love, peace and justice and never mention clean air, clean water as a right for people ... Not only that, but the intrinsic value of everything God created" (interview July 8, 2008).[2]

In the late 1980s Bingham and her family moved to San Francisco where she was again struck by her church's inattentiveness to environmental problems. She recalled that the rector of their new congregation, St James Episcopal Church, had several sons, one of whom was a river guide.[3] Bingham remembered saying to him, "Your kids are out there river guiding ... aren't they seeing what's happening? And why don't you talk about it from the pulpit?" His answer: "Why don't *you* go to seminary and find out where the disconnect is between what we say we believe, and how we behave?" (interview July 8, 2008).

This was the impetus for Bingham's academic journey. At the age of 45 she enrolled in the University of San Francisco's BA program. After completing her degree in theology and religious studies, she enrolled at the Church Divinity School of the Pacific, the Episcopal seminary of the Graduate Theological Union, to pursue her Master of Divinity. She was able to convince the bishop to allow her to organize an "environmental committee" for the fieldwork component of her degree. In 1992, she traveled from church to church within the diocese, drumming up support for this Episcopal group. The end result was a group of twelve to fourteen people who met in Bingham's home on the third Tuesday of each month for five years (interview July 8, 2008).

It was never part of Bingham's plan to be ordained. Although members of the environmental committee repeatedly encouraged her to do so, arguing that she would need ordination to sponsor and vote on environmental resolutions at general conventions, she resisted. But attending chapel every morning at seminary Bingham said she began to understand the Christian message in a new way: "it was starting to assimilate into who I was as a person, and I had to begin to accept the fact that it was a call, I mean, an honest-to-goodness call" (interview July 8, 2008). This perception of a divine call, however, was not to perform weddings, funerals, or fulfill the other usual responsibilities of the clergy. Instead, it focused entirely on "saving creation." She remembers that she "felt so strongly that this [protecting the environment] was the job ... really, of anybody who professed a love of God. And we [Christians] had a responsibility, not just the opportunity, but the real responsibility—perhaps obligation is a better word—to be the leaders of the environmental movement" (interview July 8, 2008).

Bingham was ordained in 1997, the same year that California deregulated the energy industry, which meant that citizens could purchase their power from any one of a number of providers, including renewable sources. She and a lay collaborator founded Episcopal Power and Light, and went door to door among the Episcopal churches in California, promoting Christian-based energy stewardship and asking them to buy renewable energy from Green Mountain utility company.[4] In 2000 the Rockefeller Brothers Fund offered Bingham the capital to make a film of her persuasive green energy stump speech and to hire a national campaign manager, which resulted in the dissemination of Bingham's message to many more Episcopal churches.[5] The film, titled "Lighten Up," had the desired effect and by the year 2000 there were approximately sixty Episcopal churches in California buying renewable energy. The same year, however, a major energy crisis hit California, and in an effort to provide consistent power the energy industry was again regulated, which meant that the churches could no longer purchase renewable energy at their discretion.

The setback, however, also provided a new opportunity for partnership. Bingham and her supporters created an alliance with the California Council of Churches and broadened the scope of their concern to all Christian groups in California. Bingham recalled that they "were already getting calls from Unitarians and Jews, saying 'can we join this program or is it just for Episcopalians?'" (interview July 8, 2008). So in 2001 they adopted a new moniker: *Interfaith* Power and Light (IPL). Since then, Bingham's work has broadened to involve Muslims, Baha'i's, and Mormons, becoming a genuinely interfaith effort.

By 2008, IPL had doubled in size (from around fourteen chapters to twenty-eight), tripled its operating budget, and had a full-time staff of seven people. From conversations around the dining room table to a nationwide advocacy group, and Bingham's 2008 installment as canon for environmental ministry by the Episcopal Church's Diocese of California, IPL began with a grassroots initiative and went on to influence diverse faith-based and secular communities.[6] As of this writing, IPL has programs in thirty-seven states as well as the District of Colombia. Interestingly, Bingham noted that about half of the audiences she addressed were secular groups, indicating some of the broader appeal of such efforts. Their bottom–up approach has been different than the Alliance of Religions and Conservation, but both center their work on partnerships that cross faith boundaries, indicating how important such relationships are to the prospect of sustainable societies.

THE GLUE THAT MENDS THE PLATE: THE CREATION OF THE ALLIANCE OF RELIGIONS AND CONSERVATION

In 1995, HRH Prince Philip (the husband of the United Kingdom's monarch, Queen Elizabeth II)[7] convened a meeting at Windsor Castle, England with the world's major conservation groups and nine world religions to form a group specifically "to link the secular worlds of conservation and ecology with the faith worlds of the major religions."[8] It was called the Alliance of Religions and Conservation (ARC). The first steps toward the genesis of this organization, however, had occurred nearly ten years earlier.

In 1986 the World Wide Fund for Nature (WWF), at the time headed by HRH Prince Philip, brought together leaders from five of the world's largest faith traditions and several leading environmentalists to "explore how the world's religions could help in the struggle to save the natural world" (Jensen 1999: 492).[9] Assisi, Italy was the highly symbolic site chosen for the meeting, the home of thirteenth-century monk Saint Francis. Francis was well known for his relationships with non-human animals, and was nominated by Lynn White, Jr as the patron saint of ecology (White 1967). The proceedings of the Assisi conference (a) echoed White's argument that Western and Christian perspectives were largely responsible for the ecological crisis, (b) suggested that only a significant change in political processes and structures could correct the crisis, and (c) argued that epistemologies, cosmologies, and their ethical and behavioral accompaniments which are alternatives to Western worldviews should be valued as instrumental in efforts toward sustainability.[10] The WWF, World Bank, and the other non-governmental organizations present at this meeting, moreover, explicitly endorsed the idea that there was a significant, positive correlation between biodiversity and cultural diversity. Additionally, the diversity of perspectives was envisioned as a major strength. According to ARC, the special invitation received by the participants asked them to "Come, proud of your own tradition, but humble enough to learn from others," and pointed out that "this applied as much to the secular environmental groups as it did to the great faiths."[11]

Following the meeting, Prince Philip asked Martin Palmer to take the lead in proactively working with these faith groups, including Buddhists, Christians, Hindus, Muslims, and Jews, to promote conservation. Over the next ten years Palmer and other ARC leaders worked with the five groups from the Assisi meetings, and cultivated relationships with four additional faith groups, Baha'is, Daoists, Jains, and Sikhs.

Prior to the 1995 launch of ARC, each of the faith leaders was invited to elucidate what they believed to be the greatest challenges to their adherents and their faith traditions in the era of globalization. There was consensus on two points: the first was the impact of media and the global reach of communication industries that easily and rapidly disseminated Western values; second was the overwhelming power of Western economic structures, such as the World Bank, to perpetuate inequity. Thus, the event organizers ensured that World Bank officials were present at the birth of ARC, and since then, the World Bank has been an active partner with ARC in promoting biocultural and religious diversity. Palmer was asked to become the first Secretary General of ARC by the original board of directors, and he has served in that capacity since.

By 2000, Shinto and Zoroastrian religious leaders had joined the cause, bringing the total number of religious traditions represented to eleven faiths, whose adherents comprise approximately two thirds of the world's population, own around 7 per cent of the world's habitable land, and hold approximately 6–8 per cent of the global investment market (Palmer & Finlay 2003: xi). ARC primarily operates behind the scenes, brokering partnerships between international political bodies. Palmer noted,

> Some people say "Well we've never heard of you." And if you read Prince Philip's interview on our website, he makes the point: You never should! It should look as though the most natural thing in the world is that the major religions would work with the major bodies concerned with saving the planet, and preserving habitats. We're the invisible glue that mends the plate.
> (Interview May 27, 2008)

Many environmental and social justice activists have long been harshly critical of the World Bank because it was cast as the principle instrument of global biological and cultural simplification. But Palmer was more charitable, recalling that when the partnership between the World Bank and ARC began, the World Bank employed more full-time ecologists and spent more money on understanding ecosystem ecology than any conservation group in the world (interview May 27, 2008).[12] While Palmer and others who would later form ARC were forging relationships with the Bank, other groups with whom they worked broke off relations. According to Palmer, some environmentalists felt that working with the World Bank amounted to abetting the enemy. Clearly, sometimes new relationships exact a cost on older partnerships. This is part of the risk of cultivating relationships in a pluralistic world.

THE ETHICS OF RISKY PARTNERSHIPS: A MARRIAGE OF INCONVENIENCE

"Partnership is actually about the risk you might change," Martin Palmer said when discussing how ARC has been able to effectively bridge gaps between religious and secular groups across the globe. "If you're not prepared to take that risk and to do so with integrity, we can't work with you. It's very much like a marriage in that sense." He went on to say that many development or conservation oriented groups believed they already had the answers to how to provide development, sustainable agricultural regimes, new political structures (or what-have-you), and merely presented these ready-made answers to peoples from other cultures or backgrounds (interview May 27, 2008). To the extent that they were unwilling to risk changing their pre-existing plans or take the time to hear what problems were most pressing for local residents they were not participating in a sustainable "marriage," a two-way relationship that attended to the needs of the "other." Risky partnerships need not only involve interactions with cultural others. According to Palmer, interactions with peers and colleagues in the global North also require risky partnerships where people express deep beliefs and core values.

For example, Palmer recalled his brief involvement with Friends of the Earth (FOE), a well-known conservation organization which entered a tumultuous period when their policy platform and administrative direction were uncertain.[13] The head of the organization decided that the ten division heads would benefit from a retreat where they could work through the emotional obstacles in the way of positive progress toward policy agreement.

According to Palmer, for the first two days, nothing happened. Negative feelings seemed to weigh on the participants and almost no progress was made in congeniality let alone policy agreement. Finally, one night, it came out that one of the leaders was a Christian. Once this admission was made, conversations were jump started, and it turned out that most of them were Christians, and that many of them had ultimately joined FOE *because* of their faith. Not one of them had ever spoken to their co-workers of it until then. But after that night they were able to move forward productively because for the first time they understood *why* their peers were engaged in this particular career path. The foundations of the values that motivated their chosen occupation were laid bare.[14]

Engaging neighbors

One of the ideas that my informants most frequently noted was the idea that protecting the environment was in an important sense protecting one's self.

Fred Kirschenmann, director of the Leopold Center, called it developing our "ecological conscience," drawing directly from Aldo Leopold's insistence that in order to be in an ethical relationship with the land one's moral imagination must include ecological systems. Sally Bingham, Richard Cizik, and others I interviewed voiced a parallel idea when they reinterpreted an important Christian story as illustrating that all peoples (sometimes including non-humans) are neighbors, and that Christians ought to love their neighbors as themselves.[15] Bingham put it this way: "I had a cousin who went off to Vietnam,[16] quite regretfully, who said that when you kill a person, you kill part of yourself ... It's that way with the earth, I think. When you harm any part of the earth, you harm yourself. What we're doing now is trying to save ourselves from ourselves." An exploration of the concept of "neighbor" is part of Bingham's usual speech for both faith groups and secular audiences. She attempts to persuade her audiences that the concept should include the next generation, and "people on the other side of the world who are affected by every single thing we do here" (interview July 8, 2008). The expanded meaning of neighbor is a metaphor for expanding the boundaries of morality. In this, it parallels the environmentalist metaphor that describes the actualization of an ecological conscience through an expanded sense of self. These metaphors can be used across several Christian constituencies, and seemingly also resonate with those (such as Leopold and Seed) who are not Christian. This ability to engage others by finding common stories is, for Palmer, central to moving toward sustainability. He suggested that one central task of his work was "to get religions to remember they're storytellers, and [to] get the inspirers of the environmental movement to remember they ought to be poets. Then they can talk. Otherwise, they're just wearing the armor of their impenetrable language" (interview May 27, 2008).

Palmer confided that conservationists too often use language that is not meaningful outside of their own in-group. Likewise, religious groups often couch their motivations in terms that are not meaningful for others. Words like sustainability, Palmer noted, are problematic precisely because they can mean so many things to so many different people or groups. They are of little use unless the values that go along with any particular deployment of the term are made explicit. "For example, biodiversity" Palmer argued, "means almost nothing to anybody outside [conservation biology and the biological sciences] ... The point is that we use language that people don't understand. You have to challenge people to use terms that the other side can understand" (interview May 27 2008).[17] Palmer went on to say that, when dealing with such "concept-words," he often asks people to "Show us a poem in which that word has been used ... If you can't show us a poem, then it's not a word that people love enough that they want to *play* with it.

If you can't show us a poem, it probably means it doesn't mean anything." As illustrated in Chapter 6, biodiversity was intentionally coined to gain political and public traction for conservation. It is a word designed to make complex ideas easier to grasp and to reference. Rather than teaching people who receive development aid new words to describe ideas already embedded in their religious world model, Palmer suggested that his goal is to draw out and highlight extant values.

Walking between two worlds: world model interpretation and sustainability

According to Palmer, Bingham and others, building consensus and making progress on policy issues requires translating value sets and worldviews between different constituencies. Once Episcopal Power and Light became Interfaith Power and Light their task was to investigate what resources different faith traditions already possessed for promoting beneficient stewardship of creation, and then effectively market those resources to the tradition's participants.[18] Thus, in some cases, IPL representatives were "outsiders" intent on "selling" new interpretations of traditional stories to those inside that tradition. Bingham was also able to make a stronger case for reducing energy consumption and making renewable energy choices within her own tradition by noting that other faith leaders and traditions were already making progress. For Bingham, the formula for translating the IPL message to secular groups (for example, university audiences) is relatively simple: (a) quote "experts" in other denominations and religions (Joel Hunter [an evangelical], the Dalai Lama [a Tibetan Buddhist leader], and the US Catholic bishops were all examples provided by Bingham) who argue that their tradition demands environmental responsibility (often couched in terms of stewardship); and (b) outline what sorts of behaviors should follow from these ecologically friendly readings of these traditions.[19] For the insiders (those within the particular faith traditions) it is a way of reading the traditional texts in a way that is relevant to contemporary concerns. When broadcast to groups outside those faith communities the task is to explain why people of faith are legitimately concerned with environmental issues. For Palmer the task is similar, but the groups for whom ARC acts as a translator are large scale international groups such as the WWF, the World Bank, and the United Nations. Palmer noted, "Because we're able to speak the language of both sides ... we are a trusted mediator" (interview May 27, 2008).

The translation of one group's values into language that other peoples can understand is a difficult and time-consuming task. Beginning with such a slow and unwieldy set of processes is problematic when most conservation and development organizations have project goals, timelines, and budgets which discourage a slow process of community-based engagement. But as John Smith, director of ARC's Sacred Land Project said, "The downside is that some projects take longer, but the benefit is (a) the people believe that they did it, and (b) they therefore are much more protective of it" (interview May 29, 2008).[20]

THE PITFALLS OF PARTNERSHIP

Smith recalled that many times when ARC proposed a project to local residents the first question locals asked was "Who's going to pay for this?" Smith reported his response was usually the same: "We're not going to talk about that for the first six months." Instead, that time was spent learning what each particular stakeholder brought to the table and what they sought to change. Conservation and development, Smith emphasized, cannot be a one-size-fits-all solution to what are typically complex contextual problems. In Smith's experience many organizational participants, although their intentions are good, are not willing or able to undergo such a lengthy courtship period. That is why some partnerships fail.

Among the problematic relationships they have encountered, both Smith and Palmer noted the deeply unsatisfying relationships formed with academics. Palmer remembered the gradual engagement of religious scholars in conservation and development work beginning around 1989. Specifically he noted Hans Kung's work advancing a "global ethic" which inspired an exhibition on religions and ethics in Washington, DC (Palmer & Finlay 2003). For Palmer, Kung's grand global ethic is "academically interesting, but ultimately irrelevant to the world I work in … That's not what I'm dealing with when I'm in Indonesia working with single mothers running a logging operation according to the Qur'an" (interview May 29, 2008).

While acknowledging that most academics get involved for the right reasons, their strategies are often misguided, according to Fazlun Khalid, director of IFEES. In response to questions about the possibility of such a global ethic, Khalid described it as an academic fantasy:

> I like small. If it's global somebody's got to control it … So who's going to decide this ethic? We going to have a new global pope for everybody? Maybe Mary [Evelyn Tucker] wants to be the global pope! (laughs).[21] We cannot have academics in Yale, or Harvard, or Oxford, or Cambridge or wherever … thinking for the rest of the world. (Interview May 28, 2008)

The problem with academic approaches, according to these and other activists, is that they are top–down: academics and policy experts decide on a set of global principles, then disseminate them to the masses. The perception is that the values of individuals on the ground are never vetted, they remain private while the public global ethic extols a diluted set of values. The emphasis in sustainability oriented work is often on publications (for academics) and deliverables (for conservation and development organizations), but this does not account for peoples' motivations, which is the focus of groups like ARC and IPL. The goals of groups like IPL and ARC is, in a sense, "allowing the private to become public again," providing a venue for people to express their deep seated values and beliefs, which are tied to particular religious or community narratives, in the public sphere (Palmer's wording, interview May 29, 2008). According to Palmer a global ethic is empty of content because it is not significantly tied to particular community narratives, and thus perpetuates the notion that such particularistic beliefs should remain within the private sphere (see Palmer & Finlay 2003: 17–21).

In such cases, partnerships can sometimes hamper positive progress. Engaging groups with different value preferences and goals is no easy task. ARC was perhaps the first religious NGO to cultivate a relationship with the World Bank, but the partnership was rooted in ARC's honest rendering of the complicity of the Bank in the destruction of ecosystems and cultures. At ARC's launch in 1995 at Windsor Castle, one of the Bank's bureaucrats had given a presentation with the usual statistical and graphical representations of data which prompted a response from ARC's poet, who was present at the event.[22] The poem read:

Somewhere between Christ and Lucifer
with your silver-grey hair and your quick, silver tongue,
as you slide the transparencies over each other,
Mercurial in the projector's glow.

And your shadow, as your rapid, polished monologue lulls us
into believing, into hoping even, beyond the figures
you skate over like thinning ice,
smiling, energizing as you
arabesque and spin and stop dead
with your hand outstretched to grasp.

And I could, we could all, almost vote for you now
for the Father of Comfort and Finance and Light,
making us feel as safe and secure as we need.

And it's not that I don't believe you, or see how easy it is
for us to distrust you.
Everything you say is right on, and good. It stands.
It's just ... that He is crucified everywhere on earth where you arrive
with your plans, and panaceas.
It's just ... you can't serve two masters without being bought,
or sold.[23]

When the World Bank refused to publish the poem, and other religious narratives, with the rest of the proceedings under the auspices of the World Bank, the poem circulated via email through World Bank employee networks. Many were astounded at how their organization appeared to others, to outsiders with whom they were attempting to forge partnerships. Palmer reported that the bureaucrat was deeply impacted by this episode, and that it helped him recover the passion that had driven him to this work in the first place. According to Palmer, "We were then able to begin working with the World Bank. Because a group that could read that poem, and go, 'Ah ... so, that's how we seem to some people' is open to thinking that, maybe, there are other ways, that there are other stories" (interview May 29, 2008). This story is an example of how costly some partnerships can be, but for Palmer it is also an example of the potential that such personal risk has for fostering partnerships that last.

It was at that time rare (at best) for a multilateral development organization to consider poems as a source of data. But in this case, a poem effectively caused a policy shift in one of the world's most politically insular institutions. According to Palmer, the World Bank employee was living without a "story," that is, he had no guiding narrative that informed his perception of his purpose in the world or within his organization. All of my informants, and particularly those involved in ARC, were excellent story-tellers. It is no coincidence, however, that the leaders in these relatively successful organizations tell good stories. Telling and listening to stories, particularly other peoples' stories, is increasingly cited as the most important ingredient in sustained collaboration, through which security and smart subsistence within habitats can develop.[24]

FROM PARTNERSHIP TO STORIES: THE IMPORTANCE OF NARRATIVE FOR SUSTAINABLE COLLABORATION

Storytellers all

According to Martin Palmer and Victoria Finlay, humans interpret their worlds "through stories even if we sometimes like to call them facts" (Palmer

& Finlay 2003: 51). The environmental movement in particular retells a series of stories that various participants endorse and recall as authoritative. When these stories draw on metaphors of apocalypse or green utopias, valorize earlier or alternative cultural mores and practices (such as the wisdom of indigenous peoples), and endorse Christ-like visions of spotted owls and polar bears, they are religious (or at least religion-resembling) stories. Oftentimes though, secular groups do not realize that they are manufacturing narratives. The crucial task, according to Palmer, is to help secular groups understand that they are also storytellers. In his eyes, the secular environmental movement "has clothed itself in the garments of religion, [but] claims to be scientific." Reflecting on engaging with secular conservation organizations, Palmer stated that

> one of the first tasks we've had to do is to help [them] recognize that *they function symbolically, metaphorically, and so to some degree quasi-spiritually,* and that the science bit is pretty much irrelevant. That's not why they're there. And once they get to the point that they recognize that they tell stories, then you can introduce them to other groups that tell stories.
> (Interview May 29, 2008, emphasis Palmer's)

Stories that do not inspire: environmental apocalypticism and negative affect

Many environmental activists, particularly those whose motivations are primarily religious, shy away from the more negative imagery and argument of the environmental movement. Both ARC employees and Bingham reported that positive stories tend to fare better with audiences, but also resonate more with their personal sentiments. Most religions have ritual fasts, but they are typically followed by feasts. Some religions have a doctrine of sin, but also deal in forgiveness. Thus, according to ARC, "balancing the need for repentance with the need to party is a central insight into human psychology that the faiths can bring to the environmental and developmental movement" (Palmer & Finlay 2003: 34).

On the other hand, stories that *do not* "work" according to these thought leaders include those that use terror or fear to promote action, or those that eschew democratic solutions in favor of quicker, more authoritarian options. For example, John Smith of ARC stated that most of the conservation organizations he has worked with believed so deeply in their programs that they assumed they had the "right" answers. Beneath the surface, Smith believes, such overconfidence stems from an implicit religious story, derived from "quietly religious attitudes, like 'we are the saviors of the planet.' It [environmentalism] was sort of like a 'new religion'" (interview May 29, 2008).

Palmer recalled that during the question and answer period following a panel in which he participated, a well-known ecologist insisted that the urgency of the ecological crisis required humans to bypass democratic means of change, and suggested that we should "stop nine-tenths of what people are doing and it has to be done, if necessary, by military force" (Palmer's recollection, interview May 28, 2008). Oftentimes such extreme positions are accompanied by what Palmer termed "Neo-Puritanism." He meant that some use the ecological crisis as a means of demonstrating their superior moral fiber through abstention from some aspects of Western culture. For example, that scientist later informed Palmer in conversation that he and his wife had vowed never to fly in an airplane again because of the large carbon output. Unfortunately, this well-intentioned act of self-limitation had caused them to miss both their sons' weddings, and prevented them from ever meeting their grandchildren. In Palmer's view, the scientist had forgotten "how to party"—the repentance, in this case, did not fit the crime. Palmer recalled an old Jewish proverb he believed was relevant: "On the day of judgment, you'll be judged—and condemned—for every legitimate pleasure that you could have taken, and did not" (interview May 28, 2008).

For Palmer, negative stories are capable of inspiring fear but not of producing positive change. The environmental movement, said Palmer, cloaks its religious stories behind secular science, and because science is presumed to be value free it is incapable of providing positive large-scale guiding metaphors. Environmentalism, he said, "can bring us to the moment of crisis, it can bring us to the foot of the cross, it can bring us to Auschwitz, but what it can't do is take us to the transforming, or transcending experience" (interview May 28, 2008).

HOW TO PARTY, OR, LEARNING HOW TO DANCE IN THE EARTHQUAKE: THE POWER OF POSITIVE NARRATIVES

Palmer and the others at ARC call positive narratives "wonder-ful" stories— tales that depend on messages that inspire not just hope but responsible environmental behavior (Palmer & Finlay 2003). There are narratives in nearly every one of the world religions that remind people to work hard, but not too hard, and to celebrate what they have, not weep for what is gone (Palmer & Finlay 2003: 23–36). The report from a UNESCO conference on faith-based organizations' contributions to education for sustainability noted that the world's current problems of "overdevelopment and under-nourishment, overconsumption and undereducation, overpopulation and underemployment, overmilitarization and undersecurity" are contrary to values that have been upheld by religious communities for thousands of years. Quoting Rabbi Arthur Waskow, the report's editor stated,

> The whole world today is in an earthquake: politics, economics, sexuality … People look for something that isn't quaking … and so they don't pay attention to the state of the Earth. Our calling today, as Rabbi Waskow emphatically put it, is like "learning to dance in an earthquake." This quaking will transform everything, including religions. (Pigem 2007: 1–19)

According to Waskow and others, religions are adapting their message to the ecological crisis and one of their primary contributions can be to remind people how to celebrate each other, and life in the midst of these "over–under" crises.

"You protect what you love"

The positive narratives provided by informants characterizing their engagement in sustainability advocacy almost always included either emotively intense personal experience in nature, or an intense concern for social equity. Sally Bingham was one of those who traced her environmental awareness to profound childhood experiences in nature. She believed, moreover, that if I were to ask all of my respondents "when was the first time you ever had a sense of the divine, or of something bigger than you are?" I would invariably be told that it had occurred "in nature" (interview July 8, 2008). Her own account of the emergence of her "ecological conscience" is worth retelling:

> I used to lie on the ground behind our house … It's not totally country anymore, but sixty years ago it was. We bordered on … property where they had herds of cattle out in the fields. And I would lie on the ground, sort of underneath this willow tree where I'd built a fort, and I had my ear to the ground one day, and I could *hear this earth beating!* I mean I heard the heartbeat of the earth. And I went, wow, this is *alive!* And I stayed with that for a long time.
> And then, when I was older, I realized what I was listening to was cattle in the field … But never mind! For me, it was so real.

It gave me this really innate sense that the earth is alive with this beating heart. And of course, people say that now. Carl Sagan said [the earth] is a living species. And so that's been with me all my life. And I did grow up in a place where we played outdoors. With chickens, and dogs and cats, and foxes eating the chickens, and chasing coyote, and you know, that is who I am.

Who's going to protect our parks? Our beautiful wildlife refuges? Who's going to protect those things when my generation is gone? A few people in your [the author's] generation, my children, for example, are nature lovers, and two of them [Bingham's children] work in the environmental community. But after them, if children want to be indoors playing with electronic toys as a preference over being outside, who's going to love nature? You protect what you love!   (Interview July 8, 2008)

John Smith told me that his love and respect for place grew out of a deep belief in the importance of social justice, indicating the primacy of the human dimension of sustainability. One story he told illustrated his claim that respectful partnerships comprised of people from widely divergent backgrounds was the key to sustainability. Smith recounted one instance when ARC decided to provide funding to a Buddhist group that had purchased an old building previously used by the Irish Republican Army in an area of town with no "self-esteem."[25] The Buddhists turned the building into a monastery, and constructed a garden in the surrounding space. Although Smith admitted that they never achieved the full scope of what they envisioned, "what went on was enough." The monks turned the facility into an educational establishment, community meeting place, ran a café that promoted healthy lifestyle choices, and brought in students from schools across the region. The director of the monastery was Buddhist by conversion, Smith told me, and still sang in the local Christian church choir every Sunday. "It [the monastery] became the center of economic regeneration in that area," Smith said. Overall, Smith estimated that they probably spent around one million pounds on the project, a figure he noted was remarkable given the usual budgets of community redevelopment groups: "No authority in the country could spent a million pounds and make such a change! They could spend ten million and not get the return." It was particularly interesting because it was not a faith that was native to that part of the world. As Smith put it, "Something quite exotic, and unusual, and completely outside their experience had got people thinking, 'we are worth something!'" (interview May 29, 2008). If Bingham's awareness of "something bigger" first came to her alone in the fields, awareness of accountability can also arise among groups of people who engage each other in novel, and mutually beneficial ways. In these cases, religious beliefs, far from being confined within particular communities, become the primary motivations for engaging with others.

Religious metaphor and language are often the primary means of communication between these disparate groups. Follow-up work by ARC in instances like the one above illustrate that in some cases environmental protection may derive from an expanded sense of self and a moral sensibility that extends the concept of neighbor to include people or groups who hold significantly different worldviews and values. To stimulate community-level change, as in the story Smith related, interpersonal interaction is of paramount importance. Smith believes that the most effective way to enact change is one on one with individuals, in discussions of values, priorities, and short- and long-term goals.

Smith, who describes himself as an atheist, told me that these are the sorts of projects that work and that there are more success stories from faith communities than from any other group. These examples alone should make a convincing argument for at least revisiting the arguments of those who, like Norton (2005), would evacuate religion from the public sphere, for in many cases it is the primary motivation for peoples' engagement in activities that could be considered sustainability advocacy.[26] To illustrate how the process of worldview translation occurs, another example, this one not related to the global North, is helpful.

Islam in action in Zanzibar

In keeping with the philosophy that solutions to environmental, social, and development problems should be local, and not imposed from the outside, ARC often recruits others to help them fulfill their goals. For example, in a much-celebrated conservation victory, ARC and WWF teamed up with Fazlun Khalid and the Islamic Foundation for Ecology and Environmental Sciences (IFEES) to halt the destruction of the reefs around Zanzibar, endangered because of non-traditional and unsustainable dynamite fishing.

Khalid, whose father was an Islamic theologian, created a set of workbooks with accompanying visual media in the local language (Swahili) detailing Muslim resources that promoted awareness of ecological limits and intergenerational obligations. Khalid's first step was to gather with a group of Qur'anic scholars. He offered the workbooks and accompanying materials with passages of text from the Qur'an and asked the scholars to interpret the text with an eye to the environmental problems prevalent within their communities. According to Khalid, many of these scholars told him, "we read these verses every day, and we've never thought of them that way before!" These religious leaders agreed to help Khalid spread the message to the community fishermen.

With the authority of these community leaders behind him, Khalid engaged the local fishermen in a series of workshops. The workshops were a tremendous success: "The result was that in twenty-four hours they stopped dynamiting the coral reefs. Which CARE International, which WWF couldn't do for 3–4 years. They just couldn't stop them. In twenty-four hours, over-night, they stopped dynamiting the coral reefs!" (interview May 29, 2008).[27] In suggesting to these scholars a new interpretation of traditional texts he is assisting with the manufacture of an ecologically aware Islam, and thus with the manufacture of the religious dimensions of sustainability.

Worldview translation is thus a laborious process. It requires engaging citizens who are the targets of sustainable development, discernment of their interests, and the creation of materials and programs that foster their actualization. In this case, it required that two western NGOs leverage their collective resources (financial and theological) to access a community whose values were ecologically problematic. The solution was not to impose a management scheme on native populations, but to help them use their own religious resources in new ways.

Tending the garden in a tough neighborhood: cultivating love in place

Smith talked of another garden in the middle of a series of high rise flats in the UK where only the most desperate people lived. Between these high rises was an old Anglican church with a crumbling school long since abandoned by the church. A friend of Smith's, Reverend Canon David Wyatt, decided that school yard would be a fine spot for a garden, but had no money to bring that dream to fruition.[28]

Out for a walk one day, Wyatt discovered some young men vandalizing a bus stop. Wyatt stopped, observed them for a moment, and asked the boys, "Do you like doing that?"

"Well, yes!" the boys chimed, although puzzled they were not admonished by the older gentleman.

"Come with me," Wyatt said, and they followed him to the old playground. "Do you think you can destroy that?" Wyatt asked the boys, pointing to the abandoned play structures?

The boys, of course, took him up on his offer, gradually tearing down the old bars, pulling out the old concrete, as Wyatt collected and recycled newspapers (long before it was common practice). With the small allowances of money from the newspapers, they built a garden together. Smith told me,

> The outcome of it was: That [the garden] was the catalyst that completely changed that area ... when I [Smith] interviewed him [Wyatt], there was actually a waiting list to get into those flats. And the only, you know, real visible change you could see was this garden. It had a nice high wall around it, and it was very much sort of a quiet, open space. He had built the respect at all levels of the community, huge numbers of which had never stepped foot in the church.

Smith used this as an example of grassroots processes that create genuinely sustainable positive outcomes. Even when religion is not the catalyst for positive action, it often provides resources that can facilitate positive community formation (like the old churchyard). When such initiatives work well, Smith concluded, "they work *really* well" (interview May 29, 2008).

Transformational leaders in sustainable partnerships tell such stories to their collaborators and those outside their communities. Part of the reason such stories are often not influential among World Bank and other development and political institutions' officials is that they do not provide hard data and are infused with ethical and often spiritual language. Large institutions such as the World Bank, or the five-year plans preferred by many international bodies, typically have concrete goals which are ideal for governments and institutions. But Smith is convinced these strategies are not very effective on the ground (interview May 29, 2008). When Palmer, Smith, and others brought these and other stories to the World Bank for publication in their planned, jointly published report, the World Bank editors balked, stating that there were not enough "facts" in the stories. As a multilateral development institution beholden to a variety of stakeholders, they could only publish facts. Palmer and his colleagues pleaded with them: "that's not how religions work," and they informed the Bank that if they wanted to genuinely engage with the world's faith traditions, they were going to have to listen to such stories. Palmer told this story with some satisfaction: "In the end, they passed an editorial decision. That is, according to the World Bank, *myths, legends, and tales are facts*. And on that basis, they were able to publish the book" (interview May 28, 2008).[29] By deciding to listen to the stories of some of the world's faiths, the World Bank was also helping to broaden the scope of its own story by raising the possibility that new sorts of information, such as religious narratives, could provide data for normative decision-making.

ETHICS AT WHAT SCALE?

The above stories revive significant questions, first raised in Chapter 1, about the scale at which values should be included in deliberations about conservation, development, and sustainability. Smith and Palmer both believe that sustainable partnerships are created when they fit with the values of individuals at the most local level, not when they match the broad agendas of external agencies and organizations. This is part of the rub between NGO employees and academics, who are perceived by many of these NGO operatives as threatening the world's cultural diversity by promoting a common set of foundational ethical principles to guide the world's diverse cultures.

Hans Kung's universal ethic, first articulated in the 1980s and presented at the Parliament of World Religions in 1993, continues to be popular with some religious studies scholars, and its elucidation is still mentioned as a formative event for the field of religion and ecology (see for example Golliher 1999; Tucker 2006: 404). Mary Evelyn Tucker, in her survey of the field (2006), mentions Kung's work and the Earth Charter as important contributions. Tucker and her husband John Grim have shaped the international dialogue on sustainability, providing the most visible link between the academic community concerned with religion and environmental issues and international political bodies such as the United Nations. They launched the Forum on Religion and Ecology (FORE) in October of 1998 at a United Nations Press Conference held to report on the series of conferences at the Harvard Center for the Study of World Religions (CSWR) between 1996 and 1998.[30] Beyond their ongoing monthly report of religion and ecology oriented news bites from UNEP, Tucker and Grim have participated in many other programs. In the published report from a United Nations Educational, Scientific and Cultural Organization (UNESCO) event at their Catalonia, Spain location (UNESCOCAT), Tucker is cited no less than half a dozen times, and her idea that there is an "emerging new sensibility" related to sustainability provides the structure for the report (Pigem 2007).[31] "Sustainability," Tucker is quoted as saying, "needs to be placed in a larger, spiritually inspired context that includes the following major elements: (1) planetary awareness; (2) caring for future generations; (3) nurturing bioregional cultures and local knowledge; (4) expanding our ethical horizon; and (5) celebrating life" (Pigem 2007: 8).

To some extent, such global ethical formulations act as a religion (Taylor 2010), and in most cases such efforts were criticized by my informants. Ethics cannot be generated *ex nihilo* (from nothing), Palmer argued. They must be grounded in a world model, and a global ethic necessarily has no common community or life experience in which an ethos could be plausibly grounded. Palmer was especially critical of the Earth Charter: "I don't know anybody apart from those who promote it who's even heard of it. I mean, what does it *do* other than state the obvious in a somewhat bland way? People do not do things because they're the same. They do things because they have something distinctive to give" (interview May 28, 2008). The critics believe that these global ethics schemes basically promote a new, less specific sort of faith without attending to the rich possibilities that extant faiths already possess for creating positive change (see for example the critiques of the Earth Charter reviewed by Taylor 2010: 185–6).[32] Fazlun Khalid called such ethical systems "mega-ethics," and argued,

> The people don't want an earth religion, they want their own reli-
> gion. These things are coming from academics ... For them [the
> people on the ground], this kind of language would be alien, anath-
> ema to their own beings ... It's alright as a debating point, which
> is what the academics like, but ... who wants to create another
> religion? We've got enough religions!   (Interview May 29, 2009)

Sally Bingham noted that she did not see evidence that people were turning toward a global ethical system but believed that people were finding *within and through* their own traditions new strength, new stories, and new partners.

Interestingly, although these thought leaders disagree about the value of universal minimum standards of earth citizenship and responsibility such as the Earth Charter, they generally agree that the preservation of bioregional and indigenous languages, lifeways, world models, and narratives is centrally important to sustainability. So while there is agreement on some ultimate goals, there is some disagreement about the appropriate scale of ethical formulations in an interfaith context. Some believe that different faiths can assent to sets of common principles while others are convinced that any ethic that operates at such broad scales is useless, top-heavy, and thus unstable.

If Palmer is correct, and he is well placed to have a good grasp of the prevalence of such ideas in interfaith NGOs, then efforts such as the Earth Charter neither filter down to the typical citizen with whom they work (especially ARC's partners in the non-industrialized world), nor convince people in leadership roles in sustainability initiatives.[33] The high-profile position of Tucker and Grim at Yale University's School of Forestry, however, and their working relationship with UNEP suggest that the Earth Charter's exposure may continue to increase, and may become more widely appreciated. Moreover, it is possible that the less doctrinal universe story promoted by Tucker and Grim could appeal to more people, including those (in the global North, for example) who shy away from institutionalized religions in favor of a more personalized form of spirituality.

DIFFERENCES THAT MATTER: FROM GLOBAL ETHICS TO LOCAL PRAGMATISM

There are three primary and related themes which require further comment. The first is the idea offered above that an expansion of ethical concern is important to sustainability advocacy. The inclusive understanding of who is a "neighbor" (offered by Bingham, Hunter, Kirschenmann, and Cizik) parallels ideas drawn from scientists and activists involved in sustainability. For example, recall that the idea that defending the environment is actually defending one's self as articulated by the deep ecologist John Seed. Clearly the idea of ethical extension has manifested in significant ways in radical environmental circles, among mainstream sustainability advocates, and even in evangelical circles. But more important to the argument here, the extension of moral consideration by stretching the "self" to include others (ethnic, cultural, ethical, or non-human), or through an expanded understanding of "neighbor," is an important ingredient of interpersonal empathy and risk. It is the foundation upon which genuine engagement with others begins in these faith and interfaith communities. Ideally, individuals treat themselves and their neighbors with care and respect and demonstrate openness to their ideas and worldviews. It is often difficult to encourage individuals or groups, particularly ones that disagree profoundly on particular issues, to participate together in a way that exposes core values and beliefs, and holds them up for scrutiny. But according to the high level actors highlighted here, when it does work, the outcomes are much more sustainable. Progress toward sustainability is ultimately generated through these risky partnerships, where people with differing foundational values work together toward their common interests.

Second, the disagreements among informants regarding the usefulness of a global ethic are worth greater scrutiny. Both sides have made plausible arguments for their cause. But interestingly, this may be an instance where the clarification of terms and motivations could prove helpful. For example, Palmer and Khalid both expressed reluctance about common or global ethics because they have witnessed what they believe to be a significant danger of "green fascism" within environmentalist movements.[34]

Calvin DeWitt, on the other hand (in agreement with Kung, Earth Charter supporters, and UNESCOCAT conference participants), explicitly extolled the virtues of a global conservation ethic (interview April 8, 2008; for more on DeWitt see Chapter 7).[35] Whatever sort of global ethic UNESCO, the Earth Charter, DeWitt, Kung, and Tucker advocate, when unpacked, it includes provisions for grounding ethics in local communities, and deliberately attempts to avoid imposition of a one-size-fits-all ethic. For instance, the UNESCOCAT conference discussed above, which essentially promoted a schematic definition of global sustainability, included in its recommendations to the UN that "fostering local knowledge and nurturing local cultures and languages is part ... of preserving the ecological integrity of a bioregion," and that "sustainability and environmental ethics must be place-based rather than universal" (Pigem 2007: 18). Further, the conference participants believed (along with, according to my interviews, Palmer, Khalid, Bingham, and Laushkin [see Chapter 7]) that "most of the damage to the Earth is done by 'believers' in the secular modern worldview, with its ingrained 'faith' in endless economic growth and consumerism" (Pigem 2007: 18).[36] For these critics, this expansionist secular modern worldview is precisely the problem. It would seem then that a new global ethics derived from this secular modern worldview cannot provide adequate correction.

Thus, whatever sort of ethic is suggested by the UN, the religious scholars who participate with them (such as Tucker and Grim) and some civil society representatives, it is not intended to be an ethical panacea to be successfully applied everywhere. As Tucker and Grim put it in the foreword to the FORE volumes, they were "not looking for a unified worldview or a single global ethic," rather they were seeking a minimum global standard for environmental conduct and believed the affective power of religious rhetoric to be the best means of achieving it (Tucker & Grim 1997: xxiv). They intend to graft this ethic of reverence for life and the cosmos onto existing religious cultural production, not to replace existing traditions wholesale. For example, the UNESCO publication specifically noted that religious traditions are crucial to providing education for sustainable lifeways, and assented to the idea that our culture requires "a re-evaluation of our place in the cosmos" and awareness "that human solidarity and kinship with all life is strengthened when we live with reverence for the mystery of being, gratitude for the gift of life, and humility regarding the human place in nature" (Pigem 2007: 11). This universal spirituality of connection and its accompanying kinship ethic (consonant with the themes highlighted in Chapter 6) is certainly a religious vision, and may be integrated with extant religious narratives, a global civic earth religion, or personalized forms of generic spirituality.

In short, there is some disconnect here, for these global spiritualities of connection aim for universal ethical tropes and visions while also promoting the preservation of place-based and context-dependent lifeways. The question of whether promotion of such universal ethical systems obscures or even erodes cultural difference, particularly when deployed in sustainable development schemes, remains a question on which more empirical evidence could shed additional light.

Third, and related to the search for a global ethics, is the extent to which the religious themes within ethical discourse reflect the narratives, practices, and worldviews of diverse peoples. The editors of the FORE volumes use as a framework for their project a suggestion attributed to J. Baird Callicott (1994) that scholars and others should "mine the conceptual resources" of the world and traditional religions to generate a global environmental ethics (Tucker & Grim 1997: xxii).[37] There have been significant criticisms of this approach (see Larson 1989). Such endeavors are often envisioned by critics as erosive of traditional worldviews, diluting or adapting them to such an extent that they lose their distinctiveness.[38] As the preceding discussion of the religious dimensions of sustainability advocacy demonstrated, however, at the international level there are resonances between the metaphors deployed by representatives of the world religions, indigenous groups, NGO advocates, and international political regimes. The convergence of narratives from different groups does not necessarily constitute the imposition of a global ethic. Rather, it reflects, in part, a pragmatic, strategic approach to furthering the aims of particular communities.

Many international aid and development organizations focus on raising standards of living (however defined). Conservation groups primarily aim to preserve biodiversity (and more recently, cultural diversity). Indigenous advocacy groups have focused on gaining political traction and retaining traditional land tenure. Each of these groups and their differing aims can be roughly sketched for other groups using the discourse of sustainability.[39] In many cases the language, metaphor, and ideas frequently used by the Forum to describe the reasons why individuals and governments ought to care for biocultural diversity are increasingly exercised by indigenous and traditional peoples themselves in international venues. If such a broad spirituality in practice does little to erode existing religious beliefs or practices, and instead promotes bridge-building and collaboration with cultural, ethnic, or ethical others then it achieves the collaborative outcomes aimed at by Palmer and Bingham. But even if there is little doubt that these themes are in some way present within both global and indigenous religions, little or no research has investigated what these metaphors or themes *mean for those people* (particularly in the case of indigenous or traditional cultures engaged in sustainable development projects).[40] For example, participants within some religiously inspired grassroots efforts may be adopting and adapting sustainability-related concepts for their own political ends, while scholars who analyze them imagine that such values and themes are central to their religious lives. This is a potentially fruitful area of further research.[41]

Although there is some disagreement regarding the appropriate scale for ethics, in any case a distinction should be drawn between metaphors and tropes that work on an international level and those that are efficacious on the ground. Even if ideas related to a global ethics are unrelated to the moral reasoning of individuals across the globe, stories of local success are transmitted (through organizations such as IPL and ARC) into international political venues where they perform political work. The preceding analysis has only begun to tease out some of the cognitive tools used in these national and international political venues by leaders in civil society segments of sustainability movements. Take for example the importance of narrative in imagining and transmitting ethical norms. The formation of strategic partnerships based on an ethic of personal risk and recognition of deep interdependence are common attributes of sustainability advocates, and these are also important themes that are transmitted to other constituencies in stories.

The existence of a global ethic grounded in sustainability is not *necessarily* fascist or oppressive, but the possibility that it could be so remains.[42] Just as indigenous peoples may adopt and adapt the affective dimensions of sustainability discourse, governmental, corporate or other entities may also adapt it to promote their own ends. A spiritualized global ethic, or what some have pointed to as a global civic religion, may provide a unique opportunity for "greenwashing" on a global scale.[43] While a dark green civic earth religion may not promote the exploitation of resources or other peoples, it may be that a sustainability-oriented civic religion (which contains light green and light brown hues) could have other negative impacts, which are explored in Chapter 10.

TRACING THE LINES OF FORCE

At the close of this chapter, two things should be clear. First, there are many metaphors and themes that are shared by the evangelical communities of Chapter 7 and the multi-faith groups discussed here. For example, the extension of the concept of "neighbor," the belief in the importance of including religious discourse in the democratic arena, and the centrality of story and narrative are all common themes. In addition, it is possible to begin to see some of the connective threads between these expert networks. Through these open-ended interviews it was sometimes difficult to establish the origin and direction of transmission of certain ideas, but some of the pathways for transference are apparent.

For example, like some of the evangelicals I interviewed, Bingham cited E. O. Wilson as one of her inspirations. Others she cited as influential to her thinking about the relationship between religion and sustainability included the Union of Concerned Scientists (also cited by at least one evangelical respondent), Al Gore, the poet Mary Oliver, and Mary Evelyn Tucker. Bingham recalled that early in her career as a religious environmental advocate, she was often questioned by evangelical Christians about the rapture and what impact it had on her argument.[44] She telephoned Richard Cizik specifically to ask him how he dealt with such questions among his own constituency. "He was wonderful," Bingham recalled of their early conversation, "He said that 'there's absolutely nothing in scripture that would give you *any* indication that the destruction of our natural resources is going to bring Jesus back any faster. And people who say that are *heretics*.' So now, when I get that question, I quote him!" (interview July 8, 2008). In his explanation to Bingham, Cizik echoed something that Joel Hunter and Calvin DeWitt both said in different words: any interpretation of Christianity that devalues nature in this way denies the physicality of Jesus' supposed resurrection and eventual return. Bingham also reported that Joel Hunter was a close confidant, and that they have worked together several times. In addition, Bingham has sent sermons that addressed the concept of natural capitalism to Hunter Lovins (one of the informants discussed in Chapter 9) for her to make editorial suggestions and provide examples.[45] The two are longtime friends, and both reported that Lovins stays with Bingham when in the Bay Area.

Bingham, Palmer, and the evangelical informants I interviewed cited their parents and childhood experiences in nature as formative of their ecological conscience. Palmer's father was an Anglican priest, his mother was an amateur naturalist responsible for his respect for the environment, and his godmother taught him to read the signs of ancient landscaping (old wells, terraces, etc.) and "how to listen to the wood ... and read how it had grown" (interview May 28, 2008). Intellectually, Palmer also listed Shakespeare and Carl Jung, and cited his travels as a young man in Hong Kong, and his exposure to Daoism, Buddhism, and Maoism as influences. Professionally he has relationships with officials within the World Bank and United Nations. But ARC also declared Bingham's Interfaith Power and Light initiative part of their "Sacred Gifts" program, an award that highlights IPL's ability to connect religious teaching and theology with environmentally responsible practice.[46] Palmer also worked with Ben Campbell of Conservation International's (CI) Faith-based Outreach initiative (see Chapter 9 for more details) to draw up a "handbook" for each of the world's faiths to be used in conjunction with CI's projects. Khalid began his conservation work with ARC, and after founding his own Islamic NGO, has maintained his relationships with groups such as ARC and cultivated new ones with people like Ben Campbell and CI. Campbell is also an evangelical Christian and is a regular speaker and attendee of environmentally related evangelical conferences and events (such as the C3 event detailed in Chapter 7).

Clearly these expert networks are well connected, and they depend on such relationships to broaden their appeal, sharpen the content of their messages, and to fulfill their own particular niches in the sustainability movement. It is important to note that most of these informants still believe the definition of "sustainability" to be unsettled and in some cases unhelpful to their work on the ground because it cannot be operationalized. Their work, however, cultivating partnerships with an eye to ecological and personal limits and devising strategies for how to live within them, falls under the umbrella of the broad definition utilized here. Indeed, as the following chapters demonstrate, the concept of sustainability is of central importance to many secular organizations that frame their advocacy in religious terms, or use religious narratives and other highly affective cognitive tools to describe their motivations and work.

CHAPTER NINE

THE RELIGIOUS DIMENSIONS OF SECULAR SUSTAINABILITY

INTRODUCTION

In Chapters 7 and 8, values have been couched in narratives that place ethical principles, obligations, and demands in the framework of a dynamic religious system, whether ecological, global, or cosmological in scope. The informants and the groups they represent, for the most part, work either from within a particular tradition, or begin from a multi-faith perspective. In each of the cases presented, these activists reach out to those outside their constituencies with large-scale, affectively rich narratives. This chapter reviews data gathered from high-level actors in secular organizations dedicated to the search for sustainability. The similarities between the tactics used by religious, interfaith, and secular groups will be clear. Although the religious dimensions of sustainability are perhaps more muted, and deep values and beliefs may surface further along in negotiations, religious and spiritual leaders are frequently directly mentioned as allies by those in the secular sustainability arena. Moreover, at least some of these informants consider themselves to be religious or spiritual but pursue their work through these secular venues. This attests to the fluid and permeable boundaries between religious and secular communities, at least in the United States and Europe. Finally, the examples gathered here support some theories regarding the importance of affectively tied, episodic memories in the formation of moral sensibilities. Certain modes of religiosity, which are not always confined to institutional religions or their adherents, are some of the primary vectors through which sustainability tropes are transmitted.

CONSERVATION INTERNATIONAL, NATURAL CAPITALISM SOLUTIONS, AND THE NORTHWEST EARTH INSTITUTE

Each of the organizations reviewed in this chapter has a unique history and different targets. While they share some similarities in strategy and philosophy, most of the interviewed informants envision their work in very different ways.

Conservation International

Conservation International (CI) is a large organization dedicated primarily to preserving global biodiversity with a three-pronged strategy of (a) describing the importance of biodiversity (and the dangers of loss) with cutting edge science, (b) maintaining an abiding concern for human welfare, and (c) facilitating and maintaining partnerships with businesses and nongovernmental organizations.[1] Formed in 1987 by a small group of concerned activists, the organization has grown in size and scope, and now maintains field offices and programs in Africa, Asia, North and South America, and Europe. Their focus is on biodiversity "hotspots," that is, threatened areas where genetic and species variety is especially high (for the time being). Their primary purpose is to provide scientific data to populations to help them design and implement effective conservation strategies. They have cultivated partnerships with businesses such as Citigroup, BP, Chevron Texaco, Cargill, and Conoco Phillips, and a variety of NGOs such as the World Wildlife Fund (WWF) and the International Union for the Conservation of Nature (IUCN), also including at least one explicitly religious organization (A Rocha).[2] The focus here, however, will primarily be the Faith-based Outreach Program at CI.

The Faith-based Outreach Program started in 2006. Ben Campbell was asked to spearhead the program from its inception. He was the former director of agroforestry for CI before he moved on to work for the Christian relief and development organization WorldVision, and thus had already established relationships with upper level management within CI.[3] Campbell believed that he owed his new appointment as director of the new faith-based initiative largely to his openness about being a Christian. CI began to actively pursue their vision for a Faith-based Outreach Program when the "green evangelical" movement began to gain momentum in the United States (see Chapter 7 for more details). News about evangelicals such as Richard Cizik, Joel Hunter, and others who were promoting a creation care agenda was increasingly visible in the United States, and the political power of evangelicals reached across oceans into peace negotiations (such as the ones Hunter participated in at Doha) and missionary work. As Campbell put it, "CI realized here was a whole new group of people they should be talking to, that they didn't know yet!" (interview July 29, 2008). The original vision for the program was to tap into the enormous political potential of evangelicals in the United States and secondarily to mobilize churches in the US and worldwide to get more involved in conservation efforts.

CI provides an interesting example of a secular conservation organization that is intentionally reaching out to faith groups in an effort to cultivate new partnerships which promote conservation. While the program initially focused primarily on evangelicals in the US, Campbell noted that it became interfaith and global almost immediately, since biodiversity "hotspots" are often in the tropics, places where Christians, Muslims, and other faiths must work together effectively (interview July 29, 2008).

Natural Capitalism Solutions

Hunter Lovins spoke fondly of her mentors Donella Meadows (lead author of *Limits to Growth* [1972]) and David Brower,[4] noting that one of their most important contributions to environmental movements was to talk freely about values and the "inner dimension" that provided the motivation to work for sustainability.[5] Unfortunately, Lovins noted, this inner dimension of sustainability has been separated from the technical/scientific dimension in the public sphere, leading to some disconnect for those who pursue sustainability. Although she believes it is important, Lovins does not see her role as rescuing this inner dimension from anonymity. Instead, her approach is thoroughly pragmatic: she tries to meet people where they are. If they want to talk financial bottom-line, she begins there. If they talk about values, she talks about those, too. But in many ways, even frank discussions of profitability and common sense require people to analyze what it is that they wish to maximize, and therefore require some reflection on values.

Lovins's early contributions to sustainability discourse included her work with Amory Lovins, with whom she collaborated on *Factor Four* (von Weizsacker *et al.*1998) and *Natural Capitalism* (Hawken *et al.* 1999). But earlier works included two books on nuclear non-proliferation (*Energy/War: Breaking the Nuclear Link: A Prescription for Non-proliferation* [Lovins & Lovins 1981], and *The First Nuclear World War: A Strategy for Preventing Nuclear Wars and the Spread of Nuclear Weapons* [O'Heffernan *et al.* 1983]), and about creating safe energy to enhance national security. These works were published before widespread realization in the United States that energy scarcity and dependency was a national security issue.

These books were penned while Lovins managed a non-profit organization called the Rocky Mountain Institute (RMI), a think-tank focused on strategic energy solutions.[6] After parting with RMI, Lovins founded Natural Capitalism Solutions (NatCap) in 2003, an organization dedicated to educating senior leaders in business, government and civil society "to restore and enhance the natural and human capital while increasing prosperity and quality of life."[7] NatCap provides consultations to corporations such as Royal Dutch Shell, Wal-Mart, and Interface Carpets, and has worked with the US Department of Energy, the Pentagon, and the US Environmental Protection Agency, as well as the governments of Jamaica, Australia, and Afghanistan to help promote change toward sustainability.

NatCap Solutions especially targets what Lovins calls "thought leaders"—high-level actors in these various constituencies. These leaders are highly networked individuals, and because they are often also leaders with decision-making power in large businesses, educational institutions, and governments, they are well-placed to exact large-scale change.

Northwest Earth Institute

Other groups focus on grassroots efforts, providing individuals with the tools to create change in their personal lives. The Northwest Earth Institute (NWEI) is one of those organizations.

NWEI was founded in 1993 by the husband and wife team of Jeanne and Dick Roy in Portland, Oregon with a mission to motivate "individuals to examine and transform personal values and habits, to accept responsibility for the earth, and to act on that commitment" (NWEI 2001b: 12). The Roys organized a series of what they called "discussion groups" in their home, where participants met once a week to discuss a set of readings. Soon, literally through word of mouth, the groups began to appear in local churches, homes, and in other communities. According to figures on the website, NWEI now has over 600 volunteers in all 50 states, plus Puerto Rico, Canada, Sweden, and New Zealand working to disseminate the discussion group model, with over 130,000 enrolled to date.[8]

The first discussion group module was called *Exploring Deep Ecology* and included writings from authors such as Gary Snyder, Aldo Leopold, Arne Naess, Thomas Berry, Matthew Fox, Stephanie Kaza, Brian Swimme, and many others. From there, NWEI developed modules dedicated to *Voluntary Simplicity, Choices for Sustainable Living, Discovering a Sense of*

Place, Globalization and its Critics, Healthy Children, Healthy Planet, and one dedicated to climate change called *Global Warming: Changing CO₂urse.* Each discussion group compilation includes discussion questions designed to help participants examine individual values and practices, build community, and "to take action toward creating a more sustainable future."⁹

The discussion groups are grounded in the notion that current trends are unsustainable. The Roys' prefaces explicitly state that they wish to challenge the values of the dominant consumer culture that erode traditional sources of social support for healthy living, such as extended families, neighbors, and church communities (NWEI 2007b: 10; 2001a: 10). Some of the ways in which NWEI endeavors to change personal beliefs and practices complement the other organizations discussed above. While CI focuses on collaborative partnerships with NGOs and businesses, and NatCap Solutions focuses on creating culture change through education of high-level actors, NWEI fosters grassroots-level individual changes in values and practices. Despite differences in their foci and strategy, each of these groups is working toward a more sustainable human culture.

THE "ECOLOGY" OF A SOCIAL MOVEMENT

Among the varied readings in NWEI's *Choices for Sustainable Living* module is a short piece by Buddhist scholar and activist Joanna Macy arguing that in the early years of the twenty-first century human cultures will embark on a new path toward peace, justice, and sustainability. She called it "The Great Turning" (NWEI 2007b: 20–22).¹⁰ According to Macy, the switchmen that will set humans upon this new path are the varied social movements that in different but interrelated ways work towards a sustainable society. The Turning is composed of three mutually reinforcing dimensions: (a) "holding actions in defense of life on earth"; (b) confronting the "structural causes of the global crisis and [creating] sustainable alternatives"; and (c) "a shift in our perception of reality" (NWEI 2007b: 21). The third element, Macy claimed, "is happening all around us ... Like our primordial ancestors, we begin to see the world as our body, and, whether we say the word or not, as sacred" (NWEI 2007b: 21). Public intellectual David Korten authored a book called *The Great Turning* in 2006, and his website has at least two references to Macy's use of the phrase (one of them the exact quote that appears on the cover of one NWEI discussion guide).¹¹ His interpretation of the Turning coheres with Macy's, although it is more complex. Korten repeatedly makes the point in print and in lectures that to change a culture it is necessary to change the *stories* that culture understands as normative.

Perceptual shifts are transmitted through culture from the bottom up, in the same way that a self-organizing system generates dynamic equilibrium from a period of release and reorganization phases.[12]

Examples of this perceptual shift include "cognitive and perceptual frameworks" (Macy mentions general systems theory, deep ecology, Gaia theory, and the Universe Story, "which are based on discoveries in physics and biology and reveal the radical interconnectedness of all life"), spiritual perspectives from both Eastern and Western "world religions" and from native traditions across the globe, and "new" practices and rituals (NWEI 2007b: 21). This illustrates the pervasiveness of themes introduced to sustainability movements from the natural sciences discussed in Chapter 6, and also highlights Macy's belief that all of these smaller scale movements, which can be envisioned as facets of broader sustainability movements, have significant religious dimensions. Moreover, Macy suggests that these varied movements, from direct action to New Age-style ritualizing, are working together to "re-make" the world.[13]

Cooperation between diverse sub-populations engaged in direct action for the earth, ritualized consciousness-raising, and social justice or anti-globalization resistance may be considered relatively new phenomena. Interestingly, although within the cultic and environmentalist milieus disparate groups exchanged motivational metaphors, ideas, and imagery rather freely, direct cooperation (see for example Taylor 1997) was more often the exception than the rule.[14]

It was such internecine fighting that prompted Michael Shellenberger and Ted Nordhaus to argue, in the widely read article "The Death of Environmentalism," that while the environmental movement was an important development in creating legislation and action that prevented ecological and social collapse, the movement was unable to provide a rich *positive* vision of the future based on common core values (Shellenberger & Nordhaus 2004).[15] On their account, narrowly conceived policy goals and infighting ensured that environmentalism remained a marginal movement with few positive outcomes. Note the resonance of their claim with Martin Palmer's lament (from Chapter 8) that environmentalism can "bring us to the foot of the cross" without offering any "redemption." Hunter Lovins agreed with Shellenberger and Nordhaus, and while her activist roots lie in the environmental movement (with mentors such as Meadows and Brower), she considers her current work as going beyond environmentalism.[16] Generally speaking she believes that environmentalists do not work well with others. Lovins uses the term sustainability to describe her work because, besides highlighting practices that are unsustainable, it also offers a positive vision of how to work together to reduce human disruption of ecological systems and increase social capital. In accord with Nordhaus and Shellenberger, she described some of the reasons why activists need to move past environmentalism:

> The activist community tends to act like a bucket of crabs. Anytime any one of them starts to gain any elevation, the others just pull 'em down. And that's just stupid. And we've also—'we' being those who came out of the environmental movement or the social movement—tend to look at any other movement as inferior. So [these] activists tend to look at people who are doing spiritual work as somehow irrelevant ... [But] there's work enough for all of us.   (Interview August 6, 2008)

Although she does not perceive her work as directly contributing to the religious dimensions of sustainability, she has no problem with others finding deep value, even spiritual inspiration in the hope that human production, consumption, and population could become more sustainable.

During a luncheon and roundtable discussion at the University of Florida in 2007 Lovins recalled an example of the positive outcomes that derived from cooperation. Randy Hayes and the Rainforest Action Network (RAN), a direct-action organization formed in the mid-1980s that has been calling attention to exploitation of the world's most biologically diverse rainforest habitats and the suffering of their peoples, had boycotted Mitsubushi Corporation and through direct action had drawn public attention to their contributions to deforestation.[17] Lovins recalled that Mitsubishi then approached the Rocky Mountain Institute (where Lovins was still employed at the time) and asked them to help end the boycott. On the one hand, Lovins and the RMI team provided some easy-to-implement business ideas for Mitsubishi, small sacrifices for the cessation of a negative public relations campaign. On the other hand, Lovins spoke with her old friend Randy Hayes of RAN (they had worked together as activists with Brower, and elsewhere), and asked him to end the boycott. "It was a nice one–two punch," recalled Lovins. It drove home her main point: "as a movement, we are an ecology. We need all the species [of activism and action]" (September 2007). Lovins played the role of a translator, and helped each side achieve what they wanted. Mitsubishi was able to end the boycott, and RAN saw shifts in behavior and policy at a major manufacturer.

Each of the approaches noted by Macy above, direct action, social and environmental justice activism aimed at structural inequities, and advocacy of perceptual or cognitive shifts through ritualizing and spiritual training, what Lovins would call different "species" of advocacy, were present in the

Mitsubishi campaign. Achieving sustainability requires actors who challenge to the status quo as well as actors who have the ear of the corporations and businesses that are often imagined to be the primary culprits behind ecological degradation. "Who is the enemy?" Lovins asked, reflecting on the tendency of environmentalists to simplify the "ecosystem of activism" by shutting out corporations. "Is it business [that's the enemy]? You know, when you've got Wal-Mart driving climate protection into its 90,000 supplier businesses it's hard to couch them as the enemy" (interview August 6, 2008).

While negative portrayals of corporations such as Wal-Mart by environmentalists have likely contributed to some changes in corporate culture, sustainability advocacy has typically approached such corporations with more positive messages and offers of partnership. In significant ways, sustainability has added a discourse of cooperation to the pre-existing environmentalist, social justice, voluntary simplicity, and resistance to capitalism discourses, tying them together through the recognition that there is a certain convergence of concerns despite wide general disagreement on the nature and source of the problems and their ultimate solutions. In short, sustainability is acting as a new metanarrative, a large-scale story that is able to weave together a wide variety of value sets. As in previous chapters, among secular sustainability activists there are many religion-resembling stories in which these varied value sets are encoded.

STORIES OF VALUE

"Americans, and probably everybody really, want three things: prosperity, security, and meaning," confided Lovins, drawing on David Korten's work (interview August 6, 2008). One of the major obstacles to achieving these three basic foci of human desire, Lovins says, is that there is no plausible, desirable vision that the whole world can share (discussion, September 2007). Instructions on how to achieve these basic desires for prosperity, security, and meaning are nearly always couched in stories. Cognitive science research has demonstrated that when people hear stories (particularly from people within their primary communities of accountability), they make inferences about the ideas and cognitive states of the agents in the story and construct meaningful stories that are related to particular emotional states (Atran *et al.* 2005; Wilson 2011).[18] Stories about what individuals, groups, and communities value, then, are important tools that may be adapted and deployed in the quest for sustainability.

For example, Lovins fleshed out her discussion of Korten's idea by saying, "What the neo-cons [neo-conservatives] have done is to tee up plausible stories [about how] you are personally going to achieve these three things [prosperity, security, and meaning].[19] They may be wrong, but they address them!" On prosperity, said Lovins, the neo-cons say "Don't give money to the poor, give it to the rich, because they won't squander it. Maybe untrue. But it's plausible." When addressing security, Lovins added, "neo-cons say it's the individual white male on the big horse, and so we elect people like the Terminator to be governor.[20] And the progressives say, 'make love not war,' but not much about how we're going to stay secure in an insecure world." When it comes to meaning, perhaps the dimension most obviously relevant to religion, Lovins stated that "the neo-cons say 'my President speaks to God on Friday,' and the rest of the country says, 'thank God somebody does.' The progressives say separate church and state, and are completely unresponsive to [the question of] 'What is meaning?'" Lovins' conclusion is that "until the progressives come up with a plausible set of storylines about how you're going to achieve prosperity, security, and meaning, they're not going to get a lot of traction" (interview August 6, 2008). Lovins was suggesting that these stories are *cognitive tools* for encouraging a mindset that promotes more sustainable societies.

Andrés Edwards suggested that the "principles" of sustainability are best imagined as stories, or better yet, Songlines (Edwards 2005). Edwards drew the idea from the Australian Aboriginal use of Songlines, narrative tracks through particular landscapes, passed down orally, slightly different with each telling as new generations add layers of understanding to a mythologized landscape. "The principles of sustainability," stated Edwards "represent the footprints of the various groups that make up the Sustainability Revolution. Like the Songlines, these statements of principles articulate a group's values, archive its history, and indicate the future direction of its actions" (Edwards 2005: 26).[21] Songlines are religious stories and like others (including those tied to sustainability advocacy) they are "deep" narratives that transgress temporal and political boundaries by trafficking in affectively oriented protagonists and plotlines. There are biophilic stories, ones drawn from the life sciences, which provide a new set of stories about how and why humans ought to preserve biodiversity (see the discussion in Chapter 6). As David Orr reminds readers of the NWEI's *Exploring Deep Ecology* module, biophilia is actually "a series of choices, the first of which has to do with the conduct of childhood and how the child's imagination is woven into a home place" (NWEI 2001a: VI-11). For Orr, without profound experiences with nature in childhood, human survival is in question: "We will not enter this new kingdom of sustainability until we allow our children the kind of childhood in which biophilia can put down roots" (2001a: VI-12).[22]

168

In addition there are cosmophilic stories which draw on the "Epic of Evolution," a phrase popularized to refer to the awe and reverence for the cosmos engendered by the recognition of its long history of increasing complexity, which contribute to sustainability. The Northwest Earth Institute volumes weave together stories from science (from authors such as Fritjof Capra, Thomas Berry, Brian Swimme, James Lovelock, and others), articles depicting quantum mechanics as morally instructive, selections from Native American cultures (from authors such as Black Elk, Winona LaDuke, Sun Bear, and Gary Snyder), as well as teachings from Christian mystics (Meister Eckhardt, Matthew Fox) and Buddhist scholars (Macy and Stephanie Kaza). These are all tied together and imagined as working toward a convergence where the evolution of the universe itself is seen as morally instructive. In a section of one NWEI module entitled "A New Story from Science," Brian Swimme admits that,

> the Epic of Evolution is definitely mythic. But it's … a form of myth that comes along with this mode of inquiry we call empirical or scientific … Within the evolutionary point of view, you realize—holy Toledo!—the mind itself is just an expression of the powers of the universe. And then you have that non-dualistic, hand-in-glove realization that Newton couldn't have and that Darwin enables us to have but that he didn't fully have.[23]
>
> (NWEI 2001a: V-10)

Or, as Lovelock put it,

> Ancient belief and modern knowledge have fused emotionally in the awe with which astronauts with their own eyes and we by indirect vision have seen the earth revealed in all its shining beauty against the deep darkness of space … Like a religious belief, it is scientifically untestable and therefore incapable in its own context of further rationalization.[24]   (NWEI 2001a: II-5)

Each of these is a tale that provides a different set of ethical foundations, and thus a different perspective on how humans can access to prosperity, security, and meaning. They are stories about healing the earth and about the relationships between people. These stories explain what is ultimately good (relationship with others, humility regarding the human place in the world, and respect for and preservation of cultural and biological diversity), and what is ultimately unsustainable (short-term vision, stories of domination and oppression, and the idea that humans are bounded, self-interested cost–benefit calculators).

169

As Lovins noted, these stories are tools, forged for the quest toward sustainability. She elaborated on her strategy when she gives public talks: "I very consciously address these issues of prosperity, security, and meaning, but I do so without calling them out. So I end my talks with pictures of the Lord of the Rings, and Gandalf, which is mythic, good vs. evil, and the role of little people and individuals in tackling the great challenges" (interview August 6, 2008).[25] She relates these affectively rich tales to what she believes are real-life evils: "the evil that I've been talking about throughout the talk is the loss of all major ecosystems on earth, and climate crisis, and peak oil, etc." (interview August 6, 2008). In a roundtable discussion at the University of Florida Lovins also pointed toward the polar bear as the newest martyr of the evil, unsustainable facets of society.[26] Polar bears make good icons for sustainability movements because their disappearance illustrates the interdependence of biological life, since localized but widespread human behaviors impact the habitats and food sources of the planet's most remote species.

In NEWI's *Global Warming: Changing CO$_2$urse* module, Lovins's mentor Donella Meadows contributed a short piece entitled "Polar Bears and Three-Year-Olds on Thin Ice." There Meadows recalled her friends' reaction when faced with biologists' predictions that the polar bear's demise was imminent: "in response to this news, she [Meadows' friend] did the only appropriate thing. She burst out weeping. 'What am I going to tell my three-year-old?' she sobbed. Any of us still in contact with our hearts and souls should be sobbing with her, especially when we consider that the same toxins that are in the bears are in the three-year-old" (NWEI 2007a: 4).

CLASHING VALUES: TALKING THROUGH AND ACROSS VALUE STRUCTURES

I asked Ben Campbell, head of CI's Faith-based Initiative, about his impression of the phrase sometimes discussed in evangelical circles (and which provided the title for Chapter 7) that participants in the sustainability movement were "walking together separately." His answer, I believe, is an important lesson in how people within different sectors of the sustainability movement are working together.

Campbell told me that as a Christian, working within an organization that included and interacted with a variety of faiths was challenging both professionally and personally. He recalled that his wife once wondered if his exposure to a multi-faith atmosphere required that he actually endorse Muslim or Buddhist (or other) practices in some way. Campbell's answer was a qualified "no." He recalled telling his wife

Do I believe they're correct? Do I believe in their eschatology? Do I believe their ultimate ... what happens in terms of an afterlife, in terms of a belief system? No, but ... it is really very much the "walking together separately" concept. I know what motivates them, they know what motivates me, and through our various belief systems [we] have different reasons why we are concerned about the current state of the world right now.

(Interview July 29, 2009)

Campbell noted that because he is rather open about his faith, he is faced with questions from colleagues in the conservation profession about his beliefs, and from his fellow Christians about the centrality of science to his work. One of the most frequent lines of questioning, he said, comes from Christians who want to know if he believes that the earth was really created in seven days, with its full complement of animals.[27] Campbell's answer:

Well, I don't have to [believe in seven day creation]. And it doesn't change my relationship with Jesus Christ. It doesn't change anything about what I think about the importance of the Bible as a narrative of our society and God's role in our understanding of society. If you're going to get hung up on that, honestly, that will be something that will prevent a scientist in our office [CI] from ever even considering Christianity as an option. If that is an obstacle to belief, we are doing a disservice to Christ.

(Interview July 29, 2008)

Campbell's thoughtful answer emphasizes his belief that many people are driven away from the church precisely because they perceive the church to be anti-scientific. Moreover, he suggested that the church has made little effort to acknowledge and validate peoples' affinities for living things, and broader ecosystems. That is one of the fundamental shortcomings of contemporary Christian churches, in Campbell's view.

Campbell's perspective recognizes that there are features of the biblical narrative that, if taken literally, are problematic for contemporary Christians intent on reaching across religious and political boundaries. He recognizes the theological import and historical context of such narratives, but still claims to treat the Bible as the literal word of God. His views are consciously formulated with an eye to maintaining relationships with others.

Campbell and many others emphasized that they actively cultivate partnerships *not* because they have similar worldviews, or even because they have found some ethical common ground, but rather precisely because they have been explicit about the differences between them and have offered up their different worldviews and value sets for scrutiny. They have attempted to engage others recognizing the mutual vulnerability and risk such engagement entails.

Here there are clear resonances with the notions of development offered by Martin Palmer and John Smith in Chapter 8, where development actually meets the needs of the people receiving aid. They emphasized that conservation and development agencies ought not to assume that peoples' goals and values—their particular visions of sustainability—are universal. Recall Smith's suggestion that ARC typically spent six months with a particular group before they even spoke about which programs and ideas they wished to fund. Likewise, Campbell noted that he believed spending time with, and understanding the religious beliefs and practices of others was essential to his work: "you have to understand the respective worldview of the religion ... how their unique belief system frames how they understand their relationship, not just with other humans, but with nature itself. Unless you can do that, chances are you're speaking at odds to most people" (interview July 29, 2008). Lovins echoed this when she told me that sustainability is not achieved when consultants come in with answers. Rather, they ought to "come in with questions and ... sit with, for example, elders in the village, to have a conversation about 'what is it that you want?' [Lovins says to them] 'Is there anything in what I have [skill sets and success stories] that can help you achieve what you want?'" (interview August 6, 2008). The common element here is that none of these thought leaders claim to have the best definition of sustainability, or best set of practices applicable to most situations. Deciding what sustainability ought to be in these cases depends upon what people imagine are the central values that they wish to preserve or sustain within their community into the foreseeable future.[28]

While less attuned to the importance of explicitly religious beliefs and practices in sustainability, Lovins also noted that people respond best when you tell stories (such as the Lord of the Rings narratives) that touch upon deep-seated values. For example, she told me that "Americans and western Europeans tend to value the individual choice, the law of small business, academic freedom, ideas. So a lot of what I talk about [when giving presentations in those places] is within that context." But she noted that the idea of natural capitalism, which plays upon these largely American and western European sentiments, when exported, must undergo a facelift: "In Serbia, people hated the idea of natural capitalism, because they think that capitalism is the enemy. They had a visceral reaction against capitalism" (interview August 6, 2008). The relatively simple solution, to re-frame natural capital as human well-being, makes the rather profound point that, as Lovins put it, "if you look at what's driving unsustainability, it is largely, I think, *the absence of these conversations across values structures*" (interview August 6, 2008). In at least a limited way this talk across value structures is occurring within the sustainability milieu, increasing not only the frequency but the complexity of conceptual and practical transmission across these borders.

SUSTAINABILITY FOR A GLOBAL COMMUNITY

Values clash and must be negotiated within and between personal and professional lives, and larger communities of accountability. The importance of acquiring the language necessary to speak across these value systems is especially important in a world characterized by rapidly contracting spatial and temporal scales. If Lovins is correct, and the failure to talk across these value structures is the primary driver of unsustainability, then the partnerships that individuals and groups form are pivotal because they provide linkages that facilitate such communication.

Lovins made her comment above, regarding conversations across value structures, in the context of the tenuous relationship between the United States and Near or Middle Eastern nations. She noted her perception that "the US is now blowing over a billion dollars every day and a half in part trying to secure access to oil, but even more so, for a neo-crusade against Islam." Meanwhile, "theologians in Islam are trying to destroy the Western ideology. That sort of battle needs to become a conversation ... talking with people whose religious underpinning is different than the predominant one in the West. There are sincere value differences, but shooting each other isn't solving it at all" (interview August 6, 2008).

Such conversations often begin through the high-level actors that are the focus of this study, who are highly motivated to promote cooperation, are in the unique position of having access to and understanding of two or more sets of community values, and who can effectively play the role of a translator between individuals or groups. But their longevity and effectiveness depend upon the partnerships they are able to cultivate and sustain. Ben Campbell told me that when he has been responsible for international projects, while he may engage to some extent with the religious leaders in that place, he does not attempt to instruct them about their religious values. "I would never presume to go out and talk about the Qur'an in Indonesia," Campbell told me frankly. He continued,

> if I were going to talk to Muslims, I wouldn't go myself, I'd find a
> partner with whom I share, let's say, a concern about conservation
> ... our partner in Indonesia is IFEES ... Fazlun is one of our main
> contacts. I would actually work for Fazlun ... [and] basically, he
> would know what parts of the Qur'an to appeal to in making the
> case for Muslims.   (Interview July 29, 2008)

Perhaps such relationships require interlocutors, translators, or go-betweens
precisely because risky relationships require trust. The best intentions do
not automatically overcome a lack of trust. Unfortunately, in many cases,
partnerships are difficult to create and sustain precisely because international-level negotiations and policy-making rarely proceed on the basis of
trust. For example, Lovins was attempting to act as a "translator" at a United
Nations sponsored meeting just days before the United Nations Climate
Change Conference in Bali, and was describing to international governmental officials her successes in local redevelopment work in south Asia.[29] She
and others working in India had built what she believed was a solid case for
the proliferation of village-based technologies, and for rethinking energy
production from the bottom up. After two days of presentations, she recalled
that the Pakistani diplomat stated simply "we're just going to burn coal. We
need to develop and you can't tell us not to" (Lovins's recollection, interview
August 6, 2008).

Lovins exclaimed, "Have you not been listening? If what you want is
development, you'll get it better, faster, cheaper through these sorts of technologies [village-scale energy production] than you will through using last
century's technologies." The diplomat's reply: "I don't trust you." He then
proceeded to point in sequence to the others sitting around the room, saying
"I don't trust you, and I don't trust you, and I don't trust you ... [across the
room]." Lovins recalled responding with vehemence:

> Tell a Colorado cowgirl you don't trust her you better be ready
> for a fight! 'Cause frankly, we're either all in this together, and the
> world's going to solve this problem [together], or there's going
> to be winners and losers. And frankly, bud, you're going to be a
> loser! Me? I'm rich, I live in Colorado. You want warming? Bring
> it on, we'll have oceanfront property. In Pakistan the glaciers are
> melting: you're not going to have water. Growth zones are shift-
> ing: you're not going to have agriculture. Your country's going to
> dry up and blow away and frankly I don't give a damn!
>   (Interview August 6, 2008)

Lovins may have been unduly provocative but her point is a good one. She had exposed his distrust by making clear what conflict resolution specialists call the "best alternative to negotiated agreement." If the scientists who describe and predict global climate change are acknowledged as authoritative then their claim that developing countries such as Pakistan and others whose economies are shifting rapidly will bear the brunt of change must be given credence also. Lovins and those like her who live relatively insulated from the dangers of climate change clearly have different motivations for engaging in such international discourse. In a very real sense Lovins's near-term survival does not depend as much on these negotiations as do the citizens in nation states to whom translators such as Lovins are trying to market strategies and technologies for sustainability.

Campbell also noted that appreciating pluralism does not necessarily mean that he does not challenge different people to think critically about their faith and its relationship to conservation. Campbell was involved in a project in Bali, for example, focused on sea turtle conservation. Sea turtles have long been harvested by the local population for religious ceremonies. At the time, however, the turtles had been over-harvested and were on the verge of extinction. Campbell recalled that one of his colleagues gathered thirty-seven Hindu theologians and asked them to go back to their sacred writings and look at whether "bringing a species to the brink of extinction [was] a value held by Hinduism" (interview July 29, 2008). The theologians reviewed their own writings, and parallel to Khalid's recollection of how religious leaders helped halt the destruction of Zanzibar's reef structures, these Hindus adapted their ceremonies to crises within their habitat. Campbell told me,

> They were forced to go back and look at their own texts ... their own belief system ... they [their religious myths] *are stories that form peoples' value systems, and how they view their relationships with the world.* Now there's almost no trafficking of sea turtles, there's almost no sea turtles in ceremonies that are sacrificed. Instead they've developed a bit of a ceremony where they find sea turtles on the beach, they turn them around and help them get back out to sea. And there's another ceremony blessing the earth. That was done exclusively by them, we didn't ask them to hold these ceremonies ... [it represents] *a re-discovery of their own deep values.* (Interview July 29, 2008, italics mine)

The sea turtles might have been driven to extinction without the intervention of this external NGO. But these new interpretations of the same religious texts also did not come without prompting. NGOs clearly have a pivotal role in the emerging quest for sustainability, as institutional actors that translate the concerns of different constituencies in respectful ways (at least ideally). In a way, one of the tasks of NGOs in cases like the ones above is to generate something like what Berkes, Folke, and Colding called for when they suggested that sustainability requires the development of contemporary versions of "taboos" and "social sanctions" (Berkes *et al.*1998: 430). These nongovernmental bodies are providing the impetus for the creation of internal sanctions and the pursuit of behaviors and perceptual frameworks that are beneficial to the persistence of people in their habitats.

MARKETING THE MYTH OF SUSTAINABILITY: PROSPERITY, SECURITY, AND MEANING

If, as Korten and Lovins have argued, generating widespread acceptance of the quest for sustainability depends on linking it to human desires for prosperity, security, and meaning, then references to these desires should repeatedly bubble up when people advocate sustainability. The religious dimensions of sustainability are perhaps less apparent when discussing the economic arguments for sustainability (which are central to the ideas of prosperity and security), although talk of values is common. There are several organizations and groups that begin sustainability dialogue with these practical economic arguments. In what follows I will explore how certain narratives related to economic arguments, environmental justice, and indigenous cultures are deployed by secular sustainability-oriented groups to address the basic needs for prosperity, security, and meaning.

Economic arguments for sustainability

It may now be easier to make a convincing case for sustainability within the business sector than anywhere else. If so this is ironic because many of those in environmental movements, one of the significant tributaries to sustainability, often pin the blame for environmental degradation on capitalist mentalities generally and corporate entities in particular. But the popular persuasive power of the term sustainability has recently prompted even businesses that have little or no understanding of what the word means to adopt sustainability plans and clauses in their mission statements. Lovins recalled several examples of businesses that are "going green" in order to "make more green." She cited a major whiskey distillery controlling 40 per cent of the global spirits market and Wal-Mart as two examples of organizations where positive change driven by the integration of a values-based perspective is occurring. Marketing sustainability as economic good sense does not typically require deep discussion of stakeholder values. In some sense, it is the hook that brings people to the negotiating table with others, so that deeper work toward long-term relationships can occur. As Lovins put it, "In what we do, we don't lead with values ... until someone we're working with raises that, I won't" (interview August 6, 2008).[30] For Lovins and others, making the economic case for sustainability can be a gateway for understanding other dimensions of sustainability, including the importance of social equity and justice, the apprehension of interconnectedness and the adoption of practices that reflect it. This is one key ingredient—visions of prosperity—in fulfilling the basic desires of all citizens.

Environmental justice and sustainability

"Markets were never intended to take care of grandchildren," Lovins told me. Indeed, as Lovins and her collaborator Bob Willard argued, the current form of capitalism is unsustainable, and by most projections future generations will have a less stable and secure world.[31] Markets can certainly be effective in facilitating technology transfer from the industrialized to the developing world, disseminating public health education, monitoring and fulfilling consumer demand, and reducing the material throughputs required to sustain the economy. Markets cannot (and should not be expected to) act as formulators of values, as exemplars of future ideal social states, or moral frameworks.

The symptoms of the failure of our current economic system cited by sustainability advocates such as Willard and Lovins are most evident in encounters with ecological limits (i.e. water scarcity, the collapse of global fisheries, the increase in greenhouse gas emissions, the disappearance of coral reefs, the fragmentation and simplification of terrestrial habitats), and in recognition that the consequences of encountering limits tend to affect the poorest members of the global community first and most. The inability of many of the world's individuals to access and utilize global markets to facilitate their movement out of harm's way illustrates the market's limitations when it comes to solving social issues.

"In the long run," Lovins commented, "Malthus was right. It's just a question of how much human misery we want in the interim" (roundtable discussion, November 2007). It was this realization that the world was changing, that human societies were exceeding their carrying capacities, and that the

177

poor were bearing the brunt of that change that contributed to the emergence of environmental justice movements related to sustainability. Ben Campbell told me that he came to conservation and development work largely because of a strong interest in protecting human rights. It was his concern for human rights that led him to understand environmental issues as centrally related to social justice. "It's kinda funny," he told me, "Christianity is layered over a deeper value system for the environment. I've found ... that they're not at odds" (interview July 29, 2008).[32]

CI attends to the justice component of development, and its work occurs primarily in the developing world. Environmental justice, however, does not only concern marginalized peoples on other continents. NWEI's climate change module includes a selection from Van Jones's contribution to *Orion* magazine detailing some of the justice issues brought to the surface in the wake of hurricane Katrina.[33] Jones suggests that "in the new century, the only way to survive will be to help each other more—and judge each other less" (NWEI 2007a: 10). The editors of *Orion* suggested that those who lived in the lower ninth ward of New Orleans, the hardest hit by the storm, were the first North American refugees of climate change, and that "we're all neighbors of New Orleans now" (reprinted in NWEI 2007a: 9). Jones suggested that the best metaphor for how humans ought to journey into the uncertain future may well come from the biblical story of Noah, who in the midst of an increasingly chaotic world, had a simple aim: "their [Noah and his family's] aim was ... to survive together, while protecting as many family members and fellow species as they could" (NWEI 2007: 10).[34]

Certainly the federal response to natural disasters is a matter of national security, for miscalculated or feebly executed response plans erode confidence in government, and create vulnerabilities in national infrastructure. Environmental justice, as one dimension of sustainability, is often tied to religious imagery or commitments, and crucially related to fulfilling the needs tied to security and meaning.

Sustainability as a sacred duty

In *Blessed Unrest* (2007a) Paul Hawken posed a question to the reader:

> It has been said that we cannot save our planet unless human kind undergoes a widespread spiritual and religious awakening. In other words, fixes won't fix unless we fix our souls as well. So let's ask ourselves this question: Would we recognize a worldwide spiritual awakening if we saw one? Or let me put the question

another way: What if there is already in place a large-scale spiritual awakening and we are simply not recognizing it?

He goes on to discuss the "Axial Age," an era when many of the "world religions" were born in a geographically compact region in a short span of time (see for example Armstrong 2007).[35] Hawken suggests that there is a sort of Axial Age currently emerging, whose first birth pains are the formation of a massive, fluid, and loosely interconnected set of movements that Hawken refers to collectively as "the largest movement in the world."[36] Hawken argued that "at the core of all organizations [involved in the movement] are two principles, albeit unstated: first is the Golden Rule; second is the sacredness of all life, whether it be a creature, child, or culture" (Hawken 2007a: 186).

Such pronouncements clearly draw on religious imagery. It is important to note, though, that Armstrong's project has been critiqued by Russell McCutcheon, who stated that "comparative religion practiced in this manner is more akin to a theology of religious pluralism than the academic study of religion" (McCutcheon 1997: 105; see also 123). Hawken's project might be critiqued on similar grounds, for his assumption that there exists some essential feature (or set of features) that is definitive of sustainability illustrates that he is promoting the set of values that he would like to see sustained over the long term. If Armstrong (according to McCutcheon, like Mircea Eliade and Rudolph Otto before her) is advancing a theology of religious pluralism, then Hawken might be said to be advancing a theology of sustainability that has a particular set of goals related to defending particular values. As geographer James Proctor and religion scholar Evan Berry and their collaborators have illustrated, environmental behaviors are more strongly correlated with political affiliations than with religious commitments (Proctor & Berry 2005). The use of religious imagery and metaphor then is certainly religious, but it is also, particularly in cases related to environmental issues, more than likely also political.

During participant-observation in one of NWEI's discussion circles, the facilitator for our group, a long time veteran of the discussion group model, began the first meeting with the declaration that "What unites us is our inner sense of disquiet, and a love for the earth" (spring 2005). The idea that life is sacred is woven into many of the NWEI modules, particularly the *Exploring Deep Ecology* book. One of Paul Hawken's articles, amended for the *Choices for Sustainable Living* volume, concludes by stating that "Inspiration ... resides in humanity's willingness to restore, redress, reform, recover, reimagine, and reconsider. Healing the wounds of the Earth and its people does not require saintliness or a political party. It is not a liberal or conservative activity. It is a sacred act" (NWEI 2007b: 102).[37]

Nancy Johnston, head of Operations and Logistics for NatCap Solutions, added the reminder that "The third principle of natural capitalism is actually 'being restorative,' and looking at what it takes to manage everything so that it can be prosperous in the future. And that's [also about] waking up in the morning and feeling good about yourself—not having more money in the bank" (interview August 6, 2008). She meant that the idea of sustainability drove home for her the point that *prosperity* (in the financial sense of the word) was not necessary to achieving a *meaningful* life. But her cultivation of what she believed to be a meaningful life also provided her with new resources for re-imagining what it meant to be prosperous, and for her, this was a sacred realization. Expressing her understanding of the importance of this study of the religious dimensions of sustainability advocacy, she said:

> I understand that religion is a part of ... this. In some ways ...
> having a sustainable lifestyle can become a sort of religion. To
> me, religion is a lifestyle. Sustainability is a lifestyle. There's a lot
> of crossover there, in terms of what it is you value most. If what
> it is I value most is eating peas out of my garden, and that means
> I work all day on Sunday to harvest peas, then isn't that religion?
> (Interview August 6, 2008)

These examples only briefly illustrate that even among leaders from these secular NGOs, religious imagery, language, and ideation is prevalent. Many refer to "the Great Turning" (as Macy called it), or a paradigm shift that leads humans to more humbly and respectfully engage with the non-human world, to act more mindfully, in short, to consider all actions sacred ones. Extending the scope of analysis to the broader secular manifestations of sustainability would probably yield similar results, although this is certainly an area that would be fruitful for further study.

The idea that everyday, mundane life can be filled with spiritual acts is an important ingredient in many facets of sustainability movements. Likewise, the notion that doing even small things to help reduce individual ecological footprints has motivated large cross sections of the population. Social scientific studies have demonstrated that in the United States environmental concern and behavior are strongly correlated with nature religion, if nature religion is defined as agreement with the idea that nature is authoritative or serves as the sacred locus (Proctor & Berry 2005; Taylor 2010; see Lynch 2007 for more on these trends outside the US). Even among individuals who would not consider nature itself sacred, many still consider their everyday consumption choices to be related to their spiritual well-being. For example the term LOHAS (lifestyles of health and sustainability) has emerged to refer to a powerful purchasing sector in the American economy. This primarily middle and upper middle class demographic is now the primary target audience of dozens of magazines, housing and automobile innovations, and clothing and food options. For these segments of the population, such media and material culture is often focused on spiritual practices such as yoga, meditation, organic or vegetarian food choices, natural fiber clothing, and alternative fuel and lifestyle choices.

These acts of voluntary simplicity, then, parallel the "sacred acts" of resistance and protest to consumer cultures and prevailing socio-political arrangements that Hawken suggests are the heart of sustainability movements. This analysis supports earlier studies which illustrate that focal themes, motivational metaphors, and imagery may cross political and economic boundaries, and in many cases reinforce each other (Gerlach 1971; Campbell 1972; Taylor 2010). Moreover, the idea that humans have a sacred duty or responsibility to act cooperatively contributes to two of Lovins' primary needs—the importance of meaning (by finding the sacred in the mundane) and prosperity (often by providing new visions of "the good life"). For instance, many of the NWEI books present readings, poems, or perspectives from American Indians which emphasize that attentiveness to every act cultivates a sort of spiritual awareness that is important for the sustainability transition. The climate change module, for example, includes a poem attributed to the Hopi Elders: "Gather yourselves. Banish the word struggle from your attitude and vocabulary. / All that we do now must be done in a sacred manner and in celebration. / We are the ones we have been waiting for" (NWEI 2007a: 40).[38]

Traditional ecological knowledge and sustainability

It is not uncommon for scholars to devise a model of knowledge-seeking and acquisition that imagines two modes of science: an abstract or Western tradition, and indigenous or traditional knowledge. The Western tradition is described by the modern scientific method, while indigenous traditions are often defined by the development of place-based practices. As noted in Chapter 6, J. Baird Callicott (1994), following analyses of a variety of environmental ethics "from the Mediterranean to the Australian Outback," proposed a "postmodern ecological paradigm" that would unite these varied traditional epistemologies and perceptions with Western sciences such as the "new physics" and "new ecology." Callicott's idea is that, shorn of their metaphysical baggage, many of the religious beliefs and practices he analyzed might work together toward sustainability. Perhaps ironically, it is science that has finally provided the conceptual framework through which industrialized nations can include indigenous cultures in the search for a just and sustainable social order.

Expressing some resonance with Callicott's claims, the ecologist Fikret Berkes has suggested that purely Western notions such as wilderness could not be the basis of a cross-cultural environmental ethic. Instead, he argued that "more promising is the notion of *sustainability*," quoting an important document co-authored by the International Union for the Conservation of Nature (IUCN), the United Nations Environment Programme (UNEP) and the World Wildlife Fund (WWF) called *Caring for the Earth* (1991). This remarkable document explicitly stated that its aim was to "secure a widespread and deeply held commitment to a new ethic, the ethic for sustainable living" (IUCN *et al.* 1991: 3), which included empowering people to take care of their own habitats and creating "change in personal attitudes and practices" (IUCN *et al.* 1991 : 11). Further, *Caring for the Earth* explicitly endorsed the idea that the non-human world has intrinsic value: "Every life form warrants respect independently of its worth to people" (IUCN *et al.* 1991: 14). The document called for further action to cultivate relationships with religious groups and leaders, encouraged the emphasis within these religious traditions on environmentally and socially responsible teachings and behaviors (15), and connected these aims with greater attentiveness to the needs of the world's indigenous peoples (61). This schematic for a global ethics is, according to Berkes, the best chance for generating a scientific research program that might lead to sustainable communities.

According to Berkes and several cultural anthropologists, indigenous and traditional peoples are of utmost importance in creating sustainable relationships with the natural world. For, as Berkes argued, traditional ecological knowledge (TEK) can provide a bridge between Western science and traditional lifeways. Berkes argued that certain ideas, such as "Leopold's land ethics, deep ecology, Gaia, topophilia/love of land, sense of place, bioregionalism, and biophilia/love of living beings, have explored the personal meaning and sacred dimensions of ecology that have been missing in scientific ecology" (Berkes 1999: 183). They suggest that ecological management based on traditional ecological knowledge is highly adaptable, and as such, tends to be more sustainable than Western management regimes, which are rigid and miss important features of ecosystems.[39]

Adaptive management is one place where some scholars claim there can be a mutually beneficial engagement of Western and traditional ecological knowledge (Berkes *et al.* 1998; Berkes 1999). For scholars such as Berkes, Folke, and Colding the *resilience* of ecological and social systems is the key to sustainability in a dynamic and highly interactive world. The preservation of cultural diversity, then, is important because it provides a greater number of examples of how human cultures have adapted to social-ecological dynamics over time, and thus a greater cache of strategies from which to draw when imagining how to persist within habitats (Berkes *et al.*1998: 21–2). Indeed, Berkes, Folke, and Colding suggest that contemporary versions of "rituals, taboos, and social and religious sanctions" may be necessary for the industrial world if sustainability is to become a realistic possibility (430).

Thus, in at least three ways indigenous and traditional cultures are important contributors to the religious dimensions of sustainability. First, the emergence of international indigenous resistance to globalization and capital accumulation (see the discussion in Chapter 6), and the resurgence of a North American Indian resistance movement beginning in the late 1960s (with the occupation of Alcatraz and the second stand-off with federal agents at Wounded Knee)[40] were important ingredients in the counter-hegemonic dimension of sustainability.[41] Second, indigenous cultures and the anthropologists who advocate for them have become instrumental in the development of the social dimension of sustainability within the mainstream, international political scene. United Nations declarations and World Bank programs now not only include, but often focus on empowering local communities rather than imposing prefabricated programs onto communities with specific needs and circumstances. Third, indigenous and traditional cultures have been spiritually instructive for many within the broad range of sustainability movements. It is often said that indigenous cultures have a common perception that all of life, even mundane activity, is in some sense sacred (Posey 1999: 4, 450; 2004: 64, 196–7). Although such romanticized perceptions are overly broad (Krech 1999), they are frequently championed by sustainability advocates. For example, Paul Hawken put it this way: "The quiet hub of the new movement—its heart and soul—is indigenous culture" (Hawken 2007a: 22).[42] But it is also true that indigenous individuals sometimes use (and abuse) terms such as sustainability just as those in the industrialized world might, and they do so intentionally with their own aims in mind. Typically, moreover, such aims have to do more with material security and gain than with some imagined harmonious relationship with habitats.

But such ideas, idealized or not, are impacting the sustainability milieu in significant ways, from grassroots advocacy to mainstream political bodies. While the use of the term sustainable to describe indigenous or traditional activities might resonate with the political engines that promote and fund sustainable development projects, these funding agencies and sometimes the scholars that support them tend to "view indigenous aims through Western lenses and rely on a few bicultural individuals as leaders" (Conklin & Graham 1995: 704; quoted in Wright 2009: 204). Even so, at least in theory, the preservation of traditional cultures contributes to the resilience (and thus security) of the global community, and through increasing trust and interaction across these plural values structures and epistemologies, to the fulfillment of the search for meaning (Korten and Lovins's third important feature of sustainability).

IS THE SECULAR SUSTAINABILITY MOVEMENT REALLY RELIGIOUS?

David Korten and Hunter Lovins may be correct: sustainability may ultimately be about the ability to provide for prosperity, security, and meaning over the long term. If that is the case, however, then it should be clear that the religious dimensions of sustainability are integrally involved in producing feelings of security, fulfilling the search for meaning, and answering the question of what it means to be prosperous. The examples above are drawn from secular non-governmental organizations, yet they make use of and contribute to the religious dimensions of sustainability. They pose the question: are secular sustainability movements religious?

There are some themes that are common throughout sustainability movements that are not explicitly religious but are deeply affective and tug on core values because they raise questions about the future: what sort of world do people want to grow old in, and more importantly, what sort of world would they leave for future generations? In most cultures, these questions are answered by reference to spiritual norms or religious stories. When secular sustainability organizations ask such questions, oftentimes they are not meant to be explicitly religious. But when they ask these hard questions, they help to manufacture a highly affective mode of transmitting the metanarrative of sustainability, and this highly affective mode of communication is inevitably tied to religion somewhere within the web of significations provided as answers.

The NWEI readers represent one grassroots example of this mode of transmission, asking deep questions about the purpose of human life, and questions about what it means to pursue "the good life" over the long term. The global climate-change module includes a partial transcript of a speech given at the 1992 Earth Summit by twelve-year-old Severn Suzuki (daughter of well-known sustainability advocate and author David Suzuki). Her theme resonates with Donella Meadows' earlier question about what her friend ought to tell her three-year-old about the disappearance of polar bears. The young Suzuki told the delegation "I have dreamed of seeing the great herds of wild animals, jungles and rainforests full of birds and butterflies, but now I wonder if they will even exist for my children to see" (NWEI 2007a: 54). She continued, "Parents should be able to comfort their children by saying

'Everything's going to be all right,' ... 'We're doing the best we can' ... But I don't think you can say that to us anymore ... My dad always says, 'You are what you do, not what you say.'"

"Well," concluded the young Suzuki, "what you do makes me cry at night" (NWEI 2007: 54).[43]

The United Nations represents the most obvious example of a mainstream international political body that asks similar questions, and drawing on biophilic and cosmophilic themes, deploys spiritual language and imagery to promote the global ethic they believe is required to achieve global sustainability. As an offshoot of UNEP, the Interfaith Partnership for the Environment (IPE) was founded in 1986, dedicated to "working to bring together the forces of religion and ecology."[44] In the late 1980s they began promoting an "Environmental Sabbath" day each year. In 1990, one poem from the Environmental Sabbath, published by the UN, illustrates well how secular organizations spiritualize sustainability advocacy. In an early section titled "Prayer of Awareness," the poem stated,

> Today we know of the energy that moves all things: the oneness of existence, the diversity and uniqueness of every moment of creation, every shape and form, the attraction, the allurement, the fascination that all things have for one another
> Humbled by our knowledge, chastened by surprising revelations, with awe and reverence we come before the mystery of life.[45]

Note the idea that all things have a "fascination" for one another (a biophilia), the use of the term "creation" which is in many respects a religiously inspired reference to the cosmos, and the invocation of "the mystery of life" before which humans are called to be humbled.

The "Prayer of Sorrow," later in the poem, employs a call and response pattern, with respondents repeating between stanzas, "We have forgotten who we are." This is a profound statement about the mistakes in moral anthropology that guided the modern world. The question of "who we are" is a meta-question that calls attention to the range of future options particular groups hope to leave for later generations, and how they endeavor to live well and meaningfully in the present. The "Prayer of Gratitude" which followed provided a reminder of "who we are," stating "We live in all things/All things live in us." Along with the closing stanza, "We are full of the grace of creation ... /we rejoice in all life," these lines state with clarity the themes of deep interconnectivity that have been noted within sustainability subcultures throughout this work. These narratives of relationality and cosmic affinity are one of the foundations for sustainability movements, and the strategic use of such themes within secular sustainability-oriented groups is no less spiritual than their invocation by religious groups.

To answer the question posed above—are secular sustainability movements religious?—the answer is a qualified "yes." While they are not *all about religion* they are certainly utilizing religious metaphor and imagery, and calling for a reassessment of the meta-objectives of particular cultural groups. They are not examples of what Saler might call "prototypical" religions. They are, however, both analogically related to religious movements (that is, they *resemble* more prototypical religions), and genealogically related to religious beliefs and practices (which is to say that that religious groups and movements have contributed to the present shape of secular sustainability movements).[46] They have an amazing variety of features that are themselves at least quasi-religious, implicitly religious, or related to explicitly religious values, and when deployed in public venues they are doing political and religious work. The definition of religion provided in Chapter 2, then, is central to the task of discerning the prevalence of the religious dimensions of secular sustainability organizations and groups.

To the extent that these secular sustainability-oriented groups and persons pepper their discourse with subtly or occasionally overtly religious elements, they open up the possibility of analyzing "a religious dimension in human life" without limiting the study to those features of culture that "we unhesitatingly label religion" (Saler 1993: xv). As Saler noted, while these more subtle uses of religious language, metaphor and imagery do not always fall neatly into the categories approved by scholars of religion, "segments of the general public and persons pursuing special agendas often extend the use and inclusiveness of the term [religion] beyond conventional dictionary acceptations and supporting conceptualizations [and] ... *when they do so, they are usually understood by others in the contemporary United States*" (Saler 1993: 23; italics in original, and I would add that they are generally understood, now, across the globe). Attentiveness to the religious dimensions of sustainability discourse helps to illustrate the social and political pervasiveness of religion in culture, and hopefully helps to highlight the need for sensitivity when engaging the value preferences and norms of individuals or groups from other cultures.

CONNECTING THE DOTS BETWEEN EXPERTS IN THE NETWORK: MAPPING THE "ECOLOGICAL" SYSTEM

All of the informants cited in this chapter are utilizing religious discourse at least in the broad sense that I use the term here. Daniella Dennenberg of

NWEI told me that she was spiritual, although not religious. Interestingly, Deb McNamara (also from NWEI) noted the early Latin roots of the word religion, meaning "to tie" or "to bind," and suggested that she was certainly "bound to a spiritual path." McNamara grew up a midwestern Lutheran (and said that in some sense that is still her core identity), gained a greater understanding of social equity in the Peace Corps, attended a Buddhist university, and is now a Haatha Yoga teacher and practitioner whose "connection to the earth is part of my spiritual practice as well" (interview September 17, 2008). Both claimed that they considered their spiritual lives to be important motivators for their career choices. Nancy Johnston of NatCap noted that sustainability, as a lifestyle choice that involved commitment to deep seated values, was itself a sort of religious practice.

While Lovins is less apt to talk in explicitly spiritual terms, she did with some frequency allude to the importance of spiritual work to all the other "species" of sustainability advocacy. In addition, as she noted in a public lecture, her mentors (David Brower and Donella Meadows, for example) participated in what she called the "inner" work of sustainability, namely "changing hearts and minds." Lovins told me that everybody she works with impacts how she approaches sustainability. Her adaptable approach is one of the hallmarks of successful sustainability advocates. "Sally [Bingham], for example," Lovins reported, "has helped me to understand the importance of communities of faith. And speaking to people ... whatever position they're in, whether they're a CEO or government official or whatever ... they probably have a faith, a values structure in there as well, and that it's important to speak to that as well" (interview August 6, 2008).

Reflecting on the web of relationships between leader-advocates who participate in religious, interfaith, and explicitly secular sustainability-oriented groups, it is clear that there are direct and indirect connections between all of them, providing several relatively smooth avenues for the transmission of ideas, strategies, and resources. Campbell noted that his work was similar to Martin Palmer's in many ways, and that he depended on working with Palmer in large part because of the existing network that ARC had cultivated. Campbell told me that "Martin has been instrumental in helping me to think through this from an interfaith perspective" (interview July 29, 2008). Campbell is an evangelical Christian who maintains close professional ties with Joel Hunter, Richard Cizik, Cal DeWitt, and other evangelicals. He has also produced a handbook on religions and conservation with Martin Palmer and ARC, and worked with Khalid and IFEES and other faith-based organizations to achieve CI's conservation goals. In addition, Campbell works closely with green evangelicals in the US and worldwide, while Sally Bingham remains personally close to at least Joel Hunter and

Richard Cizik. Bingham's Interfaith Power and Light was one of the honorees of ARC's Sacred Gifts program, and Bingham also maintains a close personal and professional relationship with Lovins. While the operatives at NWEI are not necessarily directly connected to this particular expert network through individuals, certainly they draw on common bodies of literature (such as those exposed in Chapters 5 and 6), and ideas championed by individuals within this network, and work toward similar goals. Recalling this complex web of relations, it should be clear that all of the informants in this study are often directly, and all are at least indirectly related through the connections of these expert networks. Each of these experts and their marketing of sustainability contribute to the idea that sustainability is not all about generating technical fixes or better management regimes. Even for those within the secular sustainability movement, the long-term persistence of humans within their habitats is, as Nobel Prize winner Al Gore put it in his award-winning documentary *An Inconvenient Truth*, "a moral, ethical and spiritual challenge" (quoted in NWEI 2007a: 53).

CHAPTER TEN
MANUFACTURING OR CULTIVATING COMMON GROUND?

This project was initiated because there was an obvious need for (a) an examination of definitions of sustainability, (b) a more robust accounting of the history of sustainability-oriented social movements and their religious dimensions, and (c) descriptions of the ways that movement leaders endeavored to improve effective communication across and between communities with different value structures, practices, and world models. It became clear that some movement leaders were attempting to re-civilize the public sphere, making it safe for the presentation and democratic assessment of community values. After reviewing the emergence of sustainability and the historical prevalence of its religious dimensions, the goal has been to map the spread of some normative and religious features of sustainability within an expert network comprised of leaders from religious, interfaith, and secular non-governmental organizations. There was significant agreement among informants about some key religious features of sustainability movements, the strategies utilized to advertise them, as well as overlap on some of the motivating factors that prompted these thought leaders to engage in sustainability advocacy.

The informants discussed here are engaged in an economy of ideas, metaphors, and imagery, and in many cases religious ideation and language is the currency for exchange. A rough summary of the data will clarify the spiritual games played by these actor networks, and how the economies of ideas and significations they perpetuate support sustainability movements. While the prevalence of the religious dimensions of sustainability are clear in the above history and the examination of this small but well-connected network of actors, another hypothesis that awaits further investigation is whether these religious dimensions will become increasingly important within broader movements related to sustainability. At this point, however, more needs to be said regarding how to analyze religious discourse within a social movement.

THE RELIGION VARIABLE IN SUSTAINABILITY-ORIENTED SOCIAL MOVEMENTS

The term sustainability and its cognate sustainable development are not etymologically derived from religious terminology, but in their deployment they do carry significant spiritual overtones. It is precisely this fact that makes the definitions of religion employed by some religion and nature scholars and anthropologists helpful for exploring the religious dimensions of sustainability advocacy and discourse. I chose to exercise definitions relying on *family resemblances*, fuzzy sets of attributes that are loosely related, although they do not share an essential substance or feature. As Benson Saler put it, "To the extent ... that we study elements that we regard as especially typical of religion in less typical settings, we attend to a *religious dimension* in human life that reaches out beyond religion" (Saler 2004: 230). Religious studies scholars should be interested in attending to this religious dimension wherever they find it, even (and perhaps especially) if it occurs outside the boundaries of what is considered typically religious.

Social movements such as sustainability can be productively analyzed with methodological lenses that perceive the spiritual or metaphysical assumptions that underlie public expressions of values and much political decision making. If sustainability is a strategy of cultural adaptation to the dynamic interplay between ecological and social systems that is often tied to religious or spiritual narratives that describe how to fulfill what is probably an innate human desire to live "meaningfully," then sustainability is necessarily normative, and inextricably tied to core values, beliefs, and practices.

The primary data for the study included historical analysis, targeted interviews with more than two dozen high-level actors from various sustainability-related movements, as well as more informal interviews with dozens of other sustainability advocates by telephone, email, or in conference and event settings. Of those who participated in the interviews, nearly all attributed their engagement in sustainability-related work either to concern for human rights and equity, or profound experiences with or in nature. In the end, 62 per cent of respondents cited experiences in nature as their primary motivation for their work, while 37 per cent cited their awareness of social justice issues. Even higher proportions of informants either communicated primarily through stories or narratives, or explicitly addressed the importance of

190

narratives for disseminating new ethical ideals and behaviors (71 per cent), while 88 per cent endorsed the tactical use of religious or spiritual language to form strategic partnerships, and leverage policy decisions.

One of the most interesting effects that emerged from the data was the strong connectivity of the network of actors despite the political, ideological, and geographical boundaries separating them. In other words, although the informants were chosen from different NGOs which operate at different scales they demonstrated direct and indirect influences on each other across these boundaries, lending at least some additional support to the idea that metaphors and motivational tropes are exchanged rather freely across sub-populations.

As suggested in Chapter 3 (in an expansion of Vasquez's version of network theory), some of the most common attributes of specific religious groups are more widespread because their actualization in behaviors "runs downhill" like a stream in a watershed, following the constraints of both biological, cultural, political, and economic "channels." Streams follow the geological features of the landscape just as understandings of sustainability and religion are dependent upon inferences about or reactions to the particular features of the national or international geopolitical powerscape. Fundamentalisms, for instance, might be more prone to develop in areas where natural resources are scarce, opportunity structures for young adults are retarded by wars or natural disasters, and politics do not represent the will of many peripheral members of a nation state or society. Conservative theologies which favor a return to traditional values, which resist economic and cultural globalization, and that reject contemporary science thrive in such a climate. If an organic landscape model imagines hydraulic flows as embedded in a broader ecological system, it is possible to investigate how people actively engage in social "engineering," building bridges to other cultural streams, often over or around the particular features of the powerscape. This is a grounded, materialist methodology that could be approached at multiple (or one of any number of) scales. Such a model does not dismiss the centrality of embodied experience but rather incorporates it as a fundamental assumption.

Experience—at once sensory, psychological, emotional, and interpretive—is one of the primary shapers of this religious landscape. Debates over values (where is the locus of value? should value be human-centered or not? monist or pluralist? preservative or restorative?) occupied most environmental ethics conversations for two decades. Other works, however, have asked what role particular behaviors might have on the formulation of values. While certain practices may cultivate awareness of new environmental issues or particular ecological relationships, they do so because they engage particular cognitive mechanisms that attach emotion, and thus moral meaning to particular experiences. Peak experiences, those that activate affective systems, are formative for perceptions, values, expectations, and especially for our decision-making. This is one illustration of why group selection models, which postulate an epigenetic (super-cultural) entity upon which natural selection acts, are problematic—cultural learning does not occur through simple, mechanical imitation. Rather, cultural transmission always involves inference, a mode of learning that is entangled with the emotional experiences of particular people in specific places. Affective stories related to protected values, then, are ecological patterns of psychological things (Sperber 1985).

Although clearly important, the experiential variable has been under-scrutinized in environmental ethics conversations. Greater attention to the ways in which experience shapes the formation of values can help to provide more data about how people interpret impactful episodic memories and translate them into narratives and practices that have moral import. The experiential variable is particularly important when analyzing values related to nature.

Among those interviewed for this research, profound experiences with or in nature were the most frequently cited catalysts for sustainability advocacy. The importance of simply "getting outside" highlights a general agreement among sustainability advocates with Richard Louv's (2005) well-known argument that experience *with* and *in* nature is necessary for a healthy, well-adjusted, and environmentally responsible culture. Unfortunately, in most of the industrialized world experiences with or in nature are on the decline. The importance of nature experiences was perhaps first advanced by the human ecologist Paul Shepard, who suggested that the human genome was formed in the Pleistocene, and that human capacity and need for relationships was still dependent on cognitive capacities that emerged when ancient hominids were both predator and prey (Shepard 1998, 1982; see also Lease 2005). More recent empirical evidence has supported the notion that reduced contact with nature leads to an impoverished capacity to recognize natural forms. This has been correlated with reduced rates of environmentally friendly behaviors (Atran & Medin 2008).

As cognitive scientists of religion might predict, there are important consonances between the religious dimensions of sustainability narratives offered by different constituencies. Certain concepts, such as the idea that there exists a deep biological or cosmological interconnectedness, and some tactics, such as the ethic of personal risk, occur in a variety of settings. These common concepts may provide a good mechanism for encouraging people to re-engage with their local habitats, recreationally or otherwise.

Recall Bingham's epiphany (from Chapter 8) that as she listened to the heartbeat of the earth, she perceived that it was alive. Bingham emphasized that her ability to "listen" to the earth had helped her to love it—and after all, "you protect what you love." Deb McNamara of NWEI told me that "you have to learn how to listen [to nature] ... if you don't have that relationship with the natural world, I don't know how I can expect someone to make choices that have the natural world in mind if they've never established that connection" (interview September 17, 2008). Similarly, Cal DeWitt recalled countless childhood hours spent with snakes, lizards, and other animals, Raymond Randall referred to the Colorado mountains where he grew up, and others cited summer or weekend camping trips as formative for their moral sensibilities. Tri Robinson's conversion moment occurred on the side of a mountain, where he perceived that God spoke to him.

Other informants suggested that empathetic engagement with other people or communities was the most important ingredient for their moral imaginations. Getting outside one's own perspective, attempting to comprehend (not endorse) the deep values and core beliefs of others means that such engagement is, as John Smith put it, "on the basis of trust, and let's *explore* what you're about, not *telling* you what you're about. And that's the key ... to faith, and recognizing how faith works" (interview May 29, 2008). Sustainability, much like faith, requires some measure of trust and vulnerability on the part of individual players, what I have referred to as an ethic of personal risk, a particular style of empathetic negotiation.

For instance, Joel Hunter suggested that it was conversations with the biologist E. O. Wilson and a fellow evangelical Richard Cizik that ultimately converted him into a leader in the creation care movement. Hunter Lovins's heated discussion with the Pakistani representative at a United Nations event (in Chapter 9) illustrated that lack of trust (which in many cases is deserved) sullies the non-hierarchical relationships that can lay the groundwork for easy technology transfer, standard of living increases, and shared fulfillment across the significant political and economic boundaries that determine access to resources.

Whether getting out of doors or getting out of one's own "skin," such encounters with nature or with the core values of others are important for priming individuals to receive messages related to sustainability. All of the informants cited either the importance of profound experiences in nature, or a deep concern for the well-being of others (whether other humans, other species, or the entire world or cosmos) as generative of a concern for long-term species survivability, and as a personal motivator for their professional lives. Ideas about deep interconnection are somewhat counter-intuitive in that they suppose an integral relationship between what we perceive to be our own discrete bodies, and human or non-human others. Likewise, ideas related to an ethic of personal risk, which requires vulnerability to the core values of others, may be imagined as ultimately dangerous to individual fitness. But such ideas and strategies are highly affective, and are thus easily recalled, and readily transmitted across different subcultures.

The important variable of experience, and the spread of sustainability-related ideas between many of these agents who have been primed to receive them, can be imagined as consonant with the above-mentioned landscape model. This can not only provide a solid theoretical grounding for further empirical research, but it may also identify how adaptation at the cultural level works. If, for example, an ethic of personal risk provides an adaptive advantage by promoting negotiation instead of warfare, dialogue rather than finger-pointing, then it may prove to be adaptive over the long run. That does not mean that *religion* is adaptive, but rather that certain human behaviors, those that minimize suffering and conflict, are adaptive, and that religions could be parasitical on them. But religion may also genuinely bolster the usefulness of such adaptive traits by facilitating experiences that act as excellent priming mechanisms which can encourage the acceptance of such ideas.

What follows highlights some more of the common elements between the religious, interfaith, and secular groups analyzed above. In addition, the discussion will interrogate the usefulness of sustainability for the respondents, and speculate about possible futures for the use of the term sustainability in national and international political discourse. The frequency of use and the general importance of the term sustainability seem to increase along a continuum from religious to secular groups, and from grassroots to international groups.

For the most part the informants did not share common value sets, and highlighting the commonalities between themes discussed by particular actors within these organizations is not intended to carelessly imply that these commonalities are a foundation for a global ethics or a common prescriptive lifestyle (indeed, most of the informants would resist such prescriptions). The importance of the term *sustainability* to the work of these constituencies varied. These differences and similarities highlight some of the novel contributions of this study.

DIGGING DEEPER INTO THE USEFULNESS OF "SUSTAINABILITY"

From the beginning I have argued that sustainability is a heuristic term used to throw light on particular sets of individual or community values. The term was used in this study to refer to a manner of engaging ethnic, cultural, or ethical others that promotes decision-making with an eye to long-term resilience, and ties these decisions to ideas about what constitutes a fulfilling life. But more should be said about the usefulness of the term to the informants and their work.

Sustainability among secular groups

For Natural Capitalism Solutions, sustainability is more than a slogan or a motto. It is a set of consequences that derive from making decisions based on information that integrates financial, social, and ecological costs and benefits with a group's mission and values. The term acts as the future horizon toward which human, ecological, and economic systems are headed. For NWEI, sustainability is also "generally accepted as a personal and cultural goal" (NWEI 2007b: 10).[1] While cautious of the term, NWEI still accepts sustainability as a widely used policy goal. Ben Campbell admitted that the use of the term was widespread in NGOs dedicated to both conservation and development. Such usages, however, tend to be highly inconsistent, leading Campbell to believe that in many cases it served more as an abstract conceptual motivator than a concrete idea (interview July 29, 2008).

For some respondents from the secular world, sustainability was envisioned as an amorphous idea. For instance, Fred Kirschenmann of the Leopold Center is an expert on sustainable agriculture and described his work primarily through stories about successful agricultural schemes (in terms of biodiversity increase, productivity and profitability, and self-sufficiency). For him, sustainability was not a reliable policy goal, but rather "a prescription ... like justice—an evolving concept ... it doesn't lend itself to definition. It's a journey, and there are always surprises along the way!" (interview December 24, 2007; see also Hukkinen 2008: 4). Community organizer Judy Skog told me she imagines sustainability in more personal terms, that "it's mostly about personal choices, and helping others see how they can do it [live more sustainably]," but acknowledged that there "are as many definitions as there are people" (interview January 3, 2008).

Ben Campbell of CI suggested that the use of sustainability as a big-picture goal for the international community had been eclipsed by *climate change*, a new threat which was performing the cultural function formerly occupied by sustainability: providing a conceptual field within which a host of complexly interconnected issues (social, political, economic, and ecological) could be talked about together, and planned for collectively. Campbell told me that "the question of sustainability is a hugely open to interpretation subject ... You use sustainability in a US context, it's radically different than you would use it from, let's say, in Latin American, African, any developing country context, where natural resources play a much greater role in livelihoods" (interview July 29, 2008). According to Campbell, however, global anxiety about climate change has created a convergence of concern for social and economic development and ecological sustainability, prompting many conservation organizations that have historically been reticent to engage faith communities to seek out novel partnerships.[2]

Sustainability among interfaith groups

Among interfaith groups, the term sustainability was frequently used, but the primary vehicles of motivational language and imagery remained explicitly religious narratives drawn from specific extant religious beliefs and practices. For these informants sustainability was a term referring to overlapping and interdependent ecological and social concerns.

The respondents and literature from the two interfaith groups used sustainability as a modifier for particular practices or goals, to highlight the long-term perspective inherent in particular faith narratives, or to tie together common elements between different faith perspectives. In the two cases analyzed here, however, the term sustainability was not the focal point of activism. For IPL, climate change (not sustainability, much as Palmer and Campbell indicated) functioned as a description of interconnected global socio-politico-ecologic-economic problems. For ARC, great emphasis was placed on honoring and invigorating existing religious narratives, using sustainability to refer to the positive outcomes of re-imagining old religious narratives and creatively interpreting them to build peace and resilience today. Martin Palmer of ARC said that,

> To a very big extent, sustainable development is a phrase that's of academic interest, primarily. Because I don't hear it being used very much by groups on the ground … For all its inadequacies, and simplicities, it [the idea of sustainable development] did at least put together the tension between sustainability and development, and recognized that it was a tension.
>
> (Interview May 27, 2008)

Like Campbell, Palmer believed that the idea of sustainability (and sustainable development) had been eclipsed by other more recent concepts such as climate change or the Millennium Development Goals.[3]

Evangelicals and sustainability

Among evangelical Christian organizations, the term was typically used in conversation casually to describe taking a long-term perspective (a sustainable building, a sustainable program, etc.), or as shorthand for general cultural goals. Most saw creation care as a specifically evangelical movement that shared some ideas and long-term goals with the larger movement toward sustainability, but these respondents still advocated independence from other social movements.

For Raymond Randall, chairperson of Northland Church's "Creation, I Care" taskforce, sustainability referred primarily to the business case for sustainability. Recall his suggestion (in Chapter 7) that climate change, sustainability, and creation care were terms deployed by different constituencies (environmentalists, businesses, and the church, respectively) to refer to the same sets of goals. Because of their intent to remain morally outside the mainstream, evangelicals perceive their advocacy for sustainability-related goals to be distinctly different in motivation from mainstream sustainability, which, according to Randall, Hunter, and others is a secular movement that stems in large part from environmentalism and secular humanism.[4] As Joel Hunter put it, the phrase creation care "came from a desire to separate ourselves, to be theologically distinct from secular environmental groups, and other religious groups" (interview May 30, 2008).

THE GROWING IMPORTANCE OF SUSTAINABILITY

If, for the sake of analysis, we classify sustainability-oriented NGOs on a continuum from explicitly religious on the one end to secular on the other, it becomes clear that the importance of the term sustainability and its deployment in more general manifestations increases as one moves from explicitly religious groups toward secular organizations. If analysis concentrates instead on the spectrum that runs between grassroots groups and international NGOs, then a similar (and perhaps related) trend emerges: frequency of the use of a more generalized understanding of sustainability increases as one moves from grassroots towards international level organizations.[5]

One hypothesis that emerges from this is that as inclusiveness increases (for example in international-level groups versus grassroots organizations) there is a greater need for a non-partisan "binding agent," an affectively grounded idea or set of metaphors that acts as a common conceptual space for initial conversation. In a significant sense, because it is tied to community and individual values, sustainability sometimes acts as shorthand for a set of value preferences that includes social equity, ecological awareness, and financial well-being.

In places where sustainability provides convincing identity markers for people who use the term to reflect particular visions of where society is headed and what values it ought to maximize, it is fulfilling the function of explicitly religious narratives—a basic companion to human culture. In many cases even secular sustainability-related NGOs disseminate moral anthropologies, using the rubric of science or social science to frame them within an evolutionary, cosmological unfolding, precisely the sort of narrative described here as religious.

The use of the term sustainability was not of principal importance to the work of some informants, but because of its widespread and rapidly increasing use in Western governance structures, higher education institutions, and corporate slogans, I believe that the concern for sustainability as well as the use of the term will persist and flourish for the foreseeable future. Although climate change is often used as a shorthand way to refer to interconnected social and ecological problems, *sustainability* is often used as a set of solutions for addressing such interconnected crises. So long, then, as environmental and social issues command public, scientific, and governmental attention, and sustainability remains a malleable and affectively charged term that facilitates blending of disparate values, it should persist within various communities and within international political discourse. If I am right, then more careful analyses of what individuals and groups mean when they use the term, and more accurate renderings of their professional networks, will become increasingly important for generating genuinely open and adaptive democratic processes.

SUSTAINABILITY SCENARIOS AND THE GLOBAL RESURGENCE OF RELIGION

International relations scholar Scott Thomas has noted that a global resurgence of religion in the past century has emerged both from the bottom up and from the top down, "a parallel development in the developed world and in developing countries that is part of a wider, already existing, critique of global modernity, authenticity and development" (Thomas 2005: 44). As alternatives to modernity, imagined authenticity, and development, many from the developing and developed world offer phrases such as *sustainability, biocultural preservation,* and *sustainable development.* Sustainability and its cognates are genetically related to the global resurgence of religion. According to Thomas, the global resurgence of religion is often imagined to manifest in "various prospects for a new global religion or 'world theology'" (Thomas 2005: 117). In such cases, Thomas offered an alternative view that the "brave new world of a global civil society [the global civil religion] is ... really part of the hegemony of Western modernity" (117).

Bron Taylor has studied one candidate for this new global religion, which he referred to as dark green religion, and which he viewed as a worldwide civil religion. But Taylor has argued that if a global religion takes on a green tint, the reverence-for-life values and anti-authoritarian sentiment within the environmentalist milieu makes it unlikely that a democratic politics based in dark green spiritual sentiment would reinforce or re-inscribe intolerance or fascism (Taylor 1998, 2003; 2010: 195). But does the sustainability milieu, which is a broader cross-section of society including many constituencies that are not dark green, have such an inherent resistance to the imposition of particular cultural viewpoints? I envision at least two possible futures for sustainability in national and international political discourse and action.

Two possible sustainability scenarios

Manufacturing sustainability The first possible scenario is that sustainability, as a human-centered and management-oriented manifestation of an ongoing Western cultural project, might continue in some cases to further colonial impulses. Sustainability has from its inception owed much to its close association with utilitarian resource management, business and government sectors, and the military industrial complex. The First and Second World Wars and the Cold War, for example, provided fertile cultural ground for the emergence of new sources of inspiration and experimentation with sustainability-related practices (see Chapters 4 through 6 for further discussion). So while sustainability discourse integrates perceptions and metaphors from alternative and even oppositional sub-populations, it is also closely tied to traditional sources of power and status, raising the possibility that the sustainability narrative may actually work against the ongoing manifestation of a civic earth religion on the global scale. In such a scenario the existing nodes where power dwells would domesticate environmental themes, allowing them to appear green while advancing an international development scheme in which "experts" from the global North spread economic growth and well-being by benevolently sharing their cultural products.[6]

Within this scenario it would be reasonable to expect an increase in the use of the term sustainability by industrial, government, and military actors and a concomitant assessment by these parties that they are the only bodies in a position to be able to engineer sustainability on a societal or cultural scale. In such cases, what sustainability *is*, is manufactured by cultural elites or powers and disseminated through tightly integrated economic and socio-political levers. One of the most telling signals of this scenario would be a continued increase in rhetoric that demands protections for biological and cultural diversity coupled with a continuing integration of global economic markets that compromises such preservation. Thus far, removing constraints on the global flows of capital has reduced biological and cultural diversity, and many doubt that real biocultural preservation can occur in the midst of continued economic globalization (Worster 1993; Davison 2001).

Cultivating sustainability A second possibility is that sustainability discourse may provide an incubation place and smooth transfer point for a gradual increase in the importation of deep green themes into sustainability discourse. If this is the case, it would be reasonable to expect an increasing emphasis on shifting perception, worldview, or consciousness as central to sustainability (some early indications of which were detailed here). There may be increased attentiveness to the purpose and application of particular technologies, a transformation of the educational systems that perpetuate unsustainable cultural trends, as well as more earnest protections for indigenous peoples and their land tenure and rights to use. One of the most obvious signals that this scenario is manifesting would be some decentralization of economic activity. Alternatives to current exchange relations and political decentralization are often mentioned as prerequisites for sustainability. Indeed bioregional and other more localized forms of governance are often imagined as more sustainable political regimes. As Kenny and Meadowcroft (1999) have argued, however, the idea that greater political decentralization necessarily leads to greater environmental responsibility is highly questionable both intellectually and practically. I suspect, therefore, that economic decentralization is the more promising and more important piece of the sustainability puzzle. In such cases, sustainability is a process that develops from the bottom up, cultivated into a resilient and organic process of cultural experimentation.

Only greater epistemological scrutiny and time will tell which descriptions and understandings of sustainability are successful and thus adaptive. But if committed to an evolutionary perspective, then it is necessary to acknowledge that particular religious narratives do not necessarily persist simply because they fit scientific data or better integrate evolutionary theory. It is at best debatable whether religion itself is adaptive, although many of the "global religions" and other traditional forms of religious production extend into the deep past. While new forms of religious production undoubtedly emerge and others die off, those that perish may not do so solely on the basis of whether or not they approximate an accurate vision of reality. Even if religious production is *part of* the complex of ideation and belief that is a factor in natural selection, it is unlikely to be the lone independent variable that determines fitness within habitats.[7] The question is not which religiously-tinged stories are *correct*, but which ones *work* in place.

A LOOK TOWARD THE FUTURE

I have argued that the rich content of the idea of sustainability is comprised of contributions from a set of loosely connected social movements whose history and strongest contemporary streams cannot be well understood without attending to their religious dimensions. Historically, this religious dimension has been an important part of sustainability discourse. Pragmatically, it has been one of the primary facilitators of communication among people with differing value structures. So the first conclusion to draw is that there is a strong religious dimension to nearly all sustainability advocacy, and that the mythos derived from the collected stories that sustainability advocates project into the public sphere is itself religious.

Second, the data gathered in the ethnographic portion of this study challenges the contentions of some environmental ethicists that public philosophy should not include metaphysical speculation and religious commitments (e.g. Light 2002; Norton 2005). On the contrary, in at least some situations broad participation and inclusion of core values in public deliberation has generated better outcomes (in terms of increasing biodiversity, arresting ecological damage, or creating social resilience) (Schwartz [1991] 1996; Banathy 1997; Palmer & Finlay 2003; Willard 2005; Hukkinen 2008; Senge *et al.* 2008: 225–80). Certainly the inclusion of such religious commitments in the public sphere would require practice and nuance, particularly in countries that guarantee that no religion can be endorsed by the state or receive preferential treatment. But if core values are not allowed in the public sphere, it is unfair for "public philosophers" to expect that the public policies they advocate will satisfy the diverse needs of an increasingly complex citizenry over the long term (for discussion of environmental philosophy as an applied public philosophy, see Light & de-Shalit 2003; Light 2002).

Third, it is clear that social movements are adaptable to varying degrees. As many evolutionary psychologists and cognitive anthropologists have argued, *religion* may not be adaptive—that is, its pervasiveness and persistence in human culture does not prove that it promotes survival (for a good synopsis of those who interpret religion as being adaptive and those who reject such understandings, see Bulbulia 2004 or Dawkins 2006: 161–207). The *religious dimensions* of certain social movements, however, may be one of the features of mass movements that act as a unit of selection, for it is clear that even ostensibly secular sustainability movements utilize religious imagery and ideas to do political work. Certain social representations that have religious dimensions, such as sustainability, may act as units of cultural selection without reducing selection specifically to religion itself. We might expect that cultures that orient their production, consumption, and exchange relations around sustainability, which at least ideally is specifically oriented toward helping humans survive in particular habitats over time, will have a better than average chance of persistence. If sustainability indeed grows into a long-term cultural project, it is probable that some of the religious imagery, language, and metaphors tied to it will be some of the most successful spiritual tropes over time. This raises questions about the place of studies that seek to find evidence of environmental consciousness within existing religions, for "there is no plausible sense in which religion as a whole (or any group-level distribution of beliefs) is a group-level adaptation, like a bee-hive" (Atran *et al.* 2005: 55). Green religions may be helpful starting places for motivating adherents to begin thinking differently about individual behaviors, but green religions *themselves* are not the answers to adapting to ecological and social problems.

Importantly, the ethic of personal risk offered here differs from the global ethic of sustainability offered by others cited in this work. A minimum common denominator ethic which resonates with many of the "world religions" basically offers a substantive definition of sustainability and ethics. Such a move articulates the central principles or features of sustainability. Instead, the ethic of personal risk is, like Bryan Norton's definition of sustainability, schematic in character—that is, it focuses on particular approaches to negotiation and problem solving, rather than universal prescriptions. The schematic approach to understanding sustainability is potentially sustainable, the former, substantive approach is not.

Finally, this project provided some qualitative data that exposed some of the connections between particular leaders of sustainability-related NGOs and the pathways through which they transmit information. One of the limitations of this study is that it explored small networks. The informants, however, are well-connected individuals and they (and in most cases their organizations) are able to access the power nodes of global financial, development, and governance networks. The small networks analyzed here are related to several other networks of varying scales, and analysis of these could help provide a better picture of how sustainability discourse spreads, and what strategies generate long-term success.

Ultimately I agree with Atran and his co-authors when they stated that "cultural differences in mental models and associated values play an important role in creating intergroup conflict and, therefore, may hold the key to addressing these conflicts" (Atran *et al.* 2005: 744). Sustainability-related values and the practices that help to encourage their persistence in culture require greater scrutiny if intergroup conflict is to be minimized. We should not be surprised to find sustainability, which is a contemporary term for the now global preoccupation with species persistence, clothed in religious language. For religious language has historically been used to influence imagination, promote specific behaviors within social groups, ensure survival, negotiate peace, make war, and use and distribute resources. I suspect that as sustainability grows into the focus for global governance and development efforts as resource shortages, wars, and unexpected environmental disasters cause unprecedented destruction in an increasingly crowded world, it will be ever more important to attend to the religious dimensions of sustainability; if for no other reason, than to promote a more empathetic engagement with cultural, ethnic, and ethical others for the purpose of reducing suffering and increasing quality of life. The interdisciplinary theoretical models and the approach employed here have only begun to explore the myriad ways that sustainability is used, and for what ends. Where the religious dimension of sustainability shapes public discourse, focuses community desire, and creates and sustains new forms of exchange, it behaves in the public sphere as a political religion.

NOTES

INTRODUCTION

1. The elder was Floyd "Looks for Buffalo" Hand (Hand 1998). There were several *inipi* (sweat lodge) ceremonies, and one adaptation of a *Hunka Lowonpi* (making of relatives) ceremony, as well as feasting over two days.
2. I use the phrase "communities of accountability" throughout to refer to the various nested, hierarchically arranged communities to which individuals hold themselves accountable to differing degrees. Individuals are accountable to their own visions of self in the world (personal values), to their families, to various local groups (churches, book clubs, dining groups, etc.), to nation states, to organizations (e.g. Greenpeace, Unicef, Conservation International, etc.) and to loosely affiliated identity groups (rock climbers, surfers, peace activists, engineers, doctors, etc.) that transcend national and international boundaries. Each of these has religious dimensions, provided religion is defined broadly enough (the task addressed in Chapter 2). I picked up the phrase communities of accountability from its use by theologians who draw on narrative understandings of ethics (see for example Gula 1989), although the meaning of the phrase can obviously be extended to any number of contexts. Communities of accountability are the groups whose stories provide the framing and motivation to help individuals meaningfully navigate the worlds they find themselves thrown into. Individuals perceive differential accountability to these communities, and make ethical judgements in part by making inferences about the norms associated with these communities.
3. Indeed, the anthropologist Robin Wright noted that in many cases, religiosity may either facilitate or hamper the success of sustainable development projects, depending on the resonance of such religiosity with the values of the granting or funding bodies. In these cases, religion is certainly an important factor in sustainability.

1. THE STAKES OF SUSTAINABILITY AND ITS RELIGIOUS DIMENSIONS

1. Data drawn from the CIA Factbook, https://www.cia.gov/library/publications/the-world-factbook/rankorder/2172rank.html (accessed November 14, 2011).

2. See http://vitalsigns.worldwatch.org/vs-trend/meat-production-and-consumption-continue-grow-0 (accessed November 14, 2011).

3. It is important to note from the outset that my discussion of religion is in no way constrained by the idea of, or belief in, supernatural beings or institutionalized religious practices. As will become clear, the term religion is used to refer to a range of attributes that can manifest in individuals and social groups, and which relate to their core values and beliefs. The etymology of "religion" is typically traced to the Latin root *leig* ("to bind"), or *religare* ("to reconnect"). See Saler (1993: 64–9), Dubuisson (2003: 22-39), Thomas (2005: 21–6), and Taylor (2007: 9–14) for further discussion.

4. The most common usage of the phrase political religion refers to political ideologies which are analogous in various ways to institutional religions. A less scrutinized but nonetheless prevalent form also includes instances of institutional religions or other groups centered on naturalistic forms of reverence which focus group identity around particular political platforms or goals. Both forms are evident within the sustainability milieu.

5. Memes are hypothetical cultural units analogous to genes, except they are subject to cultural rather than genetic selection. Richard Dawkins popularized the idea in his 1976 work *The Selfish Gene*. Although there has been no empirical verification of memes, some (see Gers 2008) have suggested avenues for confirmation. However, it is difficult to see how devising lists of memes that obtain across cultures escapes existing critiques of structuralist anthropology. One problem with meme theory is its postulation of an additional level of explanation (a "cultural unit" subject to natural selection) when simpler, more materialist models account for and predict the same range of phenomena. (For further criticisms see Atran *et al.* (2002), Atran & Medin (2008), Sperber (1994), D. S. Wilson (2002: 53); Distin (2005) provides a sympathetic criticism; Blackmore (1999) and Dennett (2006) generally defend the concept.) Thus, I use the term as a descriptive metaphor rather than a scientific construct.

6. LOHAS is an acronym that stands for "lifestyles of health and sustainability."

2. DEFINING THE TERMS: RELIGION AND SUSTAINABILITY

1. As Wittgenstein put it, "How does an ostensive definition [of religion, in this case] work? Is it put to work again every time the word is used, or is it like a vaccination which changes us once and for all? A definition as a part of the calculus cannot act at a distance. It acts only by being applied" (Wittgenstein 1974: 39). Likewise, a definition of sustainability takes its meaning in large part from the specific circumstances in which it is deployed.

2. Note that I am not suggesting that the term is illuminated—that the meaning of religion is discerned—but that the application of religious language, metaphor, or perspectives to social problems indicates which problems are "deep" enough to warrant the use of religious language. Smith notes that typically, the person or group applying the labels of religion or religious are outside the communities described in this manner (Smith 1988).

3. The gendered noun is intended. I refer to scholars such as Max Müller ([1870] 2002, [1878] 2002), Karl Marx (in Tucker [1845] 1978), E. B. Tylor (1871), James Frazer ([1890] 1959), Emile Durkheim (1972, [1912] 1995), Sigmund Freud ([1918] 1998), and Carl Jung (1968). Geertz credited the fathers of the study of religion (Freud, Durkheim, and Malinowski) with creating a repetitive field of study that, drawing on Janowitz, he called an exercise of the "dead hand of competence" (Geertz 1973: 88).

4. Cases where *a priori* metaphysical assumptions guide research might include earlier scholars such as Rudolph Otto, who suggested that religious experience was grounded in a *mysterium tremendum*, or Eliade, who argued that religion was a cultural phenomenon that reflected encounters with something objectively real in nature called *the sacred*. More recent examples might include scholars who claim that followers of this or that religion (say, Islam) would naturally behave in a particular fashion if they were *authentic* believers (say, authentic Muslims). McCutcheon (2005) has provided an extended critique of overbroad and essentialist understandings of Islam following the attacks on the New York City World Trade Centers on September 11, 2001. Claims of this sort may tell more about those who imagine and endorse them than they do about those who are studied by looking through such lenses.

5. Ludwig Wittgenstein, for one, questioned whether providing a solid definition of any term is necessary for understanding: "We are able to use the word 'plant' in a way that gives rise to no misunderstanding, yet countless borderline cases can be constructed in which no one has yet decided whether something still falls under the concept 'plant.' Does this mean that the meaning of the word 'plant' in all other cases is infected by uncertainty, so that it might be said we use the word without understanding it? Would a definition which bounded this concept on several sides make the meaning of the word clearer to us in *all* sentences?" (Wittgenstein 1974: 73). Wittgenstein's—and my—answer is no.

6. Using the same theories that Saler utilized more than a decade earlier, Benthall argued that "Linguists have developed the idea of 'prototype semantics,' whereby the applicability of a word to a thing is not a matter of 'yes or no,' but rather of 'more or less,'" and further noted that "these criteria may be graded" (Benthall 2008: 21). If some aspects of human lives contain more religion-resembling features than others, we may find that "some religions, in a manner of speaking, are 'more religious' than others" (Saler 1993: xiv). This "more," however, does not refer to a greater authenticity, but rather a closer resemblance to one or more prototypes of that category.

7. Anthropologist Jeremy Benthall (2006, 2008) and religion scholar Bron Taylor (2010) use the term "para-religious" to describe these religion-resembling features. Taylor has indicated that he believes using para-religious avoids some of the potentially pejorative connotations associated with the term quasi-religious. These distinctions are unimportant to any case I wish to make here, so the terms *quasi-religious*, *para-religious* and *religion-resembling* are used interchangeably.

8. As Wittgenstein put it, "This argument [about what it means to 'understand' a concept-word] is based on the notion that what is needed to justify characterizing a number of processes or objects by a general concept-word is something common to them all. This notion is, in a way, too primitive. What a concept-word indicates is certainly a kinship between objects, but this kinship need not be the sharing of a common property or a constituent. It may connect the objects like the links of a chain, so that one is linked to another by intermediary links … Indeed even if a feature is common to all members of the family it need not be that feature that defines the concept. The relationship between the members of a concept may be set up by the sharing of features which show up in the family of the concept, crossing and overlapping in very complicated ways" (Wittgenstein 1974: 35; see also Saler 1993: 197).

9. In a later work Saler elaborated, stating that "A scholarly model of religion, as I conceive it, should consist of a pool of elements that scholars associate with religions. Not all will be found in all religions. Some will be more typical of what we mean by religion than

others, both in terms of distributions and weightings. And many will be found outside of the purview of what scholars conventionally designate as religions" (Saler 2004: 230).

10. Wittgenstein states that "the task of philosophy is not to create a new, ideal language, but to clarify the use of our language, the existing language. Its aim is to remove particular misunderstandings; not produce a real understanding for the first time" (Wittgenstein 1974: 72).

11. "Language-games, as Wittgenstein conceived them," Saler phrased it, "are exercises through which we can rid ourselves of the 'mental mist' which tends to enshroud our ordinary uses of language" (Saler 1993: 236).

12. The authors argue that their findings challenge traditional understandings of decision theory and game theory.

13. Wittgenstein suggests that concepts, propositions, and words are all part of the calculus of language, and wonders what it means to make them sensical: "how do we do it?—We can indeed turn it [the concept of religion, for example] into quite different things; an empirical proposition, a proposition of arithmetic ... an unproved theorem of mathematics ... an exclamation, and other things. So I've a free choice: how is it bounded? That's hard to say—by various types of utility, and by the expression's formal similarity to certain primitive forms of proposition; and all these boundaries are blurred." (Wittgenstein 1974: 126). Likewise, our words are defined primarily by our free use of them, whether we are using them as scholars, or in other capacities.

14. By "ethical others" I mean those who adhere to different value sets and sources of moral authority.

15. Even at the Association for the Advancement of Sustainability in Higher Education Conferences there continue to be several references to "the three E's," although mention is also often followed by another, "newer" way of referring to these three dimensions, such as the "triple bottom line," or the "integrated bottom line." But the idea of these three pillars is clearly still significant in many circles.

16. The idea that any rational moral discourse derives from within particular reasoning communities can be traced, at least within contemporary philosophy, to Alisdair MacIntyre, whose influential books *After Virtue: A Study in Moral Theory* (1981) and *Whose Justice? Which Rationality?* (1989) argued that modern moral philosophy had lost its sense of "telos," or purpose, which can only be provided by a particularistic form of reasoning imparted by participation in a community. This "narrative" approach, in which a common "story" is endorsed by a community and endowed with ethical import, was also popularized in moral theology by scholars such as Stanley Hauerwas (1981), William Spohn (2000), and many others.

17. By "purely descriptive" Norton means a concept of sustainability that uses a universal formula to achieve sustainability in particular situations, by—to use one example from environmental economics—assigning contingent values to ecological entities, and summing the costs and benefits of preserving or exploiting them. Purely descriptive definitions of sustainability may be helpful in some cases, but for Norton, they are inadequate in the long run since they do not attend to the other important types of values that he believes are essential for sustainability (Norton 2005: 379–99).

18. Given the definition of religion offered above, Norton's notion of sustainability, if implemented in a practicing community, would be doing religious work to the extent that it is forging community, shaping exchange, and focusing desire. It is important to note that I am not claiming, as Kevin Elliot has done (2007) that Norton's definition is in part "metaphysical." Norton (2007) has, I think, adequately answered Smith's charge.

Religion, as I define it here, need not imply the addition of a metaphysical layer of reality.

19. Norton's grasp of the relevant literature across a range of disciplines is noteworthy and he has a gift for building productive bridges between them. For example, he makes use of the philosophy of adaptive management, pioneered by C. S. Holling and H. T. Odum at the University of Florida (among others), with special attention to the role of hierarchy theory (derived from general systems theory) as understood by Holling. Adaptive management allows for the evolution of models over time, and the inclusion of hierarchy theory provides some sensitivity to spatial scales. They are joined with a pragmatic philosophical approach that focuses on democratic processes.

20. Wittgenstein anticipates prototype theory when he wonders what a "typical" member of a set resembles. Is it not possible, he asked, to find "say a schematic leaf, or a sample of *pure* green?—Certainly [it] might. But for such a schema to be understood as a *schema*, and not as the shape of a particular leaf, and for a slip of pure green to be understood as a sample of all that is greenish and not as a sample of pure green—this in turn resides in the way the samples are used" (Wittgenstein [1953] 2001: 15 (73)).

21. Norton is a philosopher of language, and is certainly aware of Wittgenstein's approach, although he does not deploy it specifically in his definition of sustainability.

22. By "religious" I refer to deeply felt preferences, values, and beliefs, which need not involve belief in supernatural beings or include large organizations.

23. "New" and "alternative" are terms that advocates use to express what they feel is a new set of guiding principles and values that differ in significant ways from those held by the dominant culture. For examples of this language that range from counter-hegemonic social movements to mainstream development and international political institutions, see Sumner (2005: 112), Hawken (2007a), Goldsmith *et al.* (1972: vi), Edwards (2005: 2), Golliher (1999: 446), International Union for the Conservation of Nature *et al.* (1991: 9), World Bank (2001: xxv), WCED (1987: 63; 93; 255, pagination from online document available at www.un-documents.net/ocf-02.htm, accessed August 21, 2012) (also see Davison 2001: 32).

3. SUSTAINABILITY AS A CONTAGIOUS MEME

1. Interestingly, Gary Snyder made a similar claim, but called this loose affinity of countercultures "the great underground" (see Hawken 2007a: 5).

2. Campbell contended that the concept of cult derives from a set of religious categories first proposed by Troeltsch, where a cult was associated with, and derived from the nature of mystical religions. The term was later used in a somewhat different way to refer to "any religious or quasi-religious collectivity which is loosely organized, ephemeral, and espouses a deviant system of belief and practice" relative to the dominant culture (Campbell in Kaplan and Loow 2002: 12). I believe that both definitions are descriptive of at least some features of sustainability movements.

3. Dark green religion, according to Taylor, includes the following: endorsement of the idea of a metaphysics of interconnection, which is correlated with a non-anthropocentric ethics grounded in the intrinsic value of non-human nature, and a sense of obligation to minimize damage to nature. Light green constituencies may not resonate with any of these features of dark green religion, although some are prone to agree with the idea that there is a deep biological, ecological, or cosmological interdependence.

4. This was clear from both formal and informal interviews and networking with sustainability advocates in various settings from 2001 to 2010.

5. Individuals who resonate with a "nature-as-sacred" religion generally perceive that the entities and relationships that comprise nature (typically conceived at least as all organic and living entities, and sometimes non-living entities) taken together are inherently valuable and worthy of reverence. Certain forms of pantheism and other naturalistic religions, those that do not posit a supernatural agent or agents, would fall under this category.

6. I refer to the form of weak anthropocentrism advocated by Bryan Norton (1984). Norton contended that the idea that humans can have a non-anthropocentric ethic is a confusion (let alone the best choice for a practicable environmental ethics). According to Norton, a weak anthropocentrism manifests in political outcomes that are no different than those arrived at from supposedly non-anthropocentric ethics, yet weak anthropocentrism avoids the philosophical pitfalls of attributing inherent worth or value to non-human entities (see also Norton 1991 for his "convergence hypothesis").

7. The phrase "coalitions of the unalike" is used by Edward Weber to describe collaborative conservation (2003), but I extend its usage here to groups engaged in the manufacture of sustainability discourse. I discovered Weber's work through conversations about restoration ecology with Sam Snyder.

8. The first reference is a reprint of the 1995 article in the edited volume *Green Planet Blues* (Conca & Dabelko 2004). The original article appeared in the journal *World Politics* **47**(3).

9. Here Vasquez quoted Arjun Appadurai, who suggests that these "scripts" are played out over several "scapes" that constitute the terrain of a globalizing world. Appadurai names five types of scapes: (a) ethnoscapes; (b) technoscapes; (c) mediascapes; (d) ideoscapes; and (e) financescapes. These scapes are perspecitval constructs. That is, they refer to a group of related things or features that do not look the same from every angle (see Appadurai 2003: 31). Global "flows" occur in the disjunctures between these scapes.

10. Gerlach argued that the polycentrism that characterizes SPIN movements does not imply that there are *no* leaders, but rather that there are typically *many* leaders. Such leaders tend to be more charismatic than bureaucratic, and focus more on inspiration than political systematization (Gerlach 2002: 294).

11. For Gerlach, many leaders of SPIN movements "are more accurately understood as its evangelists ... those who evangelize across the movement as a whole ... evangelists are those who zealously spread the ideology of any movement, promoting its ideas, reinforcing the beliefs of participants" (Gerlach 2002: 296). The italics appeared in Gerlach's original text.

12. Benford and Snow quote Gamson that "participation in social movements frequently involves enlargement of personal identity for participation and offers fulfillment and realization of the self" (Benford & Snow 2000: 631).

13. For example, Stern and Dietz suggest that the relationships between the values and behaviors of those who actively engage in pro-environmental behavior are significantly different than those same relationships among those who verbally support environmental advocacy, but do not themselves engage in such behaviors. They suggest that these individuals likely have significantly different value sets and social opportunities for enacting those values.

14. The "nested individual" is the agent who assimilates information from the communities of accountability to which they belong, and then acts upon this information in the world.

15. Atran and his collaborators suggest that structuralism, in the form espoused by Claude Levi-Strauss, Mary Douglas, and Edmund Leach erred by suggesting that cultural forms were somehow autonomous and separate from individuals and behaviors. Counter-currents in anthropology, typified by Marvin Harris' materialist approach, were overly-reductive, "wav[ing] away the superstructure or ideology of cultural forms as nonmaterial or epiphenomenal by-products of underlying material causes (ecological, economic, or genetic). We hold that ideas are just as material as behaviors and are indispensably constitutive of the causal chains that produce cultural regularities" (quote from footnote Atran *et al.* 2005: 748). I am generally in accord with Atran *et al.* here. For further elaboration, see the work of Michael Cole (1998, 2007), whose psychological models Atran often draws upon.

PART II THE EMERGENCE AND DEVELOPMENT OF SUSTAINABILITY

1. It is important to note that the first governance-oriented resource managers were not by any means the first to manage resources sustainably, or to manage with an eye to preserving use options for the future. Native populations in the Americas, for example, are now recognized to have engaged in beneficial modification of their ecosystems for centuries. Folk wisdom related to forest management among Europeans and those of European descent in the Americas likewise has a long history. I am grateful to Joseph Witt for this important observation.

4. THE GENESIS AND GLOBALIZATION OF SUSTAINABILITY

1. Jennifer Sumner suggests that, according to the Oxford Dictionary, the term originally derived from Thomas Sowell's 1972 book *Say's Law* (Sumner 2005, viii, 179).
2. Accessed on Dictionary.com, September 15, 2008.
3. Donald Worster declared that sustainable development "has been around for at least two centuries; it is a product of the European Enlightenment ... and reflects uncritically the modern faith in human intelligence's ability to manage nature. All that is new in the Brundtland Report and the other recent documents is that they have extended the idea *to the entire globe*" (Worster 1993: 146, italics his).
4. Susan Baker's work *Sustainable Development* suggests that the term sustainability can be traced to Malthus, Jevons, and others in the eighteenth and nineteenth centuries who first noted, and publicly worried about resource scarcity (Baker 2006: 18). Paul Hawken argued that the environmental movement was spurred by the industrial revolution in England (Hawken 2007a: 6). Hawken goes on to suggest that the three primary tributaries for the contemporary sustainability movement are environmental activism, social justice, and indigenous cultures' resistance to globalization (12). Baker does little to flesh out her claim, and then skips ahead two centuries to find the idea of scarcity re-emerging into public consciousness in the mid-twentieth century. Hawken pinpoints the first stirrings of environmentalism in reactions to the industrial revolution, but does little to connect early resistance to industrialization to the Transcendentalist movement in the United States, where he begins his treatment of environmental consciousness. In both cases, I believe, there may be more to this story.

5. Glacken suggested that Varro had an "awareness of the power of [sheep] (an extension of human activity because it is under man's control) as a destroyer of the vegetation of the farm or the mountain wilderness" (Glacken 1967: 143).

6. Nash argued that "'Romanticism' resists definition, but in general it implies an enthusiasm for the strange, remote, solitary, and mysterious. Consequently in regard to nature Romantics preferred the wild" (Nash 2001: 47).

7. Legend has it that Ludd threw a wooden shoe into the mechanized loom, destroying it. The shoes were called *sabots*, and the word *sabotage* derives from this episode. Bron Taylor pointed out to me that most likely Ludd never intended his action to be an "anti-technology" direct action, and that this was probably a later addition to the tale. But the story of Ludd's resistance later became popular within some environmental subcultures, particularly some of the more radical ones.

8. I take the phrase "wilderness church" from environmental historian William Cronon's admission, in response to critics of his well-known essay "The Trouble with Wilderness," that wild places were where he "worshipped" (1996a; for the original essay see Cronon 1996b). In a similar vein, John Gatta's *Making Nature Sacred* (2004) traces nature writing in North America from the late-1600s into the twentieth century and its consecration of the idea that nature is a *locus dei*.

9. Emerson and Thoreau also retained some ambivalence about wild nature. In the writings of both authors efforts at mediating between wild and cultivated worlds were grounded in spiritual metaphors which focused on achievement of human potential, but they also advocated a certain humility regarding the natural limits of human attempts to understand and master the natural world (Sears 1989; Gatta 2004).

10. Gatta argued that Muir's thought should not be reduced to Transcendentalism, that it differed in important ways from the prototypical Transcendentalist authors (Gatta 2004: 148–57, esp. 151). But the influence is clear. Clearly borrowing Thoreau's dictum on preserving the wildness in nature, Muir wrote that "in God's wildness lies the hope of the world—the great fresh, unblighted, unredeemed wilderness" (Nash 2001: 128, quoted from Muir [1911] 1997).

11. I agree with much of Norton's analysis, and his process-oriented, schematic definition of sustainability has been a powerful influence on my own understanding of sustainability. But I remain unconvinced by the distinctions he draws between the ideas of Muir, Pinchot, and Leopold. I suspect that they were all, to some extent, "pragmatists" (in the way he is utilizing the term), using the scientific knowledge of the day to make educated guesses about how humans interact with ecosystems, nonetheless relying on spiritualized language and rhetoric when circumstances seemed especially dire. For example, Pinchot's most dramatic spiritual language comes in his vociferous attacks on the administration officials who removed him from his post (Pinchot 1947; also see the introduction to Pinchot 1910). Muir's use of theological references certainly intensified as he watched the fight for Hetch Hetchy slip between his fingers (see Holmes 2005: 1126–7). While Norton likes to think that Leopold had moved away from utilizing such arguments, many (including Leopold's daughter) perceive in his work ethical lessons drawn from a spiritual attachment to the ecosystems with which he interacted (Meine 2005).

12. This is actually a pejorative term devised by critics in the western US who disliked federal agencies meddling in local land use matters. Their critique, according to one Pinchot biographer, stemmed from a generic "pioneer individualism," a desire to freely exploit natural resources without government intervention (Pinkett 1970: 75–80).

13. The impact of Pinchot's perspective on national resource management regimes should not be underestimated. When Theodore Roosevelt ascended to the White House in 1901, his first address to Congress outlined the creation of a Bureau of Reclamation to help develop the arid lands of the US, and more importantly for Pinchot (the son of an old family friend), the Bureau of Forestry, which was to have jurisdiction over all public forests (Pinchot 1947: 189–91; McGreary 1960: 54). As Roosevelt's premier resource manager, Pinchot wrote a great number of Roosevelt's speeches regarding resource management, and often the president sent Pinchot to negotiate on his behalf with the full power of the presidential office. As a member of his "tennis cabinet," Pinchot weighed in on every facet of federal resource management and policy (Penick 1968: 5). According to Pinchot's estimates, during Roosevelt's presidency (especially betweeen1903 and 1909), Forest Reserves increased from 62,354,965 acres to 194,505,325 acres—more than threefold (Pinchot 1947: 254).

14. As the introduction to the book stated, "Pinchot saw himself on the side of the angels, leading the forces of righteousness against dark, evil, conspiratorial influences. Reflected in what Theodore Roosevelt termed the doctrine of stewardship, Pinchot's neo-Calvinism was Puritanism placed in early-twentieth-century dress" (Pinchot 1910: xviii).

15. Making the nation into a prosperous and permanent (or sustainable) home for future generations was the focus of Pinchot's social philosophy, and in its elucidation, Pinchot drew on imagery from the Constitution and the founding fathers' vision of the agrarian, Jeffersonian ideal (Pinchot 1910: 21–39). He stated "we have a duty resting upon us … to a reasonable use of natural resources during our lifetime … for in the last analysis this question of conservation is the question of national preservation and national efficiency" (Pinchot 1910: 77–8).

16. For Pinchot conservation was a particularly democratic movement, and he "regard[ed] the absorption of [natural] resources by the special interests, unless their operations are under effective public control, as a moral wrong" (Pinchot 1910: 81).

17. As historian Donald Worster framed the greed that drove resource exhaustion, "Jesus, for instance, had declared that it was harder for a rich man to enter the Kingdom of Heaven than for a camel to squeeze through the eye of a needle. Apparently, in America, however, our camels were smaller and our needles larger" (Worster 1993: 14).

18. I am not suggesting that these two really should have "gotten along," or that they had congruent ideas about how to relate to or manage the natural world. What I am suggesting is that despite their significant disagreements, both drew on religious metaphor, language, and imagery to buttress their positions in the public sphere. This provides a good illustration of my point that sustainability movements are deeply infused with this religious dimension, and it further highlights that this is by no means a recent development.

19. Rist traces the idea of development, of somehow bettering the human condition, back to Ancient Greece (Rist 1997: 25–31) and the elucidation of the idea that there is some directionality and continuity in the process of history (27).

20. The justification for what Rist characterizes as "disguised annexations" was clothed in humanitarian and religious language that suggested that the victors held the future of civilization in their hands (Rist 1997: 62).

21. Rist's assessment of the religious status of development is negative, operating as he presumably imagines other institutionalized religions do: manufacturing consent, repressing dissent, and marginalizing minority voices.

22. As Worster put it, in "the environmental crisis of the dirty thirties ... the new profession of ecologists found themselves for the first time in service as land-use advisers to an entire nation. That episode laid the groundwork for a more scientifically fueled conservation movement in America" (Worster 1977: 253). Worster makes clear that this new science of ecology, by the 1930s, had already had an increasingly significant impact on the policy process as a direct result of a perceived environmental crisis (233).

23. Worster (1977) may be correct in tracing the first inklings of truly nation-wide concern for ecological limits and the importance of sustainable use of resources to the aftermath of the Depression and Dust Bowl. During the Second World War sustainable use and reuse and rationing of materials helped to continue this significant shift in consumption patterns.

24. This sentiment is not only proffered by environmentalists. L. Hunter Lovins, a well-known entrepreneur and sustainability consultant, argues that current energy policies in the United States, and in development schemes abroad, compromise national security by perpetuating dependence on centralized fossil-fuel-based energy production (see www.natcapsolutions.org/resources.htm#ART, especially 1982; 2002; accessed October 28, 2008).

25. The four-point plan was a platform for foreign policy. "Point Four" related to development. The first three "points" of the plan included the perpetuation of the young United Nations, the formulation of the Marshall Plan, and the formation of the North Atlantic Treaty Organization (NATO).

26. Truman mandated that "we must embark on a bold new program for making the benefits of our scientific advances and industrial progress available for the improvement and growth of underdeveloped areas. ... The old imperialism—exploitation for foreign profit—has no place in our plans ... Greater production is the key to prosperity and peace" (quoted in Davison 2001: 31).

27. The "older" primitivism was championed by the likes of Rousseau and his Romantic-era supporters.

28. Snyder was the inspiration for Japhy Ryder, the main character in Keroauc's *The Dharma Bums* (1958).

29. Kennedy called for a 5 per cent increase in aggregate income per year in the "underdeveloped" countries. Just as development was defined here as economic increase, so were later invocations of sustainable development dependent upon economic growth.

5. THE RELIGIOUS DIMENSIONS OF SUSTAINABILITY AT THE NEXUS OF CIVIL SOCIETY AND INTERNATIONAL POLITICS

1. The report was officially accepted by the WCC in Bucharest in 1974.

2. The resolution passed on July 30, 1968, see www.un.org/Depts/dhl/resguide/specenv.htm (accessed January 30, 2009). Jolly *et al.* are quoting the speech from the Secretary General U Thant (UN 1969: 4). Thant, a native of Myanmar, succeeded Dag Hammarskjold in 1961 to become the third UN Secretary General (see www.un.org/Overview/SG/sg3bio.html for a biography, accessed January 30, 2009).

3. In essence the document argued that poverty was the *causal element* in most of the world's ills, including resource shortages, violent conflict, and ecological degradation.

4. The full text is available online at www.unep.org/Documents.Multilingual/Default.asp? DocumentID=97&ArticleID=1503&l=en (accessed September 13, 2008). The quotes in this paragraph and the one following are from this online text unless otherwise noted.

5. Drawn from the text of the Declaration of the United Nations Conference on the Human Environment, available online at www.unep.org/Documents.Multilingual/Default.asp?d ocumentid=97&articleid=1503 (accessed August 19, 2012).

6. The dictionary at Dictionary.com (accessed February 12, 2009) lists six definitions of creature, two of which are based on the creature's ultimate dependence upon another being. These are relevant to the way in which the word was used here, marking an instance of an early international political venue where religious ideas were invoked.

7. From www.unep.org/Documents.Multilingual/Default.asp?DocumentID=97&ArticleI D=1503&l=en (accessed September 13, 2008).

8. This phrase was used in the opening paragraph of the Stockholm report.

9. The report was funded by the Club of Rome, a group of influential international scientists, business leaders, and public servants.

10. Dresner (2005: 25–6) suggested that strong criticisms of *Limits to Growth* ultimately doomed it to irrelevancy. He likewise dismissed other books focused on limits, such as Paul Ehrlich's *The Population Bomb* (1968), as alarmist. As I showed in the last chapter, ideas about ecological limits were common within sustainability discourse long before this, and in my judgement continue to be significant concepts. Denis Meadows's chapter in Costanza *et al.* (2007), notes that, contrary to Dresner's opinion, most of the predictions in the first edition of *Limits to Growth* have been fairly accurate, and that if anything, their models were overly conservative about the rates of change in most systems. Further, some of the protégés of these scholars, such as Hunter Lovins (heavily influenced by Meadows) continue to be influential in the implementation of sustainability globally.

11. The term "Fourth World" was coined in a book by George Manuel and Michael Posluns titled *The Fourth World: an Indian Reality* (1974). The term was quickly popularized.

12. I am deeply indebted to Robin Wright for introducing me to this literature, and for noting its significance to this history.

13. The differences between ethnodevelopment and sustainable development beg for further study. This is a potentially fruitful area for further research.

14. The Group of 77, or G-77 is the group of countries originally referred to as the Third World (the term credited to Alfred Sauvy in the 1960s). There are now some 135 countries that are part of this group. Emmerij, Jolly, and Weiss, members of the UN Intellectual History Project, suggested that the work of UNCTAD was largely focused on the G-77's critique of development and trade. Beginning in the 1980s, their *Trade and Development Reports* were envisioned as a counterpoint to the World Bank's *World Development Report*, highlighting a different set of issues (Emmerij *et al.* 2001: 54).

15. Although McNamara issued the call for the commission, the World Bank did not fund the project. The Dutch government paid for roughly half of the costs, while other nations, OPEC, and other research centers bore the remainder of the cost (Therien 2005: 31).

16. The commission proposed a four-pronged solution to development problems, which included: (1) transfer of resources from North to South, (2) a global energy policy, (3) an international food initiative, and (4) reform of international institutions. Essentially, the report recommended a global trade regime based on *rules* rather than power relations (Therien 2005: 34). This would at least make strides toward preventing powerful countries from taking extreme advantage of those with less political or economic power.

17. The participants in the Commission tended to favor the social-democratic approach advocated by the United Nations (including the Economic and Social Council [ECOSOC], United Nations Development Programme [UNDP], United Nations Conference on Trade and Development [UNCTAD], and International Labor Organization [ILO]) over the approach epitomized by the Bretton Woods Institutions (the General Agreement on Tariffs and Trade [GATT], the International Monetary Fund [IMF], the World Trade Organization [WTO] and the World Bank). While the latter are preoccupied primarily with (neo)liberalization, the UN paradigm adopts a more social-democratic view of development.
18. Another surge in oil prices in 1979 related to the Islamist Revolution in Iran, the Sandinista revolution in Nicaragua, the Soviet invasion of Afghanistan, and the election of Margaret Thatcher in the UK (1979) and Ronald Regan in the United States (1980) (both of whom supported the Bretton Woods development paradigm over the UN paradigm) all served to limit the influence of the Brandt report (Therien 2005: 30).
19. The impetus for this gathering included an increasingly frigid Cold War between the United Soviet Socialist Republics (USSR) and the US. Escalation of the Cold War was due in part to the modernization of NATO's intermediate nuclear arms in the form of Cruise and Pershing II missiles, plans to build the MX missile system (an offensive system), and a new set of strategies touted by NATO leaders that, at least to those on the eastern side of the Iron Curtain, looked like official approval of a nuclear first-strike policy (Wiseman 2005: 49).
20. Former diplomat Geoffrey Wiseman suggests that although it appeared that the Commission's recommendations fell on deaf (because overly politicized) ears, the concept of common security was "re-labeled" and re-deployed in different terms by conservative politicos on both sides of the Atlantic, and within the Soviet Union (Wiseman 2005: 53).
21. In 1990, Willy Brandt called together members from his own Commission, the Palme Commission, the Bruntland Commission, and others to generate a more effective system of global security and governance in the aftermath of the Cold War. Called the Stockholm Initiative on Global Governance, they published their results in 1995 (the fiftieth anniversary of the UN) under the title *Our Global Neighborhood* (Commission on Global Governance 1995). The title was designed to highlight the importance of security, peace, and institutional reform to the entire, interdependent global community (Jolly *et al.* 2004: 178).
22. While the Brandt and Palme Commissions were comprised primarily of a smaller number of politically important people, the Brundtland Commission was made up of environmental specialists as well as high-ranking UN and other political figures. Members, then, represented both environmental and development interests (Rist 1997: 179).
23. While many trace the term sustainability in its contemporary form to this commission, it is clear that the ideas did not emerge here. These leaders stood on the intellectual shoulders of other, earlier politicians and leaders, who had already wrestled with the complex task of combining ecological, social, and economic concern.
24. The report's basic definition is that development is sustainable if "[humanity] meets the needs of the present without compromising the ability of future generations to meet their own needs" (WCED 1987: 8).
25. The authenticity of the speech has been contested. See Michael McKenzie's entry "Seattle (Sealth), Chief" in the *Encyclopedia of Religion and Nature* (McKenzie 2005: 1511–12).

26. Philip was born Prince of Greece and Denmark, but renounced these titles when he married Elizabeth in 1947, becoming the Duke of Edinburgh, the Earl of Merioneth and Baron Greenwich (see the information on Philip on the royal family's website at www. royal.gov.uk/OutPut/Page5551.asp, accessed January 20, 2009).

27. See for example Lynn White's now famous article "The Historic Roots of the Ecologic Crisis" (White 1967).

28. "Life," as Haudenosaunee faithkeeper Oren Lyons reminded the gathered peoples, "is community" (quoted in Hart 2005: 1763).

29. The principles were explicitly normative and prescriptive, recommending that national governments take responsibility for wise resource use and conservation, and endorsing the precautionary principle and notions of both inter- and intra-generational equity (Baker 2006: 55).

30. Moreover, it created a Commission on Sustainable Development (CSD) which was to report to the Economic and Social Council of the UN (Rist 1997: 190; Baker 2006: 56).

31. Five years down the road, this body created an international set of standards in Japan, referred to as the Kyoto Protocol, which every major industrialized nation signed with the exception of the United States. The US refused to be bound by specific emissions-reduction goals, and thus the framework agreement was signed by over 150 countries, but without any concrete binding commitments.

32. President George H. Bush and the US representatives at the summit refused to sign the CBD, which Bush claimed would cause financial strain to the US biotechnology industry (Baker 2006: 96; Rist 1997: 189).

33. This summit is sometimes referred to as Rio+10.

34. Taylor was following the political theorist Daniel Deudney in calling this "terrapolitan earth religion." For Deudney's use of the phrase, see Daniel Deudney (1998).

35. Such ideas vetted in international venues are difficult to enact because each is a non-binding resolution, which means that even countries that endorse their principles cannot be held legally responsible for not adhering to them. Moreover, all such negotiations at the international level have honored the principle of subsidiarity, which suggests that decision-making and binding laws should be left to the smallest (most local) constituent legislative body.

36. For example when earlier cognates of sustainability were related to personal consumption choices and resource use during the Second World War.

37. Concern for clean water and air, for example, became a national issue in the decades after the Second World War when increasing consumption, encouraged by the federal government, was found to have detrimental environmental costs.

38. Although the Stockholm convention is often noted as the first "international" recognition of sustainability, similar ideas were vetted earlier by religious groups, as noted above.

39. It is important to note that Darrell Posey, who has played an important role in popularizing traditional ecological knowledge and the importance of indigenous peoples to sustainable development and conservation has been criticized by other anthropologists for helping to perpetuate rather romantic portraits of indigenous peoples (see Parker 1993, and the discussion in Chapter 6 of this work). To the extent that such criticisms are correct, the idea that a global sustainability ethic is directly related to indigenous cosmologies or some traditional ecological ethics may help perpetuate a colonialist impulse within international sustainability circles.

40. This is in addition to the usual "three pillars of sustainability," the ecological, social, and economic dimensions.

41. Like many in northern Europe and the United States in recent decades, he generally identifies religion with institutional structure and hierarchies, but believes that spirituality is more personal, and avoids some of the pitfalls of organized religion.
42. Susan Delgado's book *Shaking the Gates of Hell* (2007) focuses on faith-based resistance to corporate globalization, but I am more interested in this section in instances of cooperation and support.
43. The invocation of global civic nature reverence at UN sponsored events such as the Rio de Janeiro and Johannesburg Earth Summits is probably a relatively new sort of religious production. I treat it here as but one stream of religion that exercises influence on the sustainability metanarrative, along with the world religions which have been active in sustainability for decades. Other subcultures of resistance which resonate with non-mainstream religious traditions are discussed below.
44. Pigem stated in a footnote that religious groups have been involved since 1972, but UN Secretary-General Ban Ki-moon has pointed out that faith-based NGOs were present at the organization's founding. These are drawn from combined press releases offered by the Forum on Religion and Ecology (FORE) each month. This particular communiqué from FORE was received on October 14, 2007.
45. Available at www.time.com/time/magazine/article/0,9171,1810321,00.html (accessed October 9, 2011). Blair identified resource access and use as the heart of the world's social problems, and therefore a key focus for religions aimed at promoting social justice.
46. See www.gci.ch/ (accessed October 31, 2011).
47. Press release received from the Forum on Religion and Ecology.
48. The verse reads "If you offer your food to the hungry and satisfy the needs of the afflicted, then your light shall rise in the darkness and your gloom be like the noonday" (New Revised Standard Version).
49. In UNEP news clippings, forwarded by FORE, November 1, 2007.
50. She defines the "civil commons," drawing on McMurtry, thus: "*it is society's organized and community-funded capacity of universally accessible resources to provide for the life preservation and growth of society's members and their environmental life-host*" (Sumner 2005: 96, italics in original).
51. There is significant resonance here with Gare's claim (1998) that various intellectual streams must join together to create a new metanarrative.
52. Such violations have always been ongoing, but they came into international political consciousness around the late 1960s.
53. The first contribution from Wounded Knee to the American moral imagination (or conscience) came in 1893 when over 200 women and children and men were killed by federal soldiers for their persistent practice of the Ghost Dance, a millenarian religious movement that enjoyed pan-Indian popularity in the late 1800s. The 1973 incident recalled this deep wrong in profound ways, bridging past events with (then) present affect.
54. Received in collated UNEP notes from FORE (October 14, 2007).

6. THE CONTRIBUTIONS OF NATURAL AND SOCIAL SCIENCES TO THE RELIGIOUS DIMENSIONS OF SUSTAINABILITY

1. Their thought experiment postulated that two particles, having once interacted, continued to display instantaneous correlated behavior even when separated by such

a distance that they could not be causally related according to relativity theory. For the experimental "singlet" state, the statistical predictions of quantum mechanics were incompatible with separable predetermination. Either the particles were exchanging information faster than the speed of light, or the quantum mechanical explanation must be considered incomplete. EPR assumed relativity theory was correct, and that what Einstein called "spooky action at a distance" was illogical, thus concluding that the quantum mechanical description of reality was *not* complete. As EPR put it, "No reasonable definition of reality could be expected to permit this [the correlation of two distant particles without direct causal relationship]" (Einstein *et al.* [1935] 1983: 141).

2. By sustainability-related sciences I refer generally to particular interpretations of phenomena observed within the life and physical sciences that inform, whether explicitly or implicitly, various efforts toward sustainability. The most obvious examples are certain understandings of ecology, systems science, and what some have called the "new physics."

3. It is perhaps telling that Killingsworth and Palmer use the term "evolution" to describe the development of environmental politics, for they certainly do not use the term in the sense that most biologists would. Their uncritical use of a scientific term to describe social phenomena is illustrative of the pervasive (and often uncritical) use of scientific language, metaphor, and imagery to convey ideas related to the environment and sustainability.

4. It should be noted that the authors refer to "deep" and "social" ecology more casually than would many who study such movements. The authors use social ecology to refer broadly to those who perceive a close relationship between social injustice and ecological degradation. Others use it more specifically to refer to a political philosophy advanced most notably by Murray Bookchin. The authors use deep ecology to refer to biocentric or ecocentric environmental stances, not to refer specifically to the philosophical system developed by Arne Naess, or his intellectual offspring.

5. Joanna Macy, for example, was one scholar who intentionally combined general systems science with religious belief and practice, specifically Theravada Buddhism, to analyze a different sort of approach to "development" (Macy 1991). On-the-ground practitioners are also aware of systems theory. For example, it makes frequent appearances in the literature related to the Northwest Earth Institute discussion groups (see Chapter 9 for more details about NWEI).

6. Conservation biologists generally advocate holistic landscape planning schemes with the aim of restoring or reinvigorating ecosystem diversity, and part of their aim is to point up instances where human activities hamper achievement of those goals.

7. Information about the foundation of the Society for Conservation Biology, the affiliated journal, and Soulé's Buddhist practice comes from a series of talks at the University of Florida in autumn of 2004.

8. Given the normative character of the term biodiversity, Takacs noted that "it is ironic … that the term *biodiversity* and the politics it has engendered sprang from this august and cloistered institution [the NAS]" (Takacs 1996: 36).

9. Patten's book includes contributions from many well-known scientists such as Thomas Lovejoy and Vandana Shiva, and political personalities such as Gro Brundtland and HRH Prince Philip.

10. Stephen Kellert defined biophilia as "The idea that people possess a genetic inclination, grounded in the quest for individual and collective fitness, to attach physical, emotional, intellectual, and moral meaning to nature" (Kellert 2005: 185).

219

11. *Moby Dick* is a saga about a whaling vessel. Removing the blubber from a kill could be dangerous, one of the reasons shipmates were tied together.

12. For a book length treatment, see Mark Bekoff, *The Emotional Lives of Animals* (2007).

13. While the bomb was being tested, Oppenheimer, speaking with another project scientist, supposedly gazed at the Sierra Oscura range in the background and muttered, "Funny how the mountains always inspire our work" (Fiege 2007: 579).

14. This quote refers to a well-known chapter of Leopold's *Sand County Almanac* titled "Thinking Like a Mountain" (Leopold 1949: 129–33). There, Leopold discussed his belief that "fewer wolves meant more deer, that no wolves would mean a hunter's paradise" (130). On one occasion, however, Leopold shot a she-wolf and watched as a "fierce green fire" died in her eyes. This mysterious fire represented "something new" to Leopold, "something known only to her and the mountain" (130).

15. Macy was an activist working with Tibetan refugees when she was exposed to Buddhism. After obtaining a doctorate by exploring the resonances between general systems theory and Buddhism (Macy 1991), she worked for the Sarvodaya Shramadana movement, a movement for sustainable communities in Sri Lanka (see Strobel 2005 for more details). She has been influential in Buddhist environmentalism, environmental ethics, and deep ecological thought and practice, and has thus contributed to ideas related to sustainability.

16. Much of this background was discussed during lectures at the University of Florida by Heart Phoenix, longtime radical environmental activist (spring 2005), and John Seed (spring 2005). For more see Taylor (2001: 229).

17. Seed's observation was stimulated by participation in a direct action to stop logging in a rain forest. He talked about this experience during lectures at the University of Florida in the spring of 2005. In print, Seed described his meditative technique: "[I] lie down in the forest … cover myself in leaves, and imagine an umbilical cord reaching down into the earth. Then I visualize myself as being one leaf on the tree of life, both as myself personally and as a human being, and I realize that the sap of that tree runs through every leaf including me, whether I'm aware of it or not" (Seed 2000: 288–9).

18. Einstein believed this signaled that quantum mechanics was an incomplete theory. Bohm recognized that such epistemological uncertainty could in theory be overcome with more powerful tools or logic, and suggested new interpretations of quantum mechanics that imagined it to be a complete theory. There are many interpretations of quantum mechanical phenomena that can fit the data. For example, Hugh Everett proposed a "many-worlds" interpretation of quantum mechanics which posited multiple parallel universes (Everett 1957).

19. I spell "wholism" with a "w" here to follow Bohm, although elsewhere I use the more conventional spelling.

20. The volume edited by Griffin, titled *The Reenchantment of Science* (1988), included contributions by life scientists Charles Birch (with whom Cobb published an influential volume called *Liberation of Life* [1981]), Rupert Sheldrake, and physicists Bohm and Brian Swimme.

21. Capra stated that Western culture was lopsided because it had been preoccupied with the "yang," or masculine energy. He believed "the rising concern with ecology, the strong interest in mysticism, the growing feminist awareness, and the rediscovery of holistic approaches to health and healing are all manifestations of the same evolutionary trends" (Capra [1975] 1984: xvi).

22. According to Chas Clifton, "'entheogens' is a term that refers to drugs which provoke ecstasy and have traditionally been used as shamanic or religious inebriants … The

term's Greek roots translate as 'god generated within'" (Clifton 2005: 596). Capra stated that "in the beginning, I was helped on my way by 'power plants' which showed me how … spiritual insights come on their own … emerging from the depth of consciousness … it was so overwhelming that I burst into tears, at the same time, not unlike Castaneda, pouring out my impressions on to a piece of paper" (Capra [1975] 1984: xx).

23. Callicott asked the reader to assume "a) with Shepard and Capra that nature is one and continuous with the self, and b) with the bulk of modern moral theory … that self-interested behavior has a *prima facie* claim to be at the same time rational behavior." Following this logic to its conclusion, "the central axiological problem of environmental ethics … may be directly and simply solved" (Callicott 1985: 275).

24. In this essay, Callicott is not defending *objective* intrinsic value (as Holmes Rolston III often does [see Rolston III 2002 for an example related to biophilia]), but rather a *subjective* intrinsic value, where human valuers are required to encounter nature before considering it to be valuable for its own sake. In essence, Callicott is really making two points: (a) first, that quantum mechanics helps to overcome the fact–value dualism by positing emergent complementary properties; and (b) that quantum theory offers a new "cosmological–metaphysical" interpretive frame that transcends traditional rationality (here I draw on Michael E. Zimmerman [1988] 1995).

25. From the official website www.whatthebleep.com/index2.shtml (accessed April 23, 2008).

26. For example, Einstein, Capra, Carson, Leopold, and many other ecological "heroes" are honored with pages in the Better World Project's Earth Day coloring book. The Better World Project is dedicated to the "diverse movements for change" toward a "just and sustainable world." For more information about Better World, see www.betterworld.net (accessed June 18, 2008).

27. Lecture, fall 2002.

28. The full text is available in several languages at the UN website: www.un.org/esa/socdev/unpfii/en/declaration.html (accessed November 6, 2011).

29. Berkes, Folke, and Colding suggest that it is not historical continuity that is most important. Experience, observation, and attentive learning from particular places constitute the essential ingredients in traditional or neo-traditional management (Berkes *et al.* 1998: 5).

30. Four US-owned passenger jets were hijacked, and two of the jets were flown into the twin towers of the World Trade Center in Manhattan, New York. The full speech is available at www.whitehouse.gov/news/releases/2001/09/20010920-8.html (accessed June 10, 2008).

31. One of Bush's calls for aid went to "banking systems around the world" (www.whitehouse.gov, accessed June 10, 2008).

32. On September 15, 2001 Bush was asked at a press conference: "Sir, how much of a sacrifice are ordinary Americans going to have to be expected to make in their daily lives, in their daily routines?" His reply was "Our hope, of course, is that they make no sacrifice whatsoever. We would like to see life return to normal in America." Full text available at www.whitehouse.gov (accessed June 10, 2008).

33. Advocates of "weak sustainability," for example, might allow the replanting of logged old-growth forest with a single high-pulp species, noting similar levels of net primary productivity, and arguing that this is an appropriate substitute. Some strong sustainability advocates, on the other hand, might draw stricter boundaries on what sort of resource substitutions would be allowed.

34. Former World Bank economist Hermann Daly refers to this diversification without increasing throughputs as "development" (Daly 1996).

35. Their official measurement is gross national happiness, or GNH.
36. The reader is introduced to the bishop quite suddenly, with no real explanation of who he is, or why he is important to the authors.
37. The etymology of the term "economics" derives from the Greek *oikos*, and literally refers to the process and means of exchange within the "house."
38. Daly grounds his argument on what he calls a biblical basis, which provides a particularly cutting commentary on the ideas of equity and economics.
39. Drawing on Habermas's work, Norton states that "discourse ethics promotes multilayered communication channels that are unshaken by substantive beliefs or personal values" (Norton 2005: 288).
40. Fazlun Khalid, founder and director of the Islamic Foundation for Ecology and Environmental Sciences (IFEES) told me that "working with other people helps us to educate the Muslims." He went on to say that this was a crucial piece of faith-based environmental protection, particularly in areas where Muslims engaged in violent conflict were unable to see "the issues that lie beneath their feet! [environmental issues]" (interview with Khalid, May 29, 2008). Muslims, then, were also learning from those outside of their own communities.
41. David Chidester notes that a now out-of-date guidebook for Christian missionaries put the number of "animistic" peoples on the planet, those who do not resonate with traditional Western categories and concepts, at roughly 40 per cent (Chidester 2005b: 78, study referenced from 1991). Anthropologist Darrell Posey suggested that, excluding urban populations, indigenous peoples could amount to 85 per cent of the world's population (Posey 2004). One publication from the IUCN, UNEP, and WWF put the number of indigenous peoples at about 200 million, or approximately 4 per cent of the (then) global population (1991: 61).
42. Public policy expert Michael Redclift notes that "What is required is the admission that we are dealing, when we observe local resource management strategies, with *multiple epistemologies* possessed by different groups of people" (Ghai & Vivian 1992: 35, italics in original).
43. For example, traditional Western democratic theory assumes that the primary economic unit of analysis is the individual, who is, at least in the process of making rational decisions, a completely autonomous cost–benefit calculator (Prugh *et al.* 2000: 100; Posey 2006).
44. I do not mean to imply that those groups that are explicitly religious do not interact with other religious groups. On the contrary, they do partner with others with different religious beliefs and practices, but they do so because of teachings *within* their own tradition. The interfaith groups analyzed here are groups whose primary aim is to facilitate interactions across faiths. The secular groups also work with various religious groups. Their explicit goals are not framed religiously, but in terms of sustainability and conservation.

PART III THE ETHNOGRAPHIC DATA AND SUSTAINABILITY CASES

1. For the small-scale study in Gainesville (UFIRB # 2005-U-945) I participated in a discussion group facilitated by the Northwest Earth Institute (one of the organizations detailed in Chapter 9), and also circulated a survey instrument to participants in my own discussion group and participants in several other groups. In-depth interviews were

conducted with all participants in my own discussion group, and several others from different discussion groups. Participants were asked to affirm one or more of the nine ways of valuing non-human nature proposed by Kellert (1993b), or to select a category labeled "other," indicating that none of the proposed ways of valuing resonated with them. Kellert's categories of valuation included: utilitarian, naturalistic, ecologistic-scientific, aesthetic, symbolic, humanistic, moralistic, dominionistic, and negativistic. I also asked the participants to which communities of accountability they attributed their concern for the environment and their activism. The communities of accountability were differentiated by scale, and included: self, family, municipal, regional, national, international, global, and other.

7. WALKING TOGETHER SEPARATELY: EVANGELICAL CREATION CARE

1. From the Hebrew Bible's book of Job 38:4. In the passage God is reminding Job that a mere mortal could never know the deep history of the cosmos, or understand the mind of the Creator.
2. Evangelical Christians believe it is important to distinguish themselves from scientists who resonate with religious naturalism, and from other religion scholars such as Thomas Berry who advertise a scientifically grounded "universe story" (see Swimme and Berry 1994).
3. Illustrations abound in the popular press. During my residence in Gainesville, FL, the local newspaper *The Gainesville Sun* included frequent opinion pieces which insisted that the United States is a Christian nation founded on Christian values, and that these values ought to play a significant role in setting policy. These local voices grew louder and more frequent when public disputes arose about including evolution in public school curricula or about which public areas could display religious symbols and texts. For example, in 2007 there was significant controversy in Florida when one school board attempted to remove all mention of the age of the earth and of macroevolution from high school science textbooks. To further illustrate, in 2003 an Alabama judge was ordered by a higher court to remove a large-scale model of the Ten Commandments from his courtroom. For a period, citizen support for the judge's cause (in defense of the "Christian nation") was demonstrated by the rash of plastic placards that bore the commandments that appeared in yards across the nation.
4. Pew Forum on Religion and Public Life, http://religions.pewforum.org/ (accessed July 1, 2008). Evangelical Christians are the largest single religious group in the US, according to the Pew Study, nearly 2.5 per cent larger than Catholics, and a full 8 per cent larger than the mainline Protestant Christian denominations. Although not all who are classified as evangelical Christians in the Pew study would resonate with the views of those I discuss here, in many cases many would agree on other legislative matters, including life and death and marriage issues.
5. For good introductions to the emergence of evangelicalism in the United States, a topic which is not my concern here, see Mark Noll's *The Scandal of the Evangelical Mind* (1995) and Marsden's *Understanding Fundamentalism and Evangelicalism* (1991).
6. The term "evangelical" derives from the Greek *euangelion*, meaning a bearer of good news. DeWitt detailed this etymology in two public addresses in Gainesville, Florida April 7 and 8, 2008 (see also DeWitt 2006: 572).

7. DeWitt noted that their distrust of authority has also prevented many evangelicals from embracing biblical teachings on environmental degradation, and from understanding the content of early Hebrew or Greek biblical texts (DeWitt 2006: 573).

8. I first heard this phrase used by Alexei Laushkin, Program Assistant for the EEN, in our interview on May 13, 2008. When I used that phrase to describe evangelical environmentalism to Jim Ball, executive director and president of the EEN, he agreed that it was an apt characterization of the way that evangelical Christians relate to non-evangelicals. Ben Campbell, another evangelical respondent employed by Conservation International (see Chapter 8), also agreed that it was an appropriate description for how he viewed his spiritually centered life in relation to secular conservation advocates.

9. Jim Ball, founder and director of the EEN suggested that it was important to clarify what I meant by "creation care," since many Christians, as well as people of other faiths, use it to describe their activism for the environment. I use it here to refer to a specifically evangelical Christian understanding of creation care that views this activism not as *environmental* activism, but as advocacy for God's whole creation. There is no distinction in this cosmovision between advocacy for the poor ("the least of these") and advocacy for the environment, for both are undertaken in obedience to God (not in response to some perceived ecological crisis).

10. The intention here is to highlight significant benchmarks in the development of creation care, not to offer an exhaustive history of its emergence. David Larsen's two-volume dissertation through the University of Chicago, titled "God's Gardeners: American Protestant Evangelicals Confront Environmentalism, 1967–2000" (2001), provides such a history with a detailed account of the tributaries and main events in the emergence of what he termed "evangelical environmentalism."

11. The title of the chapter is "Our Fair Sister," drawn from the lyrics, "What have they done to the earth? / What have they done to our fair sister?" Schaeffer's use of this song is delightfully ironic, for The Doors were important purveyors of the music that was an integral part of the subcultural milieus that Schaeffer collectively and pejoratively referred to as "hippies" and "pantheists." To add to the irony, Jim Morrison, The Doors' lead singer, once famously called out to a crowd gathered outside a Los Angeles nightclub that he was "the Lizard King" and "could do anything." This demonic moniker is now frequently associated with Morrison in memorabilia.

12. The italics in this paragraph are from the original text. Schaeffer's work is one early illustration of the idea that non-human nature possesses intrinsic worth ("nature was valuable *in itself*") without depending on bio- or eco-centric ethics. In this case, recognition of intrinsic value derives from a theocentric viewpoint that retains a strong human exceptionalist component, not from the perceived sacredness of nature itself.

13. Their focus was on what was then called "Christian environmental stewardship" (interview with DeWitt, April 8, 2008). David Larsen, in his authoritative excavation of evangelical environmental concern from 1967 to 2000, termed this movement *evangelical environmentalism* (Larsen 2001). DeWitt seemed uncertain about the value of the term "environmentalism" to describe evangelical motivations, but has used the term in print (DeWitt 2006). He has emphasized that evangelicals are not sympathetic with the claims typically advanced by environmentalists, and evangelical care for creation should not be confused with environmentalist sentiment (2006: 571; personal communication).

14. If the influences of dark green religion reach as deeply and broadly into environmentalism as Taylor (2010) believes they do, then these evangelicals' fears may be warranted.

15. Obviously not all Christians immediately distance themselves from such ideas. See for instance Wallace (2005), who offers an animist Christianity.

16. According to these Christians, humans are born with an inherently degraded spiritual and emotional capacity as a result of Adam and Eve's original act of disobedience in the Genesis narrative. This act of rebellion, partaking of the fruit of the tree of knowledge of good and evil, is often (particularly after Augustine's work in the fourth century CE) referred to as "the Fall."

17. Richard Cizik, Joel Hunter, and Jim Ball all cited this as central to their understanding of creation care.

18. The magazine was later called *Green Cross*, and later still, *Creation Care*. According to DeWitt, Bob Carling was active from the early days of evangelical environmentalism and remained active in the EEN after its founding.

19. From their website, www.ausable.org/au.ourmission.cfm (accessed August 7, 2008). According to DeWitt the apparent dearth of practicable environmental ethics is a direct result of the fragmentation of knowledge. That is, the division of the Academy into distinct disciplines has encouraged the erosion of constructive fields of study whose task was, at least until the end of the nineteenth century, to provide some connective tissue between different areas of inquiry. Theology, in this understanding of educational history, held the curriculum together and provided it with purpose, ensuring that education was used for the public good (from interview with DeWitt, April 8, 2008).

20. All of the participating institutions are Christian colleges and seminaries in the US.

21. David Larsen reports that the EEN was a ministry of Evangelicals for Social Action (ESA), a group spearheaded by Ron Sider. DeWitt, both in our interview and in print (2006) has described the genesis of the EEN the way I have here, as derivative from the IEEN. There is no information on the websites of ESA or IEEN that describes the EEN as a partner or offshoot. Alexei Laushkin of EEN reported that he thought that the EEN derived from a joint ministry of ESA and WorldVision, a Christian development organization. Thus, I have been unable to determine if there was, or continues to be any relationship between ESA and IEEN, but neither of these groups claims the EEN as a derivative. Interestingly, this piece of the emergence of evangelical environmentalism appears to be contested.

22. See www.creationcare.org/ (accessed August 7, 2008). The editor of *Creation Care* was Bob Carling, whom DeWitt credits with the name that eventually stuck to this Christian social movement (interview April 8, 2008).

23. See www.creationcare.org/resources/declaration.php (accessed August 7, 2008).

24. For instance, in 2008 Jim Ball was one of the keynote panelists for a session on faith and climate change at Florida Governor Charlie Christ's Climate Change Summit, attended primarily by business and industry leaders. This illustrated the powerful national political voice of evangelicals.

25. The Circle Church was envisioned as a progressive church. It was mentioned in a 1969 article in *Time* magazine which described a pervasive existential need for Americans, and particularly youth, to seek out a vibrant, living spirituality rather than the institutionalized religions of their parents (Fri., December 26, 1969, available online at www.time.com/time/printout/0,8816,941816,00.html (accessed February 4, 2009).

26. A more detailed accounting of Northland's history than can be provided here is available at their website, from which the information included here was drawn: www.northlandchurch.net/about_us/Our_History/index.html (accessed January 10, 2009).

27. Bingham is the founder and director of Interfaith Power and Light.
28. This quote was taken from *Creation Care* magazine, published by the EEN, which printed an excerpt of Hunter's *Right Wing, Wrong Bird* (2006). The article was on the EEN's website (www.creationcare.org/magazine/winter07.php, accessed September 9, 2008).
29. Randall was quick to point out that there was no ill will between IPL and him.
30. Bryan Norton's well-known work *Toward Unity Among Environmentalists* (1991) argued that although anthropocentric and non-anthropocentric ethical theories might differ on the ultimate source and locus of value, they would typically concur on practical recommendations for environmental policy. In this case, practical convergence might be prevented by underlying value commitments, suggesting that in many ethically rich situations practical convergence may not be possible without negotiation at the level of core values and deep beliefs.
31. Dr Hunter's mention of parthenogenesis (a natural phenomenon where birth results from an unfertilized egg) interested me greatly, for I had never heard that mentioned in the context of explaining the supposed virgin birth of Jesus. I have found no evidence that indicated that it was possible for mammals to give birth from an unfertilized egg, but the implication was that this idea was circulating in evangelical Christian constituencies. Some evidence, however, has pointed to this phenomenon in at least two captive sharks (see www.cnn.com/2008/US/10/10/shark.virgin.birth.ap/index.html, accessed October 10, 2008). Parthenogenesis is also thought to occur under population duress in certain birds, amphibians, and reptiles. It is interesting to ponder the effects that a scientific explanation for Jesus' birth would have on Christian theology. Presumably it would still be considered miraculous. But if so, this would likely require a revision of the popular understanding of *miracles* as events which suspend or overrule natural laws. Several theologians have advanced complex models of divine action in which God is "non-interventionist" and works *through* the forces and relationships of nature, not instead of them (see for example Murphy & Ellis 1996; Russell 1998). It is possible that Hunter was expressing affinity for such positions.
32. A series of meetings occurred in Thomasville, GA from November 30 to December 2, 2006 sponsored by the Center for Health and Global Environment at Harvard Medical School and the National Association of Evangelicals. See their press release, accessed through the "Evangelicals and Scientists United to Protect Creation" website at www.creationcareforpastors.com/PDF_files/creationcarepressrelease.pdf (accessed February 4, 2009). Their joint statement was released in January of 2007.
33. Michael Guinan's *The Pentateuch* (1990) stresses the strong presence of stability and order within the natural realm during the creation, and uses the idea of *shalom* to describe them. Although he does not use the term *shalom*, Theodore Hiebert's *The Yahwist's Landscape* (1996) also discusses the Israelite relationship with the land and the natural order.
34. This metaphor was first invoked by the economist Kenneth Boulding in the early 1970s.
35. Cizik is no longer in this position, although he continues to advocate for evangelical action on climate change.
36. The title of the talk was "For God's Sake: Literally."
37. The term "inject" is DeWitt's language. As the discussion above noted, evangelical environmentalism goes much deeper than Cizik's work, but DeWitt was here crediting Cizik with effectively bringing creation care into the public sphere and making it a political issue.
38. Testimonies at www.creationicare.net/2007/05/why_i_care_dan_.html (accessed March 2008). This page does not seem to be active any longer.

39. This question comes from Luke 10:29. Jesus supposedly summarized the Christian message as "love the Lord your God with all your heart, and with all your soul, and with all your mind; and your neighbor as yourself" (Luke 10:27). When asked by a lawyer, "and who is my neighbor?" Jesus replied with the parable of the good Samaritan.

40. Dr Hunter did refer to Augustine as "Saint Augustine." I was not able to confirm that this quote came from Augustine, but this was Dr Hunter's recollection.

41. By "Process-oriented" I refer to those theologies, such as Berry's, that were influenced by Alfred North Whitehead's "Process philosophy" (see his *Process and Reality* [1927] 1978). While Berry does not necessarily declare allegiance to Whitehead's philosophy, he retains many features of Whitehead's thought, including the temporally dependent nature of the divine (God does not "know" the future before it happens), and the notion that cosmological unfolding is a sacred process. Most directly, however, Berry was influenced by the priest and paleontologist Pierre Teilhard de Chardin, whose *Phenomenon of Man* (1959) suggested an evolutionary cosmos with humans at the pinnacle of creation, able to use clarified reason to access the *noosphere*, a transcendent realm where human consciousness could reunite with God. In either case, the sort of divinity implied by this cosmological model is not one that resonates with most evangelicals, which is DeWitt's point, and crucial for distinguishing between these different forms of cosmocentrism.

42. In the Genesis account, after almost every stage of the creation, God declares the work He has done to be "good." This is a frequently cited passage in eco-theology circles.

43. The title of his speech at the C3 event was "Earthkeeping and God's Love: Biblical Teachings on the Care of Creation." This point resonates with some economists also. See for example Herman Daly's "On Economics as a Life Science" and "The Steady-State Economy: Toward a Political Economy of Biophysical Equilibrium and Moral Growth," both in Daly ([1973] 1980).

44. A press release from the Oxford Climate Forum was available online (www.jri.org.uk/news/statement.htm) through the John Ray Initiative website (accessed February 6, 2009). The John Ray Initiative is a nonprofit educational organization focused on integrating Christian teachings with scientific knowledge.

45. The full text is available at www-tc.pbs.org/now/shows/343/letter.pdf (accessed August 12, 2008). Unless otherwise noted, all quotes in this paragraph are drawn from the full text document available at the PBS website.

46. He stated that he was uncertain how his congregants would respond to what he perceived was an atypical Christian message.

47. Other things, such as beginning and end of life issues and marriage are not generally considered part of these individual liberties for evangelicals, but rather are issues they perceive to have been decided upon by a higher power.

48. As will become clearer in Chapters 8 and 9, positive messages, myths, and narratives are more memorable, and more frequently cited by interview subjects than are the more pessimistic assessments of humans' place in the natural world.

49. A flyer from Tri Robinson's church phrases their theocentric motto this way: "We do this [advocate for environmental justice] not because of Mother Earth, but because it belongs to Father God" (see www.vineyardboise.org/garden/, accessed August 12, 2011). Joel Hunter specifically used the term theocentric to describe the evangelical Christian perspective at the C3 event.

50. Note his invocation of the principle of quantum entanglement, discussed in Chapter 6.

51. Campbell is an evangelical Christian employed by a secular conservation organization. See Chapter 8 for further discussion of CI and of Campbell.

52. Campbell is referring to the account in Genesis where the cosmos was created in six days, with God resting on the seventh.

53. Gould coined the phrase in his book *Rocks of Ages* (1999). For a clever if not altogether convincing critique of this idea see Dawkins' *The God Delusion* (2006: 54–61). Dawkins points out several problems with the NOMA approach, although his primary concern is that Gould is "bending over backwards" paying "lip service" to "completely impartial agnosticism" (2006: 55, 54). Interestingly the crux of Dawkins' argument depends upon a theistic belief in supernatural miracles and an interventionist perspective on divine action. Such an interventionist perspective on divine action may not characterize all, or even most Christians.

54. Holden is referring to a decade or more of research that continues to suggest that close to half of the US public has serious doubts about evolutionary theory and agrees with ideas related to a "young earth." She includes as evidence reports that even college science students do not differ much from the general public, noting studies conducted by Edward Crisp (geology professor at West Virginia University) and James Colbert (biology professor at Iowa State University) who found that about 32 per cent and 25 per cent of their students, respectively, expressed agreement with the idea that humans were created in their present form about 10,000 years ago. Moreover, in a survey after completing the biology class, Colbert found that the numbers declined only to 17 per cent.

55. Even if many evangelicals are willing to assent to the idea that the creation is inherently good, the source of this good is God, and not nature itself. This marks a break with those who resonate with dark green spiritualities and consider nature itself sacred, something to which these evangelicals would never assent.

56. The hypostatic union is a powerful idea precisely *because* it is paradoxical. Similarly, the idea that humans are fully soul and fully dust is counter-intuitive, but partly because of this it is a potent concept. Jesus often taught in parables that were full of paradox, the most obvious example being consistent references to the Kingdom of God, which theologians interpret as already manifesting on earth, and yet still awaiting its fulfillment in the second coming of Jesus (for a popular portrayal and examples of paradox in the parables see Borg 1994: 80–81; see also Roger Haight's [2000] discussion of the importance of paradox to understanding Jesus' ministry).

57. For a review of Sideris' book which suggests that she may be too harsh in her criticism of ecotheologians see Ferrè (2003).

58. When I attended services, those tuning in via the internet included US servicewomen and men in both Iraq and Afghanistan, viewers in Europe, Mexico, South America, and Canada.

59. The sermons are archived at www.northlandchurch.org.

8. STORIES OF PARTNERSHIP: INTERFAITH EFFORTS TOWARD SUSTAINABILITY

1. This was an Episcopal church founded by a group of veterans in 1865, just after the close of the US Civil War, as a memorial to those who had fallen. The parish was officially established in 1868. See their website for more information at www.heavenlyrest.org/html/mission.html (accessed December 22, 2008).

2. Bingham believed that everything possessed intrinsic value because everything was created by God, and declared to be "good" (see, for example, chapter two of Genesis in the Hebrew Bible). This could be considered a theocentric perspective, possessing strong

resonance with the sort of theocentrism advocated by some evangelicals in Chapter 5. Bingham's stories, however, suggested that she resonated with a slightly milder form of anthropocentrism, and certainly would not have advocated the dominion or strong stewardship themes advocated by Schaeffer (1970) or Wilkinson (1980). While she uses the term intrinsic value and even expresses sentiments that occasionally border on pantheistic perception, for the most part Bingham frames her environmental advocacy within an anthropocentric Christian perspective.

3. For more details about St James Episcopal Church see www.stjamessf.org/ (accessed January 20, 2009).

4. Vermont-based Green Mountain is an energy provider that has options for carbon-neutral energy purchase. Green Mountain does not appear to have any obvious ties to religious groups or to non-profits generally. They do, however, have an extensive code of ethics available online that refers to their expectation that all employees will act as good "stewards" of the earth, implying a softened anthropocentrism that perhaps intentionally resonates with a generic Christian sentiment (see their website at www.greenmountainpower.com/about/ethics.html, accessed January 20, 2009).

5. The mission statement of the Fund states that their goal is "Helping to build a more just, sustainable, and peaceful world." The Rockefeller Brothers Fund was founded by the children of John D. Rockefeller, Jr in 1940 to combine some of their philanthropic efforts. The major contributions to the Fund came from J. D. Rockefeller, Jr, and from his estate. The Fund did not provide further funding for Interfaith Power and Light following this initial investment. For more information see www.rbf.org/ (accessed February 5, 2009). Interestingly, Steven C. Rockefeller was one of the primary drivers behind the drafting and promotion of the Earth Charter.

6. In the Episcopal tradition, canon is a title granted to a senior clergy member of high regard, often focused on performing a particular set of tasks for the church or ministering to a particular group. The Episcopal Church website describes a canon as "a member of the clergy ... on a diocesan staff [who] assists the bishop. Members of the clergy and laity have at times been made honorary canons of a cathedral in recognition of significant service or achievement" (see www.episcopalchurch.org/19625_13888_ENG_HTM.htm, accessed January 20, 2009).

7. See Chapter 5 footnote 26 for more information.

8. The quote is from the website, www.arcworld.org/about.asp?pageID=2 (accessed August 31, 2008).

9. The faiths represented there were Buddhism, Christianity, Hinduism, Islam, and Judaism.

10. These meetings were the impetus for the Assisi Declaration, which was approved by the participants in 2002.

11. See www.arcworld.org/about.asp?pageID=2 (accessed August 31, 2008).

12. The employment of environmental economists, ecologists, and anthropologists was at least in part due to pressure from NGOs and activist groups that continually highlighted the World Bank's inability to achieve sustainable development. While the Bank continues to operate with economic considerations as its primary concern, it has at least exhibited some ability to include the perspectives of others, which for Palmer and others is a hopeful sign.

13. Friends of the Earth was founded in 1969 by David Brower (himself no Christian—a point that is important in the discussion below), longtime president of the Sierra Club (see Van Horn & Blackwelder 2005). Brower later left the organization, but Friends of the Earth continued to flourish. It is a multifaceted environmental activist

organization, with programs focused on global warming, energy, government, industry, and transportation (among others). For more information see www.foe.org/ (accessed February 5, 2009).

14. Friends of the Earth is not an explicitly Christian organization, nor is it entirely comprised of Christians. Its governance structures are rather decentralized and the constituency diverse.

15. At the Creation Care Conference in Longwood, Florida, Cizik asked the audience, who, in today's world, is our "neighbor"? His answer was detailed in Chapter 7, and followed by a story of his visit to the Arctic where he saw Native Americans whose lives were literally being washed away by rising seas. He told those gathered, "This is today's civil rights issue!" (February 21, 2008).

16. She referred to an armed conflict with communist-backed forces in Vietnam. US involvement in the conflict began with the deployment of military advisors in 1950, continued through the commitment of battle units in 1965, and ended in 1973.

17. To be fair, biodiversity has arguably had a significant impact on national environmental policy in the US (see Takacs 1996). It has also manifested in international declarations and statements such as the Convention on Biodiversity, but these measures typically depend on voluntary compliance. Palmer's point, I believe, was that while such words may be useful policy devices they do little to inform the moral sensibilities of the typical layperson. Zimmerman ([1998] 1995) has likewise suggested that concepts derived from holistic sciences (he was particularly speaking of quantum mechanics) have little bearing on people's ethical formations. The extent to which biodiversity and similar terms have shaped public understandings of nature is certainly an empirical question, but one that has not yet been tackled.

18. There has been significant resistance to the idea that specific religious traditions can and should be "mined" to get at the glimmers of "green" that appear when looking through the lenses of ecological concern (see for example Larson 1989). I am generally in accord with such criticisms. Some of the "gems" mined from particular religious traditions do, however, seem to seep into the economy of ideas that feeds the sustainability milieu.

19. See www.theregenerationproject.org/Resources.htm for film resources related to various denominations and faiths (accessed September 2, 2008).

20. Smith noted that his job title and description were highly flexible, and in large part depended on the project and the groups with whom he was working. Most of his work, however, fell under the Sacred Land Project. For more information on the Sacred Land Project see www.arcworld.org/projects.asp?projectID=9 (accessed August 15, 2011).

21. He was referring to Mary Evelyn Tucker, one of the leaders of the Forum on Religion and Ecology. Khalid had worked with Tucker on several projects previously, and stated that they were friends.

22. Palmer told me that at the founding event for ARC, and since, he has insisted that both a poet and an artist are present at all ARC events and meetings (interview May 27, 2008). They provide artists' renderings of the events through their own media.

23. This poem is unpublished. Palmer read it to me from a piece of paper.

24. There is an extensive literature on this subject from the field of strategic management. A review of this literature is beyond the scope of this study, but see for example Banathy's "Designing Social Systems in a Changing World" (1997), Schwartz's *The Art of the Long View* ([1991] 1996: 227–48), and Cowan and Todorovic's "Spiral Dynamics: the Layers of Human Values in Strategy" (2000).

25. The building had bombproof walls in some places and its fortress-like appearance did little to add to the community's esteem, according to Smith.

26. This is certainly not to argue that the inclusion of religious values in the public sphere always leads to environmentally responsible behaviors or attitudes. Many religious groups strongly resist environmental values. However, sustainable human–habitat interactions are unlikely to develop unless adaptive and empathetic relationships develop among human populations, the species with the broadest impact upon habitats. Thus, many sustainability advocates, particularly those motivated by social justice, often focus first on this human dimension of sustainability.

27. CARE is a non-profit organization founded in 1945 to provide aid to refugee survivors from the Second World War. It is now one of the world's largest humanitarian organizations, and according to their website 90 per cent of their 2007 expenditures were directly targeted at helping women (see www.care.org/, accessed February 7, 2009).

28. For more information on Episcopal canons, see footnote 6, this chapter.

29. The book was *Faith in Conservation* (Palmer & Finlay 2003).

30. The FORE is a research, education, and outreach-focused organization. The conferences hosted by the CSWR included leaders from ten of the world's global religions, as well as leaders from higher education, economists, scientists, ethicists, and policy experts. See http://fore.research.yale.edu/information/about/index.html for more information and history (accessed March 22, 2009).

31. The event was envisioned as "deepening ... the global dialogue called for by the Earth Charter" (Pigem 2007: 4).

32. Taylor's assessment (2010) is that the Earth Charter has been important in international elucidations of sustainability. Palmer's comment, however, suggests that while the Earth Charter and similar declarations are important at the international scale, most laypersons (particularly in the developing world) remain unfamiliar with them.

33. Again, this point is an empirical question, and one that begs for further clarification and elaboration.

34. This is likely, in part at least, due to the influence of Maoist ideas on both Palmer and Khalid and their long-standing concern with social equity and pluralism.

35. A caveat is in order here, for DeWitt does not endorse the minimum common denominator ethic endorsed by these others. Instead he prefers what he referred to as a "maximum" common denominator ethic.

36. For example, Palmer told me that "Secularism itself is an ideology. It seeks to impose one model upon the world, and there is no space for anybody else" (interview May 28, 2008). Laushkin said that consumerism was "the pedestal by which we measure all things," and pointed out "that's not the Christian message". He went on to suggest that "You find a lot of the things you can do to, you know, reduce your environmental impact, comport to simple living, you know, having more time for family, and community, things that are more wholesome" (interview May 13, 2008).

37. This is from the "Series Foreword" of the FORE volumes. It appears in all of the FORE volumes, but the pagination here is from *Buddhism and Ecology* (1997), the first volume of the series.

38. They may be imagined as erosive primarily because the cultural inspirations that some scholars utilize can romanticize cultural others as instructive, which raises problematic questions about indigenous authenticity, which in some cases is adjudicated by cultural outsiders (i.e. government bodies). In addition, the idea that culturally marginalized peoples can become politically efficacious to the extent that they become adept at utilizing a language and set of metaphors agreed upon in a public sphere that has typically excluded them is often raised. See Arne Kalland's "The Religious Environmentalist Paradigm" (Kalland 2005: 1369–70) for a good summary of these critiques.

39. It should still be noted that Tucker and Grim are deeply indebted to Thomas Berry and Pierre Teilhard de Chardin (who was a significant influence on Thomas Berry). Although Berry's theology dampened the overtly Christian overtones and rather extreme form of human exceptionalism endorsed by Teilhard, the worldview of both authors is decidedly Western in origin and orientation. Questions remain then about the applicability of a common denominator set of environmental obligations grounded in concepts native to the West (such as Berry's epic of evolution).

40. Although historians and ethnographers have investigated differential interpretations of the same events among American Indian and European groups (see for example Barr 2004; Griffiths & Cervantes 1999; Gutierrez 1991, especially 3–141), little scholarly attention has attended to fleshing out differences in understandings of sustainability between different cultures.

41. Robin Wright's article on the Baniwa Art Project (2009) and Teresa Trusty's dissertation "The Politics of Representing Nature, Culture, and Conservation in Northwestern Bolivia" (unpublished 2009), targeted this question.

42. Taylor has argued that dark green environmentalist sentiment, although often viewed as dangerous or harmful, is unlikely to promote oppression, violence or terror (Taylor 2004b, 2010).

43. "Greenwashing" is a pejorative term used to describe misuse of sustainability-related rhetoric to describe practices that are not actually sustainable. Recent attention to what advocates have referred to as "clean coal" is an excellent example, since many environmentalists maintain that there can be no such thing. For examples of clean coal arguments see www.americaspower.org/The-Facts/77-Percent-Cleaner (accessed January 27, 2009). This website is sponsored by a coalition of coal-based electricity producers.

44. Some Christians believe that near the eschaton ("end of times") all of the righteous souls will be lifted to Heaven to avoid the fiery fate of the rest of creation. This ascension is called the rapture.

45. See Chapter 9 for more details about Hunter Lovins and her organization Natural Capitalism Solutions.

46. For more information about the Sacred Gifts program, see www.arcworld.org/projects. asp?projectId=49 (accessed February 21, 2009).

9. THE RELIGIOUS DIMENSIONS OF SECULAR SUSTAINABILITY

1. See www.conservation.org/discover/about_us/Pages/mission.aspx for their mission, and http://www.conservation.org/discover/about_us/Pages/strategy.aspx for their strategy (accessed October 8, 2008).

2. See www.conservation.org/discover/about_us/partners/Pages/partnerslist.aspx for CI's list of partners (accessed October 8, 2008). A Rocha, Portuguese for "The Rock," is an international Christian conservation organization that provides research, community education, ecological advice, and community involvement plans for conservation of threatened habitats and species through eco-tourism or other means. Their first center was a field study site and bird observatory that drew thousands of visitors from across the world. See www.arocha.org/int-en/index.html for more information (accessed February 25, 2009).

3. WorldVision is a Christian relief and development agency primarily targeting children and families in underserved areas. Their website claims that 86 per cent of their revenue went directly to relief for children and families in 2007, and that globally they provide

relief to over 100 million people in over 100 countries (see www.worldvision.org/home. nsf/index.htm, accessed February 25, 2009).

4. Brower was elected the executive director of the Sierra Club in 1952, serving until his removal in 1967, following which he founded Friends of the Earth (1969) and later the Earth Island Institute (1982) (Van Horn & Blackwelder 2005: 225). He was often referred to as the "Archdruid" of the environmental movement (see McPhee 1971).

5. From roundtable discussion at the University of Florida, September 2007.

6. Lovins and her then husband Amory founded the RMI in 1982. For more information about the RMI see www.rmi.org/ (accessed February 25, 2009).

7. See www.natcapsolutions.org/Hunter_Lovins.htm (accessed October 8, 2008).

8. See www.nwei.org/n_american_network (accessed August 16, 2011).

9. See www.nwei.org/discussion_courses (accessed October 8, 2008).

10. Macy suggested that many activists are using that term now.

11. Korten's website describes him as an "author, lecturer, and engaged citizen" (www. davidkorten.org/home, accessed February 25, 2009). He is often referred to as an economist, but his training was in psychology and behavioral systems. He achieved the rank of captain in the US Air Force, was a research scientist with the Pentagon, taught at Harvard Business school, was a project manager for the Ford Foundation, a regional development specialist for the US Agency for International Development (USAID), has been involved in the International Forum on Globalization, and helped found the Business Alliance for Local Living Alliances (BALLE) and *YES!* Magazine, whose motto is "Supporting you in building a just and sustainable world" (www.yesmagazine.org/, accessed February 25, 2009).

12. Stories are passed through cultures, Korten believes, and eventually achieve a critical mass when they are accepted by enough of the population. According to systems theory, natural systems undergo a series of changes commonly labeled *exploitation, conservation, release*, and *reorganization* (see Gunderson & Holling 2002). This idea coheres with Korten's and Macy's idea that we are at a cultural crossroads, a moment of "reorganization."

13. Paul Hawken (2007b) used the phrase "re-making the world" to suggest, as has Macy, that these movements are cooperating in significant ways.

14. For example, deep ecology was often contrasted with "shallow" ecology. The latter was portrayed as mired in anthropocentrism and not sensitive to the spiritual or affective dimensions of species and habitat loss (Naess 1973). Such deep ecological sentiments were also criticized by many scholars (Bookchin 1987; Zimmerman 2000) as potentially fascist and inattentive to the dangers of universalizing discourse.

15. They disseminated this piece through the internet, and through sustainability and environmentalist networks and listervs. The full text is available online at www. thebreakthrough.org (accessed October 10, 2008).

16. "The Death of Environmentalism" argued that the old environmentalist paradigms based on pollution prevention and conservation were inadequate to address environmental issues at the global level, particularly climate change. The old environmentalism needed to die, they believed, before the next phase of sustainable cultural development could ensue. Nordhaus and Shellenberger went on to publish a book called *Break Through* (2007) which began with the death of environmentalism and concluded with what they called the "Politics of Possibility," an extended attempt to envision a positive political paradigm that included nature as a political entity (rather than merely a background consideration).

17. For more information on Randy Hayes and RAN see Hayes's "From Hopiland to the Rainforest Action Network" (2005). Hayes co-founded RAN with Mike Roselle, one of the co-founders of EarthFirst!, another radical environmental organization. Lovins's ability to cooperate with both the corporate entities and relatively radical environmentalists makes her a paradigm case of the new generation of sustainability activists whose allegiances are not bounded by ideologies.

18. Atran, Medin, and Ross draw on Michael Cole for some of this work. Part of Cole's research that is relevant to this discussion is his idea of *mediated cognition*, which suggests that human minds are formed in and through their interactions with others through a sort of empathetic projection and inference. Cole has suggested that "human psychological processes are acquired in the process of mediating one's interactions with others and the physical world through culture and its central medium, language. Humans are created in joint, mediated activity" (Cole 1998: 292). See also Cole's "Phylogeny and Cultural History in Ontogeny" (2007). Burgess Wilson's (2011) fascinating empathetic theory of religion also coheres in important ways with the argument advanced by Cole and this work.

19. Neo-conservative is a label used to describe people who, at least in the United States, tend toward the right of the political spectrum and attach their political perspectives to normative and often religious ideas.

20. Lovins was referring to Arnold Schwartzenegger, former governor of the state of California. Schwartzenegger previously starred in a trilogy of movies as a "terminator" robot from the future, sent to kill (and in the sequels, protect) the leaders of human resistance to robot rule in the future. He was elected governor in 2002.

21. Edwards goes on to say that, "Understanding these statements can shed light on the motivations of the groups in the Sustainability Revolution and provide a way of tracking the evolution of their core values over time" (Edwards 2005: 26–7). Such core values and their evolution and transmission are the subject of this book.

22. The selection was drawn from Orr's "The Coming Biophilia Revolution" in his book *Earth in Mind* (1994).

23. The original interview was published in 1997 as "Science as Wisdom: The New Story as a Way Forward," in a journal called *EarthLight* (**26**: 10–11, 15, 22) (see Swimme 1997 in bibliography). *EarthLight* is an eco-spirituality journal published in Oakland, California (see www.earthlight.org/index.html, accessed August 16, 2011).

24. The NWEI reader draws the selection from Andrew Dobson's *The Green Reader* (1991). The original appears in Lovelock (1979: 152, vii, 9–11, 19–20, 25–6).

25. The Lord of the Rings is a trilogy of books by J. R. R. Tolkein which depicts an epic struggle between good and evil. For more on how these myths are related to socio-political and environmental themes, see Curry ([1997] 2004).

26. Martin Palmer compared the polar bear to a Christ figure, tactically deployed by environmentalists (interview May 27, 2008).

27. A "full complement" of animals refers to the belief that all of Earth's creatures were created as they are today. This idea is a direct challenge to the scientific theory of macroevolution, where an entirely new species evolves from a pre-existing one. Campbell's perception, which was echoed by Hunter and Randall, illustrates the perception among evangelicals that many non-evangelical US citizens have a rather negative portrait of evangelicals, particularly when it comes to their acceptance of science.

28. Keep in mind that each individual is not accountable to just one community, but rather is involved in a variable set of nested communities, and thus each individual's vision of

sustainability is likely to be couched in a narrative that somehow weaves together the values of these different communities.

29. The UN Conference Climate Change Conference took place December 3–14, 2007, and was envisioned as an effort to extend the work of the Kyoto Protocol. The Kyoto Protocol, proposed by the UN Framework Convention on Climate Change (UNFCCC, a product of the 1992 Rio Earth Summit), was approved in 1997 and went into effect in 2005. The Protocol, signed by 184 countries, creates targets for thirty-seven industrialized nations for CO_2 reduction (see http://unfccc.int/kyoto_protocol/items/2830.php, accessed March 6, 2009).

30. Lovins's claim that she deploys narratives related to mythic good and evil struggles, stories with clearly spiritual undertones, however, signals that this is an important, if implicit type of religious production.

31. Willard spent thirty-four years as a top executive at IBM and has combined his business background with his interest in sustainability. He is the author of *The Next Sustainability Wave: Building Boardroom Buy-in* (2005). Willard's argument is that, in the business and industrial sectors, sustainability is no longer merely a reaction to market pressures nor relegated to passionate individuals who single-handedly implement new corporate cultures within existing organizations. Rather, in Willard's view, sustainability in business and industry is driven by an increasingly solid business case for sustainability coupled with shifting consumer attitudes, creating an ideal opportunity to couple increasing standards of living globally with good business sense.

32. Campbell told me he was an environmentalist before he accepted Christ as an adult, so he was an environmentalist before he was an evangelical.

33. Hurricane Katrina struck the US city of New Orleans in 2005, with devastating results. The original version of this article appeared in *Orion* in the 2006 September/October issue. Van Jones is a well-known sustainability and social justice activist.

34. By "family members" Jones was not referring merely to immediate family, but rather to whole communities of people who depend on each other for their well-being. Jones is referring to something akin to the long-standing idea of "mutual aid," first popularized by anarchist philosopher Peter Kropotkin ([1902] 2008).

35. The phrase Axial Age was first deployed by Karl Jaspers to refer to the period between 900 BCE and 200 BCE, during which such important figures as Socrates, Elijah, Siddhartha, Confucius, and Lao-Tzu lived. Karen Armstrong's narrative suggests that many of the world religions arose out of the socio-political matrix of that region and time and are basically context-specific enactments of a universal human religious experience.

36. This is from the subtitle to the book, *How the Largest Movement in the World Came Into Being, and Why No One Saw It Coming* (2007).

37. This selection was drawn from an article entitled "To Remake the World" in *Orion* magazine (June/July 2007).

38. This is a poem included in the volume attributed simply to "the Hopi Elders."

39. The fields of ethnobotany (Schultes 1979; Schultes & Von Reis [1995] 2008) and ethnoecology (Posey *et al.* 1984) have long histories and pioneered the theories and methods later expanded by scholars such as Berkes. The intentional blending of indigenous lifeways with the science of adaptive ecosystem management specifically, however, emerged in the 1990s.

40. See Deloria's *God is Red* (1992: 9, 21–2) for further discussion.

41. Jennifer Sumner claims that this counter-hegemonic component is one of the three primary foundations of sustainability, along with dialogue and life values (Sumner 2005: 112).

42. For a response to Krech's argument see Deloria (2000).
43. The speech was reprinted earlier in a chapter titled "A World Restored" in David Brower and Steve Chappel's *Let the Mountains Talk, Let the Rivers Run* (1995).
44. See www.nyo.unep.org/ifp.htm (accessed October 19, 2008).
45. This poem is from "Only One Earth," a United Nations Environment Programme publication for "Environmental Sabbath/Earth Rest Day," June 1990. The UN website suggested that the text would be available shortly (www.nyo.unep.org/ifp.htm). I was only able to find the text online at http://earthministry.org/resources/worship-aids/sample-worship-services/the-united-nations-environmental-sabbath-service (accessed November 15, 2012). Earth Ministry is a non-profit organization based in the Puget Sound area dedicated to promoting sustainable lifestyles and decisions for congregations and individuals.
46. Evan Berry argued that both are potentially productive ways of looking at social movements that involve religion. The analogical approach suggests that it is primarily the religious *form* that is the vehicle for cultural transmission, but according to Berry "structural functionalism and other social scientific theories of 'quasi-religions' tend to obscure the religiosity of nature religion" (Berry 2009: 13). Genealogical explanations are stronger, particularly when analyzing nature religion. Berry presented this particular article at the "Inherited Land" colloquium at Florida International University, February 28, 2009.

10. MANUFACTURING OR CULTIVATING COMMON GROUND?

1. The first pages of the *Choices for Sustainable Living* module, however, make it clear that there are a variety of definitions of sustainability used to support widely divergent sets of practices.
2. Campbell mused about how slow secular conservation organizations have been to warm to the possibility of potentially powerful partnerships with religious groups. He noted that "WorldVision [a Christian NGO] is a $2.1 billion a year organization, with 34,000 employees working in over 100 countries. By that comparison, CI ... one of the 'Big Three' conservation organizations ... [with] about 1,000 employees in 40 countries ... is a minor player" (interview July 29, 2008).
3. Palmer reported, "I think sustainable development has been superseded by the Millennium Development Goals, which are in a transition state, half about sustainable development and optimistic, and half, 'oh no, we're going to hell!' I do think this [the negative message] drives people away [from engaging in sustainable behaviors]" (interview May 27, 2008).
4. Add to it some evangelicals' perception that environmentalism is itself quasi-religious and sometimes shares affinities with pagan beliefs, and that secular humanism is also a sort of "religion," and it becomes unsurprising that they would not use the term "sustainability" to describe their manner of combining concern for financial well-being with social justice and ecological integrity. The evangelical perception that they are somehow "outside" of the mainstream culture because of their commitment to Christ, and yet called to exact positive political change through mainstream mechanisms (such as prevailing social and economic structures) begs for more careful investigation.
5. The importance of the idea of sustainability to the grassroots organization NWEI may challenge the contention that, in general, grassroots groups are less apt to utilize the

term sustainability. They are a secular organization, however, which raises the question of whether the importance of sustainability as a cognitive tool in secular organizations is able to overcome a general reticence to deploy such terms to describe local level issues. This is an empirical question.

6. Taylor has suggested that in the very long term it is possible that a terrapolitan earth religion could be grafted onto, and eventually supplant (or make less common) most theistic forms of religion, since such theistic understandings typically have at least some elements that do not resonate with evolutionary theory (Taylor 2004; 2010: 196–8). Research from demographer James Proctor and religion scholar Evan Berry, however, suggest that even an increase in nature religion may not necessarily cause a decrease in the prevalence of religions grounded in transcendent theism. Their studies have revealed that "transcendent sacredness" and "nonsacredness" represent opposing poles on the same underlying psychological factor (for a summary argument see Proctor and Berry 2005 and the suggested further readings). "Immanent sacredness," however, is a relatively separate factor: "those who believe that nature is inherently sacred thus may or may not (despite possible logical contradictions) ascribe to transcendent sacredness or non-sacredness" (Proctor & Berry 2005: 1574). Taylor's concept of dark green religion is in many ways parallel to this idea of immanent sacredness, but if Proctor and Berry are correct then dark green religion may well coexist with transcendently oriented religious ideation and practice that are decidedly anthropocentric. On the other hand, one might not resonate with immanent sacredness at all, and yet work toward sustainability.

7. There is an extensive literature debating whether religion is in any way adaptive. Others who offer a definition of religion that is not functional in the evolutionary sense include Guthrie (1993), Boyer (2001), Atran *et al.* (2002) and Dawkins (2006). On the other hand, the most sophisticated approach to explaining religion with a group adaptationist approach is David Sloan Wilson's *Darwin's Cathedral* (2002). For Wilson a religion is a set of socially defined norms that are subject to natural selection, and is thus one of the primary variables determining the survivability of that society.

BIBLIOGRAPHY

Anielski, M. 2007. *The Economics of Happiness*. Gabriola Island, BC: New Society Publishers.

Appadurai, A. 2003. "Disjuncture and Difference in the Global Cultural Economy." In *Theorizing Diaspora: A Reader*, J. Braziel & A. Mannur (eds), 23–48. Oxford: Blackwell.

Armstrong, K. 2007. *The Great Transformation: The Beginning of Our Religious Traditions*. New York: Anchor Books.

Asad, T. 1993. *Genealogies of Religion: Disciplines and Reasons of Power in Christianity and Islam*. Baltimore, MD: Johns Hopkins University Press.

Atran, S. & D. L. Medin 2008. *The Cultural Mind and the Cultural Construction of Nature*. Cambridge, MA: MIT Press.

Atran, S. *et al.* 2002. "Folkecology, Cultural Epidemiology, and the Spirit of the Commons: A Garden Experiment in the Maya Lowlands, 1991–2001." *Current Anthropology* **43**(3) (June): 421–50.

Atran, S., D. L. Medin & N. O. Ross. 2005. "The Cultural Mind: Environmental Decision Making and Cultural Modeling Within and Across Populations." *Psychological Review* **112**(4): 744–76.

Baker, S. 2006. *Sustainable Development*. London: Routledge.

Ban, Ki-moon 2007. *Ban Ki-Moon's Address to the National Association of Evangelicals*. Washington, DC, available at www.un.org/apps/news/infocus/sgspeeches/search_full. asp?statID=140 (accessed November 15, 2012).

Banathy, B. H. 1997. "Designing Social Systems in a Changing World: A Journey to Create our Future." *Systemist* **19**(3): 187–216.

Barnhill, D. L. 2002. "An Interwoven World: Gary Snyder's Cultural Ecosystem." *Worldviews* **6**(2): 111–44.

Barr, J. 2004. "A Diplomacy of Gender: Rituals of First Contact in the 'Land of Tejas.'" *The William and Mary Quarterly* (**61**)3: 393–434.

Bekoff, M. 2007. *The Emotional Lives of Animals: A Leading Scientist Explores Animal Joy, Sorrow and Empathy—and Why They Matter*. Novato, CA: New World Library.

Bellah, R. 1970. *Beyond Belief: Essays on Religion in a Post-Traditional World*. New York: Harper & Row.

Benford, R. D. & D. A. Snow 2000. "Framing Processes and Social Movements: An Overview and Assessment." *Annual Review of Sociology* **26**: 611–39.

239

Benthall, J. 2006. "Archeology and Anthropology as Religious Movements." *Anthropology Today* **22**(5): 1–2.

Benthall, J. 2008. *Returning to Religion: Why a Secular Age is Haunted by Faith*. London: I. B. Tauris.

Berkes, F. 1999. *Sacred Ecology: Traditional Ecological Knowledge and Resource Management*. Philadelphia, PA: Taylor & Francis.

Berkes, F. [1999] 2008. *Sacred Ecology*, 2nd edn. New York: Routledge.

Berkes, F., C. Folke & J. Colding 1998. *Linking Social and Ecological Systems: Management Practices and Social Mechanisms for Building Resilience*. Cambridge: Cambridge University Press.

Berkes, F., J. Colding & C. Folke (eds.) 2002. *Navigating Social-Ecological Systems: Building Resilience for Complexity and Change*. Cambridge: Cambridge University Press.

Berry, E. 2009. "Nature Religion and the Problem of Authenticity." Paper presented at the Inherited Land Colloquium, 28 February, Florida International University.

Berry, T. M. 1988. *The Dream of the Earth*. San Francisco, CA: Sierra Club Books.

Blackmore, S. 1999. *The Meme Machine*. Oxford: Oxford University Press.

Bohm, D. [1980] 2002. *Wholeness and the Implicate Order*. London: Routledge.

Bookchin, M. 1987. "Social Ecology versus 'Deep Ecology'." *Green Perspectives* **4–5**.

Borg, M. 1994. *Meeting Jesus Again for the First Time*. New York: Harper Collins.

Boyer, P. 2001. *Religion Explained: The Evolutionary Origins of Religious Thought*. New York: Basic Books.

Brower, D & S. Chappel 1995. *Let the Mountains Talk, Let the Rivers Run*. New York: Harper Collins.

Bruhenn, H. 1997. "Ecological Approaches to the Study of Religion." *Method and Theory in the Study of Religion* **9**(2): 111–26.

Buck, S. J. 2004. "No Tragedy of the Commons." In *Green Planet Blues*, K. Conca & G. D. Dabelko (eds). Boulder, CO: Westview Press.

Bulbulia, J. 2004. "The Cognitive and Evolutionary Psychology of Religion." *Biology and Philosophy* **19**: 655–86.

Callicott, J. B. 1985. "Intrinsic Value, Quantum Theory, and Environmental Ethics." *Environmental Ethics* **7**: 257–75.

Callicott, J. B. 1994. *Earth's Insights: A Multicultural Survey of Ecological Ethics from the Mediterranean Basin to the Australian Outback*. Berkeley, CA: University of California Press.

Campbell, C. 1972. "The Cult, the Cultic Milieu and Secularization." *A Sociological Yearbook of Britain* **5**: 119–36.

Campbell, C. 2002. "The Cult, the Cultic Milieu and Secularization." In *The Cultic Milieu: Oppositional Subcultures in an Age of Globalization*, J. Kaplan & H. Loow (eds), 12–25. Walnut Creek, CA: AltaMira.

Capra, F. [1975] 1984. *The Tao of Physics*. Boulder, CO: Shambhala.

Capra, F. 2002. *The Hidden Connections: Integrating the Biological, Cognitive, and Social Dimensions of Life into a Science of Sustainability*. New York: Doubleday.

Cardoso de Oliveira, R. [1964] 1972. O Indio e o Mundo dos Brancos; Uma Interpretação Sociológica da Situação dos Tukúna. [The Indian and the World of the Whites: A Sociological Interpretation of the Situation of the Tukúna], 2nd edn, São Paulo: Livraria Pioneira Editôra.

Carr, M. 2005. *Bioregionalism and Civil Society: Democratic Challenges to Corporate Globalism*. Seattle, WA: University of Washington Press.

Catton, W. R. 1980. *Overshoot: The Ecological Basis of Revolutionary Change*. Urbana, IL: University of Illinois Press.

Chapman, A., R. L. Peterson & B. Smith-Moran (eds) 2000. *Consumption, Population, and Sustainability: Perspectives from Science and Religion*. Washington, DC: Island Press.

Chidester, D. 2005a. *Authentic Fakes*. Berkeley, CA: University of California Press.

Chidester, D. 2005b. "Animism." In *Encyclopedia of Religion and Nature*, B. Taylor (ed.), 78–81. London: Continuum.

Clifton, C. 2005. "Entheogens." In *Encyclopedia of Religion and Nature*, B. Taylor (ed.), 596–7. London: Continuum.

Cobb, J. & D. R. Griffin (eds) 1977. *Mind in Nature: Essays on the Interface of Science and Philosophy*. Lanham, MD: University Press of America.

Cole, M. 1998. "Can Cultural Psychology Help Us Think About Diversity?" *Mind, Culture and Activity* 5(4): 291–304.

Cole, M. 2007. "Phylogeny and Cultural History in Ontogeny." *Journal of Physiology* 101: 236–46.

Commission on Global Governance 1995. *Our Global Neighborhood: The Basic Vision*. Oxford: Oxford University Press.

Conklin, B. A. & L. R. Graham 1995. "The Shifting Middle-Ground: Amazonian Indians and Eco-Politics." *American Anthropologist* 97(4): 695–710.

Costanza, R. & C. Folke 1997. "Valuing Ecosystem Services with Efficiency, Sustainability, and Fairness as Goals." In *Nature's Services: Societal Dependence on Natural Ecosystems*, G. Daily (ed.), 49–68. Washington DC: Island Press.

Costanza, R., L. Graumlich & W. Steffen (eds) 2007. *Sustainability or Collapse: an Integrated History and Future of People on Earth*. Cambridge: MIT Press and the Freie Universitat Berlin.

Cowan, C. C. & N. Todorovic 2000. "Spiral Dynamics: The Layers of Human Values in Strategy." *Strategy and Leadership* 28: 4–11.

Cronon, W. 1996a. "The Trouble with Wilderness: A Response." *Environmental History* 1(1): 47–55.

Cronon, W. 1996b. "The Trouble with Wilderness; or, Getting Back to the Wrong Nature." In *Uncommon Ground: Toward Reinventing Nature*, W. Cronon (ed.). New York: W.W. Norton and Company.

Crosby, D. 2002. *A Religion of Nature*. Albany, NY: SUNY Press.

Curry, P. [1997] 2004. *Defending Middle Earth: Tolkein: Myth and Modernity*. New York: Houghton Mifflin.

Daly, H. E. [1973] 1980. *Economics, Ecology, Ethics: Essays Toward a Steady-State Economy*. San Francisco, CA: W. H. Freeman.

Daly, H. E. 1996. *Beyond Growth: The Economics of Sustainable Development*. Boston, MA: Beacon Press.

Darlington, S. M. 2005. "Thai Buddhist Monks." In *Encyclopedia of Religion and Nature*, B. Taylor (ed.), 1629–30. London: Continuum.

Damasio, A. 1994. *Descartes' Error: Emotion, Reason and the Human Brain*. New York: Penguin.

Damasio, A. 2000. *The Feeling of What Happens*. San Diego, CA: Harcourt Press.

Darwin, C. [1871] 1981. *The Descent of Man, and Selection in Relation to Sex*. Princeton, NJ: Princeton University Press.

Davison, A. 2001. *Technology and the Contested Meanings of Sustainability*. Albany, NY: SUNY Press.

Dawkins, R. 1976. *The Selfish Gene*. Oxford: Oxford University Press.

Dawkins, R. 2006. *The God Delusion*. New York: Houghton Mifflin.

Delgado, S. 2007. *Shaking the Gates of Hell: Faith-Led Resistance to Corporate Globalization*. Minneapolis, MN: Augsburg Press.

Deloria, V. 1992. *God is Red: A Native View of Religion*, 2nd edn. Golden, CO: North American Press.

Deloria, V. 1997. *Red Earth, White Lies: Native Americans and the Myth of Scientific Fact*. Golden, CO: Fulcrum Press.

Deloria, V. 2000. "The Speculations of Krech." *Worldviews* **4**(3): 283–93.

Dennett, D. C. 2006. *Breaking the Spell: Religion as a Natural Phenomenon*. New York: Viking Press.

Deudney, D. 1998. "Global Village Sovereignty: Intergenerational Sovereign Publics, Federal-Republican Earth Constitutions, and Planetary Identities." In *The Greening of Sovereignty in World Politics*, K. Litfin (ed.). Cambridge, MA: MIT Press.

DeWitt, C. B. 2006. "The Scientist and the Shepherd: The Emergence of Evangelical Environmetnalism." In *The Oxford Handbook of Religion and Ecology*, R. Gottlieb (ed.), 569–87. Oxford: Oxford University Press.

Distin, K. 2005. *The Selfish Meme: A Critical Reassessment*. Cambridge: Cambridge University Press.

Dobson, A. 1991. *The Green Reader*. San Francisco, CA: Mercury House Press.

Dowd, M. 2008. *Thank God for Evolution!: How the Marriage of Science and Religion Will Transform Your Life and Our World*. New York: Viking.

Dresner, S. 2005. *The Principles of Sustainable Development*. London: Earthscan.

Dubuisson, D. 2003. *The Western Construction of Religion: Myths, Knowledge, and Ideology*. Baltimore, MD: Johns Hopkins University Press.

Dudley, N., L. Higgins-Zogib & Stephanie Mansourian (eds) 2005. *Beyond Belief: Linking Faiths and Protected Areas to Support Biodiversity Conservation*. Gland: World Wide Fund for Nature.

Dunlap, T. R. 2004. *Faith in Nature: Environmentalism as Religious Quest*. Weyerhaeuser Environmental Books, W. Cronon (ed.). Seattle, WA: University of Washington Press.

Durkheim, E. 1972. *Selected Writings*, A. Giddens (ed.). Cambridge: Cambridge University Press.

Durkheim, E. [1912] 1995. *The Elementary Forms of Religious Life*, K. E. Fields (trans.). New York: Free Press.

Edwards, A. 2005. *The Sustainability Revolution: Portrait of a Paradigm Shift*. Gabriola Island, BC: New Society Publishers.

Ehrlich, P. 1968. *The Population Bomb*. New York: Ballantine.

Einsten, A., B. Podolsky & N. Rosen 1935. "Can Quantum-Mechanical Description of Physical Reality be Considered Complete?". *Physical Review* **47** (10): 777–80.

Eliade, M. 1959. *The Sacred and the Profane; the Nature of Religion* [1st American edn]. New York: Harcourt.

Eliade, M. 1964. *Shamanism: Archaic Techniques of Ecstasy* [rev. and enl. edn]. New York: Bollingen Foundation.

Elliott, K. 2007. "Norton's Conception of Sustainability: Political, Not Metaphysical." *Environmental Ethics* **29** (2007): 3–22.

Elliot, M. 2008. "Tony Blair's Leap of Faith." *Time* **171**(23): 26–30.

Emmerij, L., R. Jolly & T. G. Weiss 2001. *Ahead of the Curve?: UN Ideas and Global Challenge*. Bloomington, IN: Indiana University Press.

Escobar, A. 1995. *Encountering Development: The Making and Unmaking of the Third World*. Princeton, NJ: Princeton University Press.

Everett, H. 1957. "Relative State Formulation of Quantum Mechanics." *Review of Modern Physics* **29**: 454–62.

Ferrè, F. 2003. "Review of *Environmental Ethics, Ecological Theology and Natural Selection*, by Lisa Sideris". *Soundings* **86**(3–4): 469–77.

Fiege, M. 2007. "The Atomic Scientists, the Sense of Wonder, and the Bomb." *Environmental History* **12**: 578–613.

Frazer, J. G. [1890] 1959. *The New Golden Bough: A New Abridgment of the Classic Work*. New York: Criterion Books.

Freud, S. [1918] 1998. *Totem and Taboo: Resemblances Between the Psychic Lives of Savages and Neurotics*. Mineola, NY: Dover Publications.

Gardner, G. 2002. "Invoking the Spirit: Religion and Spirituality in the Quest for a Sustainable World." In *Worldwatch Paper* **164**, Jane Peterson (ed.). Washington, DC: Worldwatch Institute.

Garè, A. 1998. "MacIntyre, Narratives, and Environmental Ethics." *Environmental Ethics* **21**(2): 3–19.

Gatta, J. 2004. *Making Nature Sacred: Literature, Religion, and Environment in America from the Puritans to the Present*. New York: Oxford University Press.

Geertz, A. 2004. "Can We Move Beyond Primitivism? On Recovering the Indigenes of Indigenous Religions in the Academic Study of Religion". In *Beyond Primitivism: Indigenous Religious Traditions and Modernity*, J. Olupona (ed.). New York: Routledge.

Geertz, A. W. & R. T. McCutcheon 2000. *Perspectives on Method and Theory in the Study of Religion: Adjunct Proceedings of the XVII Congress of the National Association for the History of Religions*. Leiden: Brill.

Geertz, C. 1973. *The Interpretation of Culture: Selected Essays*. New York: Basic Books.

Gerlach, L. P. 1971. "Movements of Revolutionary Change: Some Structural Characteristics." *American Behavioral Scientist* **14**: 812–36.

Gerlach, L. P. 2002. "The Structure of Social Movements: Environmental Activism and Its Opponents." In *Networks and Netwars: The Future of Terror, Crime and Militancy*, J. Arquilla & D. Ronfelt (eds), 289–310. Santa Monica, CA: RAND National Defense Resource Institute.

Gerlach, L. P. and V. Hine 1970. *People, Power, Change: Movements of Social Transformation*. Indianapolis, IN: Bobbs-Merrill.

Gers, M. 2008. "Memes vs. God: Dennett and Dawkins Take on Religion." *Journal for the Study of Religion, Nature and Culture* **2**(4): 508–20.

Ghai, D. & J. M.Vivian (eds) 1992. *Grassroots Environmental Action: People's Participation in Sustainable Development*. London: Routledge.

Gill, S. 1987. *Mother Earth*. Chicago, IL: University of Chicago Press.

Gilroy, J. M. & J. Bowersox (eds) 2002. *The Moral Austerity of Environmental Decision Making: Sustainability, Democracy, and Normative Argument in Policy and Law*. Durham, NC: Duke University Press.

Glacken, C. 1967. *Traces on the Rhodian Shore*. Berkeley, CA: University of California Press.

Goffman, E. 1974. *Frame Analysis: An Essay on the Organization of Experience*. New York: Harper & Row.

Goldsmith, E., R. Allen, M. Allaby, J. Davoll & S. Lawrence 1972. *Blueprint for Survival*. Boston, MA: Houghton Mifflin.

Golliher, J. 1999. "Ethical, Moral and Religious Concerns." In *Cultural and Spiritual Values of Biodiversity*, D. Posey (ed.), 437–48. Nairobi: United Nations Environment Programme.

Gould, R. 2005. *At Home in Nature*. Berkeley, CA: University of California Press.

Gould, S. J. 1999. *Rocks of Ages: Science and Religion in the Fullness of Life*. New York: Ballantine Books.

Griffin, D. R. 1988. *The Reenchantment of Science*. Albany, NY: SUNY Press.

Griffiths, N. & F. Cervantes (eds) 1999. *Spiritual Encounters: Interactions between Christianity and Native Religions in Colonial America*. Birmingham, AL: University of Birmingham Press.

Guinan, M. 1990. *The Pentateuch*. Collegeville, MN: Liturgical Press.

Gula, R. 1989. *Reason Informed by Faith: Foundations of Catholic Morality*. Mahwah, NJ: Paulist Press.

Gunderson, L. & C. S. Holling (eds) 2002. *Panarchy: Understanding Transformations in Human and Natural Systems*. Washington, DC: Island Press.

Guthrie, S. 1993. *Faces in the Clouds: A New Theory of Religion*. Oxford: Oxford University Press.

Gutierrez, R. 1991. *When Jesus Came the Corn Mothers Went Away*. Palo Alto, CA: Stanford University Press.

Haberman, D. 2007. *River of Love in an Age of Pollution*. Berkeley, CA: University of California Press.

Haight, R. 2000. *Jesus: Symbol of God*. Maryknoll, NY: Orbis Books.

Hall, D. (ed.) 1997. *Lived Religion*. Princeton, NJ: Princeton University Press.

Hand, Floyd Looks for Buffalo 1998. *Learning Journey on the Red Road*. Toronto: Learning Journey Communications.

Hardin, G. 1968. "The Tragedy of the Commons." *Science* **162**(3859): 1243–8.

Hardin, G. 1974. "Living on a Lifeboat." *BioScience* **24**(10): 561–8.

Harding, S. 1998. *Is Science Multicultural?: Postcolonialisms, Feminisms, and Epistemologies*. Bloomington, IN: Indiana University Press.

Harner, M. J. 1990 *The Way of the Shaman*, 10th anniversary edn. San Francisco, CA: Harper & Row.

Harris, M. 1966. "The Cultural Ecology of India's Sacred Cattle." *Current Anthropology* **7**(1): 51–4, 55–66.

Hart, J. 2005. "World Conference on Indigenous Peoples." In *Encyclopedia of Religion and Nature*, B. Taylor (ed.), 1763–5. London: Continuum.

Harvey, D. 2005. *A Brief History of Neoliberalism*. Oxford: Oxford University Press.

Hauerwas, S. 1981. *A Community of Character: Toward a Constructive Christian Social Ethic*. Notre Dame: University of Notre Dame Press.

Hawken, P. 2007a. *Blessed Unrest: How the Largest Movement in the World Came Into Being, and Why No One Saw It Coming*. New York: Viking.

Hawken, P. 2007b. "To Remake the World." *Orion* (May/June), http://www.orionmagazine.org/index.php/mag/issue/266/, accessed March 21, 2009.

Hawken, P., A. Lovins & L. H. Lovins 1999. *Natural Capitalism*. London: Little, Brown and Company.

Hayes, R. 2005. "From Hopiland to the Rainforest Action Network." In *Encyclopedia of Religion and Nature*, B. Taylor (ed.). London: Continuum.

Henning, D. 2002. *Buddhism and Deep Ecology*. Bloomington, IN: AuthorHouse.

Hiebert, T. 1996. *The Yahwist's Landscape*. Minneapolis, MN: Fortress Press.

Holden, C. 2006. "Darwin's Place on Campus is Secure – But Not Supreme." *Science* **311** (Feb): 769–71.

Holling, C. S. 1998. "Science, Sustainability, and Resource Management." In F. Berkes and C. Folke (eds.), Cambridge: Cambridge University Press.

Holmes, S. J. 2005. "Muir, John." In *Encyclopedia of Religion and Nature*, Bron Taylor (ed.), 1126–7. London: Continuum.

Hukkinen, J. 2008. *Sustainability Networks: Cognitive Tools for Expert Collaboration in Social-Ecological Systems*. London: Routledge.

Hunter, J. 2006. *Right Wing, Wrong Bird*. Longwood, FL: Distributed Church Press.

Hunter, J. 2007. *Church Distributed: How the Church Can Thrive in the Coming Era of Connection*. Longwood, FL: Distributed Church Press.

Hunter, J. 2008. *A New Kind of Conservative*. Ventura, CA: Regal.

Independent Commission on Disarmament and Security Issues 1982. *Common Security: A Programme for Survival*. London: Pan Books.

International Union for the Conservation of Nature (IUCN), United Nations Environment Program (UNEP), and World Wide Fund for Nature (WWF) 1991. *Caring for the Earth: A Strategy for Sustainable Living*. Gland, Switzerland: IUCN.

Jacobsen, K. A. 2005. "Naess, Arne." In *Encyclopedia of Religion and Nature*, B. Taylor (ed.), 1149–50. London: Continuum.

James, W. [1902] 2002. *The Varieties of Religious Experience*. London: Routledge.

Jensen, T. 1999. "Forming 'The Alliance of Religions and Conservation.'" In *Cultural and Spiritual Values of Biodiversity*, D. Posey (ed.), 492–5. Nairobi: United Nations Environment Programme.

Johnson, M. 1993. *Moral Imagination: Implications of Cognitive Science for Ethics*. Chicago, IL: University of Chicago Press.

Jolly, R., L. Emmerij, D. Ghai & F. Lapeyre (eds) 2004. *UN Contributions to Development Thinking and Practice*. United Nations Intellectual History Project. Bloomington, IN: Indiana University Press.

Jordan III, W. 2003. *The Sunflower Forest: Ecological Restoration and the New Communion With Nature*. Berkeley, CA: University of California Press.

Jung, C. 1968. *Man and His Symbols*. New York: Dell Publishers.

Kalland, A. 2005. "The Religious Environmentalist Paradigm." In *Encyclopedia of Religion and Nature*, B. Taylor (ed.), 1367–71. London: Continuum.

Kaplan, J. & H. Loow (eds) 2002. *The Cultic Milieu: Oppositional Subcultures in an Age of Globalization*. Walnut Creek, CA: AltaMira.

Kelemen, D. 2004. "Are Children 'Intuitive Theists'?: Reasoning About Purpose and Design in Nature." *Psychological Science* 15(5): 295–301.

Kellert, S. 1993a. "Introduction." In *The Biophilia Hypothesis*, S. Kellert and E. O. Wilson (eds), 20–27. Washington, DC: Island Press.

Kellert, S. 1993b. "The Biological Basis for Human Values of Nature." In *The Biophilia Hypothesis*, S. Kellert & E. O. Wilson (eds), 42–69. Washington, DC: Island Press.

Kellert, S. 2005. "Biophilia." In *Encyclopedia of Religion and Nature*, B. Taylor (ed.), 183–8. London: Continuum.

Kellert, S. R. & E. O. Wilson 1993. *The Biophilia Hypothesis*. Washington, DC: Island Press.

Kellert, S. R. & T. J. Farnham (eds) 2002. *The Good in Nature and Humanity: Connecting Science, Religion, and Spirituality*. Washington, DC: Island Press.

Kelley, K. W. [1988] 1991. *The Home Planet*. Moscow: Mir Publishers.

Kenny, M. & J. Meadowcroft (eds) 1999. *Planning Sustainability*. London: Routledge.

Keroauc, J. 1958. *The Dharma Bums*. New York: Viking Press.

Killingsworth, M. & J. Palmer 1992. *Ecospeak: Rhetoric and Environmental Politics in America*. Carbondale, IL: Southern Illinois University Press.

245

Klare, M. T. 2002. *Resource Wars: The New Landscape of Global Conflict*. New York: Metropolitan Books.

Korten, D. 2006. *The Great Turning: From Empire to Earth Community*. San Francisco, CA: Berrett-Koehler Publishers.

Krech III, S. 1999. *The Ecological Indian: History and Myth*. New York: W.W. Norton & Company.

Kropotkin, P. [1902] 2008. *Mutual Aid: A Factor of Evolution*. Charleston, SC: Forgotten Books.

Lakoff, G. & M. Johnson 1999. *Philosophy in the Flesh: The Embodied Mind and Its Challenge to Western Thought*. New York: Basic Books.

Lansing, S. 1991. *Priests and Programmers: Technologies of Power in the Engineered Landscape of Bali*. Princeton, NJ: Princeton University Press.

Larsen, D. K. 2001. "God's Gardeners: American Protestant Evangelicals Confront Environmentalism, 1967–2000." Unpublished dissertation, University of Chicago.

Larson, G. J. 1989. "'Conceptual Resources' in South Asia for 'Environmental Ethics'." In *Nature in Asian Traditions of Thought*, J. B. Callicott & R. Ames (eds), 267–77. Albany, NY: SUNY Press.

Laszlo, E. 2001. *Macroshift: Navigating the Transformation to a Sustainable World*. San Francisco, CA: Berrett-Koehler Publishers.

Latour, B. 2004. *Politics of Nature: How to Bring the Sciences into Democracy*. Cambridge, MA: Harvard University Press.

Lease, G. 2005. "Hunting and the Origins of Religion." In *Encyclopedia of Religion and Nature*, B. Taylor (ed.), 805–9. London: Continuum.

Leopold, A. 1949. *A Sand County Almanac*. Oxford: Oxford University Press.

Light, A. 2000. "Ecological Restoration and the Culture of Nature: A Pragmatic Perspective." In *Restoring Nature: Perspectives from the Social Sciences and Humanities*, P. Gobster & B. Hull (eds). Washington DC: Island Press.

Light, A. 2002. "Restoring Ecological Citizenship." In *Democracy and the Claims of Nature*, B. Minteer & B. Pepperman-Taylor (eds), 153–72. Lanham, MD: Rowman & Littlefield.

Light, A. & A. de-Shalit 2003. "Introduction: Environmental Ethics—Whose Philosophy? Which Practice?" In *Moral and Political Reasoning in Environmental Practice*, A. Light & A. de-Shalit (eds), 1–27. Cambridge, MA: MIT Press.

Louv, R. 2005. *Last Child in the Woods*. Chapel Hill, NC: Algonquin Books.

Lovejoy, T. 2002. "Biodiversity: Threats and Challenges." In *Biodiversity, Sustainability and Human Communities: Protecting Beyond the Protected*, T. O'Riordan & S. Stoll-Kleeman (eds), 33–5. Cambridge: Cambridge University Press.

Lovelock, J. 1979. *Gaia: A New Look at Life on Earth*. Oxford University Press: Oxford.

Lovelock, J. 2005. "Gaian Pilgrimage." In *Encyclopedia of Religion and Nature*, B. Taylor (ed.), 683–5. London: Continuum.

Lovelock, J. 2007. *The Revenge of Gaia: Earth's Climate Crisis and the Fate of Humanity*. New York: Basic Books.

Lovins, A. & L. H. Lovins 1981. *Energy/War: Breaking the Nuclear Link: A Prescription for Non-proliferation*. New York: Harper Collins.

Loy, D. R. 2000. "The Religion of the Market". In *Visions of a New Earth: Religious Perspectives on Population, Consumption, and Ecology*, H. Coward & D. C. Maguire (eds), 15–28. Albany, NY: SUNY Press.

Luhrmann, T. M., H. Nusbaum & R. Thisted 2010. "The Absorption Hypothesis: Learning to Hear God in Evangelical Christianity." *American Anthropologist* **112**(1) (March): 66–78.

Lynch, G. 2007. *The New Spirituality: An Introduction to Progressive Belief in the 21st Century*. London: I.B. Tauris.

MacIntyre, A. 1981. *After Virtue: A Study in Moral Theory*. Notre Dame: Notre Dame University Press.

MacIntyre, A. 1989. *Whose Justice? Which Rationality?* Notre Dame: Notre Dame University Press.

Macy, J. 1983. *Despair and Personal Power in the Nuclear Age*. Philadelphia, PA: New Society.

Macy, J. 1991. *Mutual Causality in Buddhism and General Systems Theory: The Dharma of Natural Systems*. Albany, NY: SUNY Press.

Mander, J. & E. Goldsmith (eds) 1996. *The Case Against the Global Economy and For a Turn Toward the Local*. San Francisco, CA: Sierra Club Books.

Marsden, G. M. 1991. *Understanding Fundamentalism and Evangelicalism*. Grand Rapids, MI: Wm. B. Eerdmans.

Martin, P. 2005. *Twilight of the Mammoths: Ice Age Extinctions and the Rewilding of America*. Berkeley, CA: University of California Press.

Masuzawa, T. 2005. *The Invention of World Religions, or, How European Universalism was Preserved in the Language of Pluralism*. Chicago, IL: University of Chicago Press.

Mburu, G. 2005. "Kenya Greenbelt Movement." In *Encyclopedia of Religion and Nature*, B. Taylor (ed.), 957–61. London: Continuum.

McCutcheon, R. 1997. *Manufacturing Religion: The Discourse of Sui Generis Religion and the Politics of Nostalgia*. Oxford: Oxford University Press.

McCutcheon, R. 2001. *Critics Not Caretakers: Redescribing the Public Study of Religion*. Albany, NY: SUNY Press.

McCutcheon, R. 2005. *Religion and the Domestication of Dissent: Or, How to Live in a Less than Perfect Nation*. Sheffield: Equinox.

McGeary, M. N. 1960. *Gifford Pinchot: Forester, Politician*. Princeton, NJ: Princeton University Press.

McKenzie, M. 2005. "Seattle (Sealth), Chief". In *Encyclopedia of Religion and Nature*, B. Taylor (ed.), 1511–12. London: Continuum.

McPhee, J. 1971. *Encounters With the Archdruid: Narratives About a Conservationist and Three of His Natural Enemies*. New York: Farrar, Straus & Giroux.

McVay, S. 1993. "Prelude: A Siamese Connexion With a Plurality of Other Mortals". In *The Biophilia Hypothesis*, S. Kellert & E. O. Wilson (eds), 3–19. Washington, DC: Island Press.

Meadows, D. 2007. "Evaluating Past Forecasts: Reflections on One Critique of *Limits to Growth*." In *Sustainability or Collapse?: An Integrated History and Future of People on Earth*, R. Costanza, L. Graumlich & W. Steffen (eds), 399–416. Cambridge, MA: MIT Press.

Meadows, D., H. Dennis, L. Meadows, J. Randers & W. W. Behrens III 1972. *Limits to Growth*. Seattle: Signet Press.

Meine, C. 2005. "Leopold, Aldo." In *Encyclopedia of Religion and Nature*, B. Taylor (ed.), 1005–8. London: Continuum.

Merchant, C. 1980. *The Death of Nature*. New York: Harper Collins.

Monaghan, P. 2005. "Gaia". In *Encyclopedia of Religion and Nature*, B. Taylor (ed.), 679–80. London: Continuum.

Muir, J. [1911] 1997. *My First Summer in the Sierra and Selected Essays*. New York: Penguin Books.

Müller, M. [1870] 2002. "The Science of Religion." In *The Essential Max Müller: Language, Mythology and Religion*, J. R. Stone (ed.). New York: Palgrave Macmillan.

Müller, M. [1878] 2002. "The Perception of the Infinite." In *The Essential Max Müller: Language, Mythology and Religion*, J. R. Stone (ed.). New York: Palgrave Macmillan.

Murphy, N. 2003. "On the Role of Philosophy in the Theology-science Dialogue." *Theology and Science* 1(1): 79–84.

Murphy, N. & G. F. R. Ellis 1996. *On the Moral Nature of the Universe: Theology, Cosmology and Ethics*. Minneapolis, MN: Augsburg Fortress Press.

Naess, A. 1973. "The Shallow and the Deep, Long-Range Ecology Movement: A Summary." *Inquiry* 16: 95–100.

Nash, R. 2001. *Wilderness and the American Mind*, 4th edn. New Haven, CT: Yale University Press.

Naylor, D. K. 2005. "Pinchot, Gifford." In *Encyclopedia of Religion and Nature*, B. Taylor (ed.), 1280–81. London: Continuum.

Neff, D. 2007. "My Birthday Dinner with Ban Ki-Moon." Email correspondence: UNEP News Clippings from the Forum on Religion and Ecology, received October 14, 2007.

Noll, M. 1995. *The Scandal of the Evangelical Mind*. Grand Rapids, MI: Wm. B. Eerdmans Press.

Nordhaus, T. & M. Shellenberger 2007. *Break Through: From the Death of Environmentalism to the Politics of Possibility*. New York: Houghton Mifflin Co.

Northwest Earth Institute 2001a. *Exploring Deep Ecology*. Portland, OR: Northwest Earth Institute.

Northwest Earth Institute 2001b. *Discovering a Sense of Place*. Portland, OR: Northwest Earth Institute.

Northwest Earth Institute 2007a. *Global Warming: Changing CO_2urse*. Portland, OR: Northwest Earth Institute.

Northwest Earth Institute 2007b. *Choices for Sustainable Living*. Portland, OR: Northwest Earth Institute.

Norton, B. 1984. "Environmental Ethics and Weak Anthropocentrism." *Environmental Ethics* 6: 131–48.

Norton, B. (ed.) 1986. *The Preservation of Species: The Value of Biological Diversity*. Princeton, NJ: Princeton University Press.

Norton, B. 1991. *Toward Unity Among Environmentalists*. Oxford: Oxford University Press.

Norton, B. 2003. *Searching for Sustainability: Interdisciplinary Essays on the Philosophy of Conservation Biology*. Cambridge: Cambridge University Press.

Norton, B. 2005. *Sustainability: A Philosophy of Adaptive Ecosystem Management*. Chicago, IL: University of Chicago Press.

Norton, B. 2007. "Politics and Epistemology: Inclusion and Controversy in Adaptive Management Processes." *Environmental Ethics* 29: 299–306.

Odum, H. T. 2007. *Environment, Power and Society for the Twenty-first Century: The Hierarchy of Energy*. New York: Columbia Press.

Oelschlager, M. 1991. *The Idea of Wilderness*. New Haven, CT: Yale University Press.

O'Heffernan, P., A. Lovins & L. H. Lovins 1983. *The First Nuclear World War: A Strategy for Preventing Nuclear Wars and the Spread of Nuclear Weapons*. New York: William, Morrow & Company.

Ophuls, W. 1977. *Ecology and the Politics of Scarcity: A Prologue to a Political Theory of the Steady State*. San Francisco, CA: W.H. Freeman & Co.

O'Riordan, T. 2002. "Protecting Beyond the Protected." In *Biodiversity, Sustainability and Human Communities*, T. O'Riordan & S. Stoll-Kleemann (eds), 3–29. Cambridge: Cambridge University Press.

Orr, D. 1994. *Earth in Mind*. Washington, DC: Island Press.

Orsi, R. 1997. "Everyday Miracles: The Study of Lived Religion." In *Lived Religion in America: Toward a History of Practice*, D. Hall (ed.). Princeton, NJ: Princeton University Press.

Otto, R. 1958. *The Idea of the Holy*, 2nd edn. Oxford: Oxford University Press.

Palmer, M. & V. Finlay 2003. *Faith in Conservation: New Approaches to Religions and the Environment*. Washington, DC: The World Bank.

Parker, E. 1993. "Fact and Fiction in Amazonia: The Case of the Apêtê." *American Anthropologist* (new series) **95**(3): 715–23.

Patten, C. (ed.) 2000. *Respect For the Earth: Sustainable Development*. London: Profile Books.

Penick, J. 1968. *Progressive Politics and Conservation: The Ballinger-Pinchot Affair*. Chicago, IL: University of Chicago Press.

Peterson, A. 1997. *Martyrdom and the Politics of Religion: Progressive Catholicism in El Salvador's Civil War*. Albany, NY: State University of New York Press.

Peterson, A. 2001. *Being Human: Ethics, Environment, and Our Place in the World*. Berkeley, CA: University of California Press.

Peterson, A. 2005. *Seeds of the Kingdom*. New York: Oxford University Press.

Peterson, A. 2006. "Toward a Materialist Environmental Ethic." *Environmental Ethics* **28** (2006): 375–93.

Peterson, T. R. 1997. *Sharing the Earth: The Rhetoric of Sustainable Development*. Columbia, MO: University of South Carolina Press.

Pigem, J. (ed.) 2007. "Faith-Based Organizations and Education for Sustainability." Report of the International Experts' Workshop, Barcelona, Centre UNESCO de Catalunya, March 22–24.

Pike, S. 2004. *New Age and Neopagan Religions in America*. New York: Columbia University Press.

Pinchot, G. 1910. *The Fight for Conservation*. Seattle, WA: University of Washington Press.

Pinchot, G. [1914] 1937. *The Training of a Forester*. London: J.B. Lippincott.

Pinchot, G. 1947. *Breaking New Ground*. New York: Harcourt, Brace & Company.

Pinkett, H. T. 1970. *Gifford Pinchot: Private and Public Forester*. Urbana, IL: University of Illinois Press.

Posey, D. A. (ed.) 1999. *Cultural and Spiritual Values of Biodiversity*. London: Intermediate Technologies.

Posey, D. A. 2004. *Indigenous Knowledge and Ethics: A Darrell Posey Reader*. New York: Routledge.

Posey, D. A., J. Frechione, J. Eddins, L. F. Da Silva, D. Myers, D. Case & P. Macbeth 1984. "Ethnoecology as Applied Anthropology in Amazonian Development." *Human Organization* **43**(2): 95–107.

Posey, D. A. & M. J. Balick 2006. *Human Impacts on Amazonia: The Role of Traditional Ecological Knowledge in Conservation and Development*. New York: Columbia University Press.

Proctor, J. D. 2006. "Religion as Trust in Authority: Theocracy and Ecology in the United States." *Annals of the Association of American Geographers* **96**(1): 188–96.

Proctor, J. D. & E. Berry 2005. "Social Science on Religion and Nature." In *Encyclopedia of Religion and Nature*, B. Taylor (ed.), 1572–7. London: Continuum.

Prothero, S. 2007. *Religious Literacy: What Every American Needs to Know About Religion— and Doesn't*. New York: HarperCollins.

Prugh, T., R. Costanza & H. E. Daly 2000. *The Local Politics of Global Sustainability*. Washington, DC: Island Press.

Rappaport, R. 1967. *Pigs for the Ancestors: Ritual Ecology of a New Guinea People*. New Haven, CT: Yale University Press.

Reichel-Dolmatoff, G. 1976. "Cosmology as Ecological Analysis: A View From the Rainforest." *Man* **2**(3): 307–18.

Rist, G. 1997. *The History of Development: From Western Origins to Global Faith*. London: Zed Books.

Rockefeller, S. 2005. "Earth Charter." In *Encyclopedia of Religion and Nature*, B. Taylor (ed.), 516–18. London: Continuum.

Rolston, H. III 2002. "Value in Nature and the Nature of Value." In *Environmental Ethics: An Anthology*, A. Light and H. Rolston, III (eds), 143–53. Oxford: Blackwell Publishers.

Russell, R. J. 1998. "Special Providence and Genetic Mutation: A New Defense of Theistic Evolution." In *Evolutionary and Molecular Biology: Scientific Perspectives on Divine Action*, R. J. Russell, N. C. Murphy & C. J. Isham (eds). Vatican City State: Vatican Observatory, Center for Theology and Natural Sciences.

Saler, B. 1993. *Conceptualizing Religion: Immanent Anthropologists, Transcendent Natives, and Unbounded Categories*. Leiden: Brill.

Saler, B. 2004. "Toward a Realistic and Relevant 'Science of Religion.'" *Method and Theory in the Study of Religion* **16**: 205–33.

Schaeffer, F. 1970. *Pollution and the Death of Man: The Christian View of Ecology*. Wheaton, IL: Tyndale House Publishers.

Schleiermacher, F. [1799] 1996. *On Religion: Speeches to Its Cultured Despisers*. Cambridge: Cambridge University Press.

Schultes, R. 1979. *Plants of the Gods: Origins of Hallucinogenic Use*. New York: McGraw Hill.

Schultes, R. & S. Von Reis [1995] 2008. *Ethnobotany: The Evolution of a Discipline*. Hong Kong: Dioscorides Press.

Schwartz, P. [1991] 1996. *The Art of the Long View*. New York: Currency Doubleday.

Sears, J. 1989. *Sacred Places: American Tourist Attractions in the Nineteenth Century*. Oxford: Oxford University Press.

Seed, J. 1983. "Anthropocentrism." *Earth First!* **3**(6): 15.

Seed, J. 2000. "The Rainforest as Teacher." In *Dharma Rain*, Stephanie Kaza & Kenneth Kraft (eds), 286–93. Boston, MA: Shambhala Publications.

Seed, J., J. Macy, P. Fleming & A. Naess 1988. *Thinking Like a Mountain: Towards a Council of All Beings*. Philadelphia, PA and Santa Cruz, CA: New Society Publishers.

Sen, A. [1999] 2000. *Development As Freedom*. New York: Anchor Books.

Senge, P., B. Smith, N. Kruschwitz, J. Laur & S. Schley 2008. *The Necessary Revolution: How Individuals and Organizations Are Working Together to Create a Sustainable World*. New York: Doubleday Press.

Shellenberger, M. & T. Nordhaus 2004. "The Death of Environmentalism" at www. thebreakthrough.org/PDF/Death_of_Environmentalism.pdf (accessed November 20, 2008).

Shepard, P. 1982. *Nature and Madness*. Athens, GA: University of Georgia Press.

Shepard, P. 1998. *Coming Home to the Pleistocene*. Washington, DC: Island Press.

Sideris, L. 2003. *Environmental Ethics, Ecological Theology and Natural Selection*. New York: Columbia University Press.

Sideris, L. & K. D. Moore 2008. *Rachel Carson: Legacy and Challenge*. Albany, NY: SUNY Press.

Smith, H. A. 2005. "The World Commission on Environment and Development: Ideas and Institutions Intersect." In *International Commissions and the Power of Ideas*, R. Thakur, A. F. Cooper & J. English (eds), 76–98. Tokyo: United Nations University Press.

Smith, J. Z. 1988. "'Religion' and 'Religious Studies': No Difference at All." *Soundings* **71**(2–3): 231–44.

Smith, J. Z. 1998. "Religion, Religions, Religious." In *Critical Terms for Religious Studies*, M. C. Taylor (ed.), 269–84. Chicago, IL: University of Chicago Press.

Snarey, J. 1996. "The Natural Environment's Impact upon Religious Ethics: A Cross-cultural Study." *Journal for the Scientific Study of Religion* **35**(2): 85–96.

Snyder, G. 1974. *Turtle Island*. New York: New Directions.

Sperber, D. 1985. "Anthropology and Psychology: Towards an Epidemiology of Representations." *Man* **20**(1) (March): 73–89.

Sperber, D. 1994. "The Modularity of Thought and the Epidemiology of Representations." In *Mapping the Mind: Domain Specificity in Cognition and Culture*, L. A. Hirschfeld & S. A. Gelman (eds), 39–67. Cambridge: Cambridge University Press.

Spohn, W. 2000. *Go and Do Likewise: Jesus and Ethics*. London: Continuum.

Stavenhagen, R. 1970. *Agrarian Problems and Peasant Movements in Latin America*. New York: Doubleday.

Stavenhagen, R. 1990. *The Ethnic Question: Conflicts, Development, and Human Rights*. Tokyo: United Nations University Press

Stern, P. C., T. Dietz, T. Abel, G. A. Guagnano & L. Lakof 1999. "A Value-Belief-Norm Theory of Support for Social Movements: The Case of Environmentalism." *Human Ecology Review* **6**(2): 81–97.

Strobel, C. 2005. "Macy, Joanna." In *Encyclopedia of Religion and Nature*, B. Taylor (ed.), 1019–20. London: Continuum.

Sumner, J. 2005. *Sustainability and the Civil Commons: Rural Communities in the Age of Globalization*. Toronto: University of Toronto Press.

Suzuki, D. [1934] 1964. *An Introduction to Zen Buddhism*. New York: Grove Press.

Suzuki, D. 1970. *The Field of Zen: Contributions to the Middle Way, the Journal of the Buddhist Society*. London: The Buddhist Society.

Suzuki, D. 1997. *The Sacred Balance*. Vancouver: Greystone Books.

Swimme, B. 1997. "Science as Wisdom: The New Story as a Way Forward" (interview). *EarthLight* **26**: 10–11, 15, 22.

Swimme, B. & T. Berry 1994. *The Universe Story: From the Primordial Flaring Forth to the Ecozoic Era: A Celebration of the Unfolding Cosmos*. New York: Harper Collins.

Takacs, D. 1996. *The Idea of Biodiversity*. Baltimore, MD: Johns Hopkins University Press.

Taylor, B. 1995. "Popular Ecological Resistance and Radical Environmentalism." In *Ecological Resistance Movements: The Global Emergence of Radical and Popular Environmentalism*, B. Taylor (ed.), 334–54. Albany, NY: SUNY Press.

Taylor, B. 1997. "Earthen Spirituality or Cultural Genocide: Radical Environmentalism's Appropriation of Native American Spirituality." *Religion* **27**(2): 183–215.

Taylor, B. 1998. "Religion, Violence, and Radical Environmentalism: From Earth First! to the Unabomber to the Earth Liberation Front." *Terrorism and Political Violence* **10**(4): 1–42.

Taylor, B. 2001. "Earth and Nature-Based Spirituality: From Earth First! and Bioregionalism to Scientific Paganism and the New Age" (part II). *Religion* **31**(3): 225–45.

Taylor, B. 2003. "Threat Assessments and Radical Environmentalism." *Terrorism and Political Violence* **15**(4): 173–82.

Taylor, B. 2004a. "A Green Future for Religion?" *Futures* **36** (2004): 991–1008.

Taylor, B. 2004b. "Threat Assessments and Radical Environmentalism." *Terrorism and Political Violence* **15**(4): 173–82.

Taylor, B. 2005a. "Conservation Biology." In *Encyclopedia of Religion and Nature*, B. Taylor (ed.), 415–18. London: Continuum.

Taylor, B. 2005b. "Introduction." In *Encyclopedia of Religion and Nature*, B. Taylor (ed.), vii–xvii. London: Continuum.

Taylor, B. 2005c. "Religious Studies and Environmental Concern." In *Encyclopedia of Religion and Nature*, B. Taylor (ed.), 1373–9. London: Continuum.

Taylor, B. 2005d. "Environmental Ethics." In *Encyclopedia of Religion and Nature*, B. Taylor (ed.), 597–608. London: Continuum.

Taylor, B. 2007. "Exploring Religion, Nature and Culture – Introducing the Journal for the Study of Religion, Nature and Culture." *Journal for the Study of Religion, Nature and Culture* 1(1): 5–24.

Taylor, B. 2010. *Dark Green Religion*. Berkeley, CA: University of California Press.

Taylor, P. W. 1986. *Respect for Nature: A Theory of Environmental Ethics*. Princeton, NJ: Princeton University Press. Taylor, S. 2009. *Green Sisters: A Spiritual Ecology*. Cambridge, MA: Harvard University Press.

Teilhard de Chardin, P. 1959. *The Phenomenon of Man*. New York: Harper & Row.

Therien, J-P. 2005. "The Brandt Commission: The End of an Era in North–South Politics." In *International Commissions and the Power of Ideas*, R. Thakur, A. Cooper & J. English (eds). New York: United Nations Press.

Thomas, S. 2005. *The Global Resurgence of Religion and the Transformation of International Relations: The Struggle For the Soul of the Twenty-first Century*. New York: Palgrave Macmillan.

Torgerson, D. 1999. *The Promise of Green Politics: Environmentalism and the Public Sphere*. Durham, NC: Duke University Press.

Trusty, T. 2009. "The Politics of Representing Nature, Culture, and Conservation in Northwestern Bolivia." Unpublished dissertation. Seattle, WA: University of Washington.

Tucker, M. E. 2006. "Religion and Ecology: Survey of the Field." In *The Oxford Handbook of Religion and Ecology*, R. Gottlieb (ed.), 398–418. Oxford: Oxford University Press.

Tucker, M. E. & J. Grim 1997. "Series Foreword." In *Buddhism and Ecology: The Interconnection of Dharma and Deeds*, M. E. Tucker and D. R. Williams (eds), xv–xxxi. Cambridge, MA: Harvard University Press.

Tucker, R. (ed.) 1978. *The Marx-Engels Reader*. New York: W.W. Norton.

Turner, F. J. [1893] 1956. *The Significance of the Frontier in American History*. Ithaca, NY: Cornell University Press.

Tweed, T. 2006. *Crossing and Dwelling: A Theory of Religion*. Cambridge, MA: Harvard University Press.

Tylor, E. B. 1871. *Primitive Culture*. London: John Murray.

United Nations 1969. *Problems of the Human Environment: Report of the Secretary-General*. New York: United Nations Publications.

United Nations Educational, Scientific and Cultural Organization 1988. *Man Belongs to the Earth*. Paris: UNESCO Publications.

Van Horn, G. & B. Blackwelder 2005. "Brower, David." In *Encyclopedia of Religion and Nature*, B. Taylor (ed.), 225–6. London: Continuum.

Vasquez, M. 2008. "Studying Religion in Motion: A Networks Approach." *Method and Theory in the Study of Religion* 20: 151–84.

Vasquez, M. 2011. *More Than Belief: A Materialist Theory of Religion*. Oxford: Oxford University Press.

Vilaca, A. & R. Wright 2009. *Native Christians: Modes and Effects of Christianity Among Indigenous Peoples of the Americas.* New York: Ashgate.

Vitousek, P. M. 1994. "Beyond Global Warming: Ecology and Global Change." *Ecology* 75(7): 1861–76.

Vitousek, P. M., H. Mooney, J. Lubchenko & J. Melillo. 1997. "Human Domination of Earth's Ecosystems." *Science* 277(5325): 494–9.

Von Weizsacker, E., A. Lovins & L. H. Lovins 1998. *Factor Four: Doubling Wealth, Halving Resource Use—A Report to the Club of Rome.* London: Earthscan.

Wallace, M. 2005. *Finding God in the Singing River.* Minneapolis, MN: Fortress Press.

Wapner, P. 1995. "Politics Beyond the State: Environmental Activism and World Civic Politics." *World Politics* 47(3): 311–40.

Wapner, P. [1995] 2004. "Politics Beyond the State: Environmental Activism and World Civic Politics." In *Green Planet Blues*, K. Conca & J. Dabelko (eds), 122–39. Boulder, CO: Westview Press.

Wapner, P. 1996. *Environmental Activism and World Civic Politics.* Albany, NY: SUNY Press.

Weber, E. 2003. *Bringing Society Back In: Grassroots Ecosystem Management, Accountability, and Sustainable Communities.* Cambridge, MA: MIT Press.

Weber, M. [1930] 2005. *The Protestant Ethic and the Spirit of Capitalism*, T. Parsons (trans.). London: Routledge.

Weber, T. 1999. "Gandhi, Deep Ecology, Peace Research and Buddhist Economics," *Journal of Peace Research* 36(3): 349–61.

Welch, S. D. 1990. *A Feminist Ethic of Risk.* Minneapolis, MN: Fortress.

White Jr, L. 1967. "The Historic Roots of our Ecologic Crisis." *Science* 155(3767) (March): 1203–7.

Whitehead, A. N. [1927] 1978. *Process and Reality.* New York: The Free Press.

Wilkinson, L. (ed.) 1980. *Earthkeeping: Christian Stewardship of Natural Resources.* Grand Rapids, MI: William B. Eerdmans Publishing.

Willard, B. 2005. *The Next Sustainability Wave: Building Board Room Buy-in.* Gabriola Island, BC: New Society Press.

Wilson, B. 2011. "Mirroring Processes, Religious Perception and Ecological Adaptation: Toward an Empathic Theory of Religion." *Journal for the Study of Religion, Nature and Culture* 5(3): 307–53.

Wilson, D. S. 2002. *Darwin's Cathedral: Evolution, Religion, and the Nature of Society.* Chicago, IL: University of Chicago Press.

Wilson, E. O. 1984. *Biophilia: the Human Bond with Other Species.* Cambridge, MA: Harvard University Press.

Wilson, E. O. 1994. *Biophilia.* Cambridge, MA: Harvard University Press.

Wilson, E. O. 1998. *Consilience: The Unity of Knowledge.* New York: Knopf, distributed by Random House.

Wilson, E. O. 2006. *The Creation: An Appeal to Save Life on Earth.* New York: Norton.

Wiseman, G. 2005. "The Palme Commission: New Thinking About Security." In *International Commissions and the Power of Ideas*, R. Thakur, A. Cooper & J. English (eds), 46–75. Tokyo: United Nations University Press.

Wittgenstein, L. [1953] 2001. *Philosophical Investigations*, G. E. M. Anscombe (ed.), 3rd edn. Oxford: Blackwell Publishers.

Wittgenstein, L. 1974. *Philosophical Grammar*, R. Rhees (ed.). Berkeley, CA: University of California Press.

World Bank 2001. *Making Sustainable Commitments: An Environment Strategy for the World Bank*. Washington, DC: The World Bank.

World Bank 2006. *Faiths and the Environment*. Washington DC: World Bank.

World Commission on Environment and Development (WCED) 1987. *Our Common Future*. Oxford: Oxford University Press.

World Conservation Union (IUCN), United Nations Environment Programme (UNEP), and World Wide Fund for Nature (WWF). 1991. *Caring for the Earth: A Strategy for Sustainable Living*. Gland, Switzerland.

Worster, D. 1977. *Nature's Economy: A History of Ecological Ideas*. Cambridge: Cambridge University Press.

Worster, D. 1993. *The Wealth of Nature: Environmental History and the Ecological Imagination*. New York: Oxford University Press.

Wright, R. 1988. "Anthropological Presuppositions of Indigenous Advocacy." *Annual Review of Anthropology* 17: 365–90.

Wright, R. 1998. *Cosmos, Self, and History in Baniwa Religion: For Those Unborn*. Austin, TX: University of Texas Press.

Wright, R. 2007. "Indigenous Moral Philosophies and Ontologies and Their Implications For Sustainable Development." *Journal for the Study of Religion, Nature and Culture* 1(1): 92–108.

Wright, R. 2009. "The Art of Being *Crente*: The Baniwa Protestant Ethic and the Spirit of Sustainable Development." *Identities: Global Studies in Culture and Power* 16: 202–26.

Young, I. M. 2001. "Activist Challenges to Deliberative Democracy." *Political Theory* 29(5): 670–90.

Zimmerman, M. E. [1988] 1995 "Quantum Theory, Intrinsic Value, and Panentheism." In *Postmodern Environmental Ethics*, M. Oelschlager (ed.), 277–307. Albany, NY: SUNY Press.

Zimmerman, M. E. 2000. "Possible Political Problems of Earth-Based Religiosity." In *Beneath the Surface: Critical Essays in the Philosophy of Deep Ecology*, E. Katz, A. Light & D. Rothenberg (eds). Cambridge, MA: MIT Press.

INDEX